Parti Colored Blocks for a Quilt

MARGE PIERCY

Ann Arbor   **The University of Michigan Press**

Library of Congress Cataloging in Publication Data

Piercy, Marge.
  Parti-colored blocks for a quilt.

  (Poets on poetry)
  I. Title. II. Series.
PS3566.I4P3   1982   814'.54   82-8621
ISBN 0-472-06338-3   AACR2

Parti-
Colored
Blocks
for a Quilt

Poets on Poetry   Donald Hall, General Editor

*For Jackie Shapiro, without whom
nothing much would happen around here*

Other Books by Marge Piercy:

Contents

I
Views and Interviews

Statement for *Mountain Moving Day*

I want to argue in defense equally of women who want to work to create a female culture and of those who want to contribute to what has been a male culture and change it to a broader, less oppressive culture. We have to take for ourselves the freedom to deal with what have been predominantly female concerns—subjects men define as boring—at whatever length appears to us necessary and vital and in whatever style we find natural or comely. We have to take the space and time to deal with these subjects as honestly as we can—in honesty to our perceptions. We have to insist on being judged and on judging each other, for doing our own work, not for having failed to replicate somebody else's. We have to fight just as hard to deal with subjects that appear to us to be neutral of gender, from our own perspectives. For us to feel competitive with each other is illusion left over from socialization in this society. We are not competing any more than the first two aborigines who walked into Australia were competing. We create each other. We make the space that other women will occupy. We save each other's sanity. I think probably all of the women in this book are working to make part of the same quilt to keep us from freezing to death in a world that grows harsher and bleaker—where male is the

This essay was written for the anthology *Mountain Moving Day*, edited by Elaine Gill (Trumansburg, N.Y.: The Crossing Press, 1973).

norm and the ideal human being is hard, violent and cold: a macho rock. Every woman who makes of her living something strong and good is sharing bread with us.

Inviting the Muse

Here is Henry Thoreau from his journal for October 26, 1853, although he is talking about spring. "That afternoon the dream of the toads rang through the elms by Little River and affected the thoughts of men, though they were not conscious that they heard it. How watchful we must be to keep the crystal well that we are made, clear!"

Writing poems can be divided crudely into three kinds of labor: beginning and getting well and hard into it; pushing through inner barriers and finding the correct form; drawing back and judging what you have done and what is still to be done or redone. This essay is about the first stage, learning how to flow, how to push yourself, how to reach that cone of concentration I experience at its best as a tower of light, when all the voices in the head are one voice.

I do not know how to teach that, although concentration can be learned and worked on the same as flattening stomach muscles or swimming farther. You could perhaps set someone to studying a rock or a leaf or a bird—perhaps a warbler. Nothing requires more concentration than trying to observe a warbler up in the leafy maze of a summer tree. If I were really and truly teaching poetry, I would probably drive everybody crazy by sending them off to notice the shades of sand on a beach.

Of course observation isn't concentration, but learning to do one brings on the ability to do the other. My mother taught me to observe. A woman who had not been allowed to finish the tenth grade, she had some extraordinary ideas about how to raise very young children. Later when I was grown out of dependency and highly imperfect, she had trouble with me and could not endure my puberty. However, when I was little enough to fit comfortably into her arms and lap, we played unusual games. She had contempt for people who did not observe, who did not notice, and would require me to remember the houses we passed going to the store, or play mental hide-and-seek in other people's houses that we had visited. We would give each other three random objects or words to make stories around. We would try to guess the stories of people we saw on the bus and would argue to prove or disprove each other's theories.

I suppose such training might have produced what she wanted, a sharply observant person like herself, a reporter's mentality, a little Sherlock Holmes in Shirley Temple guise. What it created in me was observation suffused with imagination, since our life was on the whole skimpy, hard, surrounded by violence outdoors and containing familial violence within, a typical patriarchal working-class family in inner-city Detroit. Blacks and whites fought; the Polish and Blacks who lived across Tireman (a street) fought the Irish who went to parochial school. The neighborhood offered the kind of stable family life writers like Christopher Lasch, beating the dolly of the new narcissism, love to harken back to. Although husbands sometimes took off and not infrequently had girlfriends on the side, women almost never walked out of their homes. Wife beating was common, child beating just as common; drunkenness, drug abuse, rape, molestation of children occurred on every block but families went on from generation to generation. In such a neighborhood where the whites were comprised of Polish, Irish, a few Italian and German Catholics, of some remaining WASP and some newly arrived Appalachian families (I divide the Appalachian WASP from the others because they were often Celts, and because they were looked down on by everybody as hillbillies and provided some of my closest friends), being a Jew was walking around with a kick-me sign. I'd say the level of tolerance for lesbians was higher than that for Jews. You learn to observe street action and people's muscular tensions and involuntary tics rather closely.

Detroit sprawls there, willfully ugly mile after flat smoggy mile; yet what saves it are trees. Every abandoned vacant lot becomes a jungle in a couple of years. Our tiny backyard was rampant with tomatoes, beans, herbs, lettuce, onions, Swiss chard. One of the earliest poems I wrote and still like is subtly about sex and overtly about peonies. Pansies, iris, mock orange, wisteria, hollyhocks along the alley fence, black-eyed Susans, goldenglow whose stems were red with spider mites, bronze chrysanthemums, a lilac bush by the compost pile. Nothing to me will ever be more beautiful than the flowers in that yard, except my mother when I was young.

You learn to sink roots into your childhood and feed on it, twist it, wring it, use it again and again. Sometimes one daub of childhood mud can set a whole poem right or save a character. It's not always a matter of writing about your family, although at times we all do that. You use your childhood again and again in poems about totally other things. You learn how to use that rush of energy and how to make sure your use transcends the often trivial and ludicrous associations you are touching and drawing power from.

Some poets get going, get the flow by reading other poets. You learn whose writing moves you to your own, whether it's Whitman or the King James version of the Bible or Rukeyser or Neruda in Spanish or in translation. Actually I've never met anyone who got themselves going by reading poetry in any other language than the one they were working in, but I'm curious if anybody does. On the other hand I have met a number of poets who use work in translation to prime themselves. It is a priming act we're talking about. You set the words and rhythms going through you and you begin to align yourself. It has disadvantages, of course; if you are the least impressionable you may produce involuntary pastiche. You may find yourself churning out imagery that is bookishly exotic, imagery culled from others and bearing the imprint of being on loan like clothes that fit badly. Some poets use poetry of another time to prime themselves, to minimize the unintentional fertilization.

This priming can happen by accident. Oftentimes I am reading poetry and suddenly a poem starts, that change in the brain, maybe words, maybe an image, maybe an idea. It need not even be poetry. That quotation from Thoreau that begins this essay instigated a poem called "Toad dreams." I remember starting a poem in the middle of reading a *Natural History* magazine or the *Farmers Almanac*.

I think of that instigation as having a peculiar radiance; that is, the idea, the image, the rhythm, the phrase—radiates. I find myself wanting to attend to it. I may not know at once, often I may not find out for several drafts, what that meaning, that implication, that web of associations and train of utterances will be or even in what direction I am being led. Sometimes the original moment radiates in many directions. Then my problem is sorting out the direction to pursue first or exclusively.

At that point if concentration is not forthcoming, the whole possibility may be blown. If you can lose a novel by talking it out, you can easily destroy a poem by not paying attention. I have lost many poems that way; I must lose one a week because I can't get to a typewriter or even to a piece of paper fast enough—sometimes can't break through to silence, to solitude, to a closed door. I am not good at working at cafe tables, as Sartre was supposed to do, although I have written on planes often enough. Even then I work only when I have a bit of space, never while wedged in the middle seat. I need at least a seat between me and any other person to work on a plane. At home, I need a closed door.

Poems can be aborted by answering the phone at the wrong moment. They can be aborted when an alien rhythm forces itself in, or the wrong other words are juxtaposed. I cannot work with a radio on loud enough to hear the words, or a television, or music with words playing. I have trouble working at all with music on, for the rhythms are much too insistent. I know other writers who work to music, but I cannot do so. Rhythm is extremely important to me in building the line and the poem, so any other insistent rhythm interferes. Irregular rhythms—hammering on a construction site nearby—have little effect.

I had a friend in Brooklyn who used to work with wax plugs in her ears, but I find that difficult. I talk my poems aloud and my voice roaring in my head gives me a headache. However, I pass on this method as it may do the trick for you. I know another writer who uses a white noise machine, the type usually purchased to help you sleep. I used to run an air conditioner to screen the noises from outside the apartment, when it seemed to me that every window opening onto the center of our block in Adelphi had a radio or a TV or both turned to top decibel.

Often I begin a poem simply by paying attention to myself, by finding what is stirring in there. I need a quiet moment. I try to use the routine of waking to bring me to work, whether into a novel I am working on or into poetry. I work best in the morning, although I started out believing myself to be a night person. I changed over during the sixties when the one quiet time I was assured of was before the rest of the antiwar movement in New York was awake. I learned to get out of bed and to use waking to move toward work.

Without the pressure on me now to work before friends are stirring, I need not rush to the typewriter but I preserve my attention. I always do some exercises in the morning and I take a morning bath. All of that routine I use to become thoroughly awake but retain some of the connectedness, some of the rich associativeness of dreaming sleep. I don't want to shed that dark energy of dreams, nor to lose that concentration and involvement in the clutter of the day. I don't think of it quite as self-involvement. I remember when a relationship that had been part of my life for seventeen years was breaking up, I would wake very early after three or four hours sleep and lie in anxiety and pain. Nonetheless by the time I rose through my morning schedule, when I came to the typewriter, I was clear of my immediate anguish and fussing and ready to turn them into work or to write about something entirely different.

I am not saying every writer should get up, eat a good breakfast, take a hot bath and do exercises without talking much to anyone, and then she will write richly. I am trying to say that you must learn how to prepare in a daily way for the combination of concentration and receptivity, a clearing that is also going down into yourself and also putting antennae out. One thing I cannot do and work well is worry about something in my life. If I sit at the typewriter fussing about where the money to pay the real estate taxes is coming from or whether my lover loves me more or less today, whether I am spending too much money on oil this winter, whether the decision taken at the MORAL meeting was correct, I will not find my concentration. I can carry emotions to my typewriter but I must be ready to use and transmute them. They must already be a little apart. It is not exactly emotion recollected in tranquility I mean, although for twenty-five years I have contemplated that phrase with increasing respect. I often feel the emotion but with less ego, less anxiety than in ordinary life. The emotion—the pain, the regret, the anger, the plea-sure—is becoming energy. I suppose whenever I find my life too much more fascinating than work, I work less and write less well. I certainly write fiction poorly in these stretches. I produce some poems, often decent ones, but my output is down.

Such periods are not frequent because I love to write more than almost anything—not essays, to be honest, but poems and novels. I am still writing in letters to friends this week that I am immensely relieved that I have finally shipped off my novel *Braided Lives* to my publisher in its last draft. I do in fact feel as if an elephant had risen daintily from its perch on my chest and ambled away. Free, free at last, oh free! Of course it will return soon enough all penciled over with the comments of some copyeditor enamored of commas and semicolons ("Fuck all that shit; we're not going anyplace," is a typical copyeditor improvement). Comes back again as gal-leys. But essentially it is gone, finished.

Then yesterday afternoon Woody and I were chatting

about the next novel I am planning to start as soon as I put this volume together and finish the next volume of poetry. Say, December? It is June now. He made a suggestion as I was mulling over something about the novel and I fell on it immediately and began chewing it, worrying it. It was just right. In the evening in the car on the way to see a movie two towns away, we began chatting again about my next novel until I shrieked that we must stop it, because I cannot get to it before December.

I try to put on with other writers how much I suffer at this excruciating martyrdom and all that posing we are expected to do, but the simple truth is I love to write and I think it an enormous con that I actually get paid for doing it. After all I did it for ten years without pay.

Find out when you work best and arrange the days that you have to write or the hours you have, to channel yourself into full concentration. If like Sylvia Plath you have only from 4:00 A.M. till the babies wake, if you have only from 6:00 A.M. till 9:00 A.M. as I did in New York, if you have only weekends or only Sundays or only afternoons from 3:30 to 5:30, you have to figure out the funnel that works for you: the set of habitual acts that shuts out distractions and ego noise, shuts out your household, your family, and brings you quickly to the state of prime concentration.

Whatever habits you develop as a writer, your ability to work cannot depend on them. I went from writing late afternoons and evenings to writing mornings because that was the only time I could be sure of. I used to smoke all the time I wrote. I imagined I could not write without the smoke of a cigarette curling around me. Then my lungs gave out. I had to die or learn to live without smoking. Given that choice I abandoned smoking rather fast. I can't say my productivity was amazing the couple of years afterwards, but that was mostly because I had chronic bronchitis and it was a while before I was not sick at least fifty percent of the time with too high a fever to work. I have had to give up alcohol at times and to give up coffee, my keenest addiction of all, for periods, and work goes on whatever I am giving up so long as I have enough strength to make it to the typewriter and sit there.

You may permit yourself any indulgence to get going, so long as you can have it: Cuban cigars, a toke of the best weed, Grandma Hogfat's Pismire Tea, a smelly old jacket: but you have to be able to figure out just what is ritual and what is necessity. I really need silence and to be let alone during the first draft. I like having a typewriter but can produce a first draft of poetry without it; I cannot write prose without a typewriter as I write too slowly by hand. My handwriting is barely legible to me. All the other props are ritual. I have my sacred rocks, my window of tree, my edge-notched card memory annex, my bird fetish necklace hanging over the typewriter, my Olympia standard powered by hand, my reference works on nearby shelves, my cats coming and going, my good coffee downstairs where I am forced to go and straighten my back on the hour. as I should. But I have written in vastly less comfort and doubtless will do so again. Don't talk yourself into needing a corklined room, although if someone gives it to you, fine. Do ask the price.

For many years I felt an intense and negotiable gratitude to my second husband because while I had supported myself from age eighteen and was doing part-time jobs, at a certain point he offered me five years without having to work at shit jobs to establish myself as a writer. I took the offer and by the end of five years was making a decent income—decent by my standards, compared to what I earned as part-time secretary, artist's model, telephone operator, store clerk and so on.

Not until I was putting this volume together and looking at my own output over the years since I began writing poetry seriously and began my first (dreadful) novel at fifteen, did I ever realize that I was less productive during those years of being supported than before or since. Women have to be very cautious with gift horses. We feel guilty. Traditional roles press us back and down. When I stayed home I was a writer in my eyes but a housewife in the world's and largely in my husband's view. Why wasn't the floor polished? What had I been doing all day?

I began to write at a decent clip again not during those two years of traditional wifehood in Brookline but in New York when I was passionately involved in the antiwar movement and working as an organizer at least six hours a day and sometimes twelve.

I am not saying we work best if we use up a lot of our lives doing other work. Some poets do; few prose writers do. It depends on the type of other work in part; I think the less that other work has to do with writing, with writers, with words, the better. I understand the temptation young writers have to take jobs associated with writing. That may be the only affirmation that you are a writer available in the often many years before publication certifies your occupation to the people around you. I don't think I could have resisted writer's residencies if they had been available when I was un- or underpublished. In an ideal world for writers we would be paid while apprenticing at some minimum wage and then encouraged to do something entirely different part-time, in work parties digging sewers or putting in gardens or taking care of the dying, at a reasonable wage.

What I am saying is that the choice may be offered to a woman to stay home (where it is much, much nicer than going out to a lousy job) and write because the amount she can earn as a part-time female worker is negligible from the viewpoint of a professional or skilled male wage earner. The offer can help but it also can hinder. You may find yourself doing a full-time job instead without pay and writing in the interstices—just as before except that you may have even less time that is really yours and you have lost your independent base of income.

Similarly a job teaching can be wonderful because it answers the questions, what do you do? If you get hired as a writer after you have published, say, five short stories, you have sudden legitimacy. If you started in workshops and got an MFA, you have more legitimacy. You have items to add to your resume. Of course once you have taken the teaching job, you may have little time to write, especially given the way the academic marketplace is a buyer's market and teaching loads are getting heavier. You're certified a writer, you deal professionally with literature and words, you make better money and are more respectable in middle-class society, but you have less time and energy to put into your own writing than you would if you worked as a waiter or secretary.

Actually sitting and writing novel after novel before one gets accepted at last the way fiction writers usually must do, or actually working and working on poems till they're right when hardly anybody publishes them and when they do you're read by two librarians, three editors, and six other poets, gives you little to put in your resume. We all make it as we can, and I do a lot of gigs. Unless writers are of draftable age, we are seldom offered money to do something overtly bad like kill somebody or blow up hospitals or burn villages, seldom paid to invent nerve gases or program data bases for the CIA. The jobs available to us range from the therapeutic to the mildly helpful to the pure bullshit to the menial and tedious; all of them sometimes prevent us from writing and sometimes enable us to write. Jobs that have nothing to do with writing often provide more stimulation to the gnome inside who starts poems than jobs that involve teaching writing or writing copy.

When I am trying to get going and find myself empty, often the problem is that I desire to write a poem rather than one specific poem. That is the case sometimes when I have been working eight hours a day finishing up a novel and have not had the time to write poems or the mental space that allows them to begin forming. That is when the writer's notebook or whatever equivalent you use (my own memory annex is on edge-notched cards) can if it is well-organized disgorge those tidbits put in it. I think of those jottings as matches, the images, the poem ideas, the lines that wait resurrection. Often lines that were cut from other poems will in time serve as the instigation for their own proper home. For me the absolute best way to get going is to resort to my memory annex. That summons the Muse, my own muse for sure.

The notion of a muse is less archaic than a lot of vintage

mythology because most poets have probably experienced being picked up by the nape of the neck, shaken, and dumped again miles from where your daily life or ordinary preoccupations could have been expected to bring you. *Duende*, Lorca called that possession. Poems that come down like Moses from the mountaintop, that bore their way through my mind, are not better or worse than poems I labor on for two days, two months, or fifteen years. Nonetheless I always remember which ones arrived that way. Sometimes in writing I experience myself as other. Not in the sense of the "I" as social artifact, the other that strangers or intimates see; the mask the camera catches off guard. When we see ourselves videotaped, often we experience a sense of nakedness and say, "so that is what I am really like," as if the exterior because we usually cannot see it is therefore the truth of our lives. Nor do I mean the artifact we construct, the "I" writers perhaps more than most people make up out of parts of ourselves and parts of our books, as camouflage and advertisement.

What I mean is simply that in writing the poet sometimes transcends the daily self into something clearer. I have often had the experience of looking up from the typewriter, the page, and feeling complete blankness about who I am—the minutia of my daily life, where I am, why. I have for a moment no sex, no history, no character. Past a certain point I will not hear the phone. I respect that self, that artisan who feels empty of personal concern even when dealing with the stuff of my intimate life. I guess the only time I am ever free of the buzz of self-concern and the sometimes interesting, often boring reflection of consciousness on itself, is during moments when I am writing and moments when I am making love. I overvalue both activities because of the refreshment of quieting the skull to pure attention.

That to me is ecstasy, rapture—being seized as if by a raptor, the eagle in "The Rose and the Eagle"—the loss of the buzz of ego in the intense and joyous contemplation of something, whether a lover, a sensation, the energy, the image, the artifact. The ability to move into the state I called concentration is a needful preliminary to, in the first and commonest case, the work that you gradually build, or in the second and rarer case, the visit from necessity, the poems that fall through you entire and burning like a meteorite.

In a society that values the ability to see visions, such as some of the Plains Indians did, many people will manage to crank out a few visions at least at critical moments in their lives; very few people will not manage a vision at least once. Some will become virtuosos of vision.

In a society where seeing visions is usually punished by imprisonment, torture with electroshock, heavy drugging that destroys coordination and shortens life expectancy, very few people will see visions. Some of those who do so occasionally will learn early on to keep their mouths shut, respect the visions, use them but keep quiet about seeing or hearing what other people say is not there. A few of my poems are founded in specific visions: "Curse of the earth magician on a metal land" which also was the seed of *Dance the Eagle to Sleep*; "The sun" from the Tarot card sequence "Laying down the tower," which was the seed of *Woman on the Edge of Time*.

That a poem is visionary in inception does not mean it comes entire. Actually writing a poem or any other artifact out of a vision is often a great deal of work. The hinge poem, for the month of Beth in *The Lunar Cycle*, called "At the well" was a case in point. I first wrote a version of that experience in 1959, when it happened. Here I am finally being able to bring off the poem that is faithful to it in 1979.

To me, no particular value attaches to the genesis of a poem. I am not embarrassed by the sense I have at times of being a conduit through which a poem forces itself and I am not embarrassed by working as long as it takes to build a poem—in the case I just mentioned, twenty years. I write poems for specific occasions, viewing myself as a useful artisan. I have written poems for antiwar rallies, for women's day rallies, for rallies centering on the rights and abuses of mental institution inmates. I have written poems to raise money for the legal defense of political prisoners, for Inez Garcia, who shot the man who raped her, for Shoshana

Rihm-Pat Swinton, for many years a political fugitive and finally acquitted of all charges. I wrote a poem for a poster to raise money for Transition House (a shelter for battered women) along with a beautiful graphic by Betsy Warrior, a warrior for women indeed. I wrote a poem to be presented to the Vietnamese delegation at Montreal, during meetings with antiwar activists.

Some of those occasional poems (as some of the category that arrive like a fast train) are among my best poems; some are mediocre. Frequently I find the necessity to write a poem for a specific purpose or occasion focuses me; perhaps coalesces is a better verb. A charged rod enters the colloidal substance of my consciousness and particles begin to adhere. "For Shoshana-Pat Swinton" is a meditation on feeling oneself active in history that I consider a very strong poem, for instance. I was, of course, to deal with the figure of the political fugitive as a paradigm of certain women's experiences as well as a touchstone for our recent political history in *Vida*; that swirl of ideas and images was obiously rich for me. What doesn't touch you, you can't make poems of.

One last thing I have learned about starting a poem is that if you manage to write down a certain amount when you begin, and failing that, to memorize enough, you will not lose it. If you cannot memorize or scribble that essential sufficient fragment, the poem will dissolve. Sometimes a couple of lines are ample to preserve the impulse till you can give it your full attention. Often it is a started first draft, maybe what will become eventually the first third of the poem, that I carry to my typewriter. But if I can't memorize and record that seed, that match, the instigating factor, then I have lost that particular poem.

Good work habits are nothing more than habits that let you work, that encourage you to pay attention. Focus is most of it: to be fierce and pointed, so that everything else momentarily sloughs away.

Circles On The Water
Introduction to the Selected Poems

An introduction might be a kind of envoi: Go little book out into the world and wheedle your way into the lives of strangers like a stray kitten. However, a selected poems is not little; and, Go big fat book out into the world and impose upon strangers like a loose elephant, lacks appeal. An introduction could be an apologia, but how redundant when the poems already coax, lecture, lull, seduce, exhort, denounce. As a poet I am bound to the attempt to capture in amber the mayflies of the moment and render them into the only jewels I have to give you. I guess I will settle for saying what I imagine I am doing.

Usually the voice of the poems is mine. Rarely I speak through a mask or persona. The experiences, however, are not always mine, and although my major impulse to autobiography has played itself out in poems rather than novels, I have never made a distinction in working up my own experience and other people's. When I am writing, I'm not aware of the difference, to be honest. I suppose that is why I have never considered myself a confessional poet. In either case I am often pushing the experience beyond realism.

I imagine that I speak for a constituency, living and dead, and that I give utterance to energy, experience, insight,

From *Circles on the Water: Selected Poems of Marge Piercy* (Alfred Knopf, New York, 1982).

words flowing from many lives. I have always desired that my poems work for others. "To be of use" is the title of one of my favorite poems and one of my best-known books—now out of print as a result of the Thor decision by the IRS to tax publisher's backlists.

What I mean by being of use is not that the poems function as agitprop or are didactic, although some of them are. I have no more hesitation than Pope or Hesiod did to write in that mode as well as in many others. The notion that poetry with a conscious rather than an unconscious politics is impermissible or impure is a modern heresy of advantage only to those who like just fine the way things are going. We are social animals and we live with and off and on each other. You would have had great trouble explaining to Sophocles, Virgil, Catullus, Chaucer, Dryden, Wordsworth, Shelley, Arnold, Whitman, Blake, Goethe that poetry refers only to other poetry and that poets are strange and special people who have no social connections, social interests, social duties.

What I mean by useful is simply that readers will find poems that speak to and for them, will take those poems into their lives and say them to each other and put them up on the bathroom wall and remember bits and pieces of them in stressful or quiet moments. That the poems may give voice to something in the experience of a life has been my intention. To find ourselves spoken for in art gives dignity to our pain, our anger, our lust, our losses. We can hear what we hope for and what we most fear, in the small release of cadenced utterance. We have few rituals that function for us in the ordinary chaos of our lives.

Although I love the work of many other poets and am always reading it and being moved by it and seeing new kinds of poems to write and new openings through the work of others, although I criticize poetry, I am not a poet who writes primarily for the approval or attention of other poets. When they like my work, I am very pleased, but poets are not my primary constituency. Poetry is too important to keep to ourselves. One of the oldest habits of our species, poetry is powerful in aligning the psyche. A poem can momentarily integrate the different kinds of knowing of our different and often warring levels of brain, from the reptilian part that recognizes rhythms and responds to them up through the mammalian centers of the emotions, from symbolic knowing as in dreams to analytical thinking, through rhythms and sound and imagery as well as overt meaning. A poem can momentarily heal not only the alienation of thought and feeling Eliot discussed, but can fuse the different kinds of knowing and for at least some instants weld mind back into body seamlessly.

Knopf has published my last three volumes of poetry. My editor, Nancy Nicholas, is extremely understanding about what I try to do with each collection. Each book is an artifact and the poems in it are placed in a particular order to work as a whole as well as individually. I may love a poem and judge it excellent and yet hold it out of book after book until at last it finds its appropriate niche. However, Nancy said to me, establish your canon thus far with this book. That I cannot do. I have left out poems I know are favorites of readers and of critics and poems I respect as well as any here. I have merely tried to select an appropriate number of poems from each volume with some kind of balance of the various sorts I have written.

I have made minor changes in some and a very few I have substantially altered. The minor changes are mostly an image, a line, a redundancy of which I have become aware over the years of saying these poems to audiences. Occasionally I am correcting an old typo that had corrupted the written text.

The poems I have rewritten are those, generally early ones, where I fudged. One poem, "Bronchitis on the 14th floor," I changed for publication into a monogamous poem. It was about the sense of being taken care of by three men while I was sick—the basic imagery of them as large strong animals (bears, horses pulling a troika) while I was extremely and vulnerably ill. I had always felt the poem under the printed poem, and suspected that the official version was weakened by being rendered conventionally.

With "Breaking camp" for instance, the prevailing patriarchal mode encouraged me to write a dishonest poem. Basically it intended to be a sursum corda of sorts, written at a time I was becoming more and more involved in SDS and the antiwar movement and we were moving from protest to resistance. I wrote the poem with the male being the leader because that was how it was supposed to be. I was basically arguing we had to live differently and be prepared to take more risks, but I cast it as if I was giving in to my husband's insistence. Without that paraphrenalia of imitation compliance, the poem is shorter, cleaner, more powerful. A kind of coyness enforced by rigid sex roles used to hurt women's work, and that poem was one of the places in my output I find it.

Except for some apprentice and overly literary work in *Breaking Camp*, my work is of a piece. I can do more and try more, but the voice is the same voice. If there is a change of substance, I would say it followed upon my moving from New York to Wellfleet after having lived in the center of cities my whole life. I moved because of bad health, so I could go on breathing, but settling here had unexpected results for me.

I live here in Wellfleet in many ways like a peasant—a middle peasant—on a couple of acres where we grow all our own vegetables and some fruit, and freeze, dry, pickle, can, rootcellar the surplus for the whole year. I fell in love with the land, in its fragility and fruitfulness, and I fell in love with this landscape. There is something of Michigan here that connects with early childhood visits in the car out from Detroit into heaven, whether heaven was two weeks in a rented cottage on a muddy lake with a rowboat, or Sundays at Lucy and Lon's tenant farm where they would kill a chicken for us to take back as our big treat.

But the ocean, the salt and fresh water marshes, the sky and the light fascinate me too. I have sunk roots and I am only really happy when I am here. I know the city—it is bred into me and for thirty-six years I knew nothing else summer and winter. Most of the year I spend a couple of days every week in Boston. Living in Wellfleet, I have learned a whole new language of the natural world that I am part of, and that has changed and enriched my work.

I have readers who love my poems about the Cape, about zucchini and lettuce and tomatoes, and simply skip or tune out the poems about an old working-class woman lying in a nursing home or about nuclear power. Then I have readers who love the poems they call feminist or political, but ask me why I write about blue heron and oak trees.

I have to confess for me it is all one vision. There are occasional poems where I try to tie it all together like "A gift of light." "The Lunar Cycle" does that on another, less individual, more complex level. (Again I have made a major attempt in the "Elementary Odes" section of *Stone, Paper, Knife*, since the publication of this particular collection.)

I have included poems in this volume in a very long line, in a very short line, in a line that hovers around iambic pentameter or tetrameter, in verse paragraphs, in undifferentiated columns, in stanzas. I haven't put any rhymed poems into this collection, although once in a great while, I do work in rhyme. If I rhyme, I mostly do so in the center of lines rather than on the end, where to my ear it sticks out and chimes.

Since every time I put together a collection, I leave out as much as I put in, this is very much a selection of a small piece of a number of selections. I apologize if your favorite poem is not here. Some of mine are also missing.

Interview with Karla Hammond

A sunny early afternoon in September. Wellfleet, Massachusetts. Marge Piercy, dressed in a brightly colored peasant dress, welcomes me into her house. Set high above the road, her house is surrounded by scrub grass, flowers and pine. In some respects it is a typical Cape setting. In other ways, the house expresses a certain modernity (split level) and the taste and charm of its inhabitants. Books and literary magazines abound. There is an air of industry. While Marge and I conduct our interview upstairs in the living room Jackie, Marge's close friend and secretary, types and answers the telephone downstairs in the office. There is, as well, a sense of ease and the interview progresses smoothly and uninterrupted. Before long there is laughter and smiles. Marge Piercy is a warm, animated, attractive woman who speaks with the candor and honesty her work manifests. When the question of the relationship between life and art arises, she responds quickly: "Poems are poems. I think a confusion between life and art does courtesy to neither of them. I have enormous respect for the richness and unknowableness and variousness and orneriness of living and great respect for the richness and clarity and beauty of art. I think they're very different!" This consciousness—a sharp and lively sensibility—where life and art are concerned made for a memorable conversation.

First published in *Pulp* 4, no. 1 (1978).

In a review of Carol Muske's Camouflage *and Carolyn Forche's* Gathering the Tribes, *Wendy Knox remarks: "Poets deal with their lives. It's not so much the forms that are revolutionary, as the revelation of the thoughts, emotions, concerns, and mythologies drawn from a world formerly repressed or ignored" ("Relatedness and Ritual"* Moons and Lions Tales *2, No. 2 [1976]). Would you agree?*

Yes, that's what I was talking about: the buried lives. I have the sense that there are many lives that articulate themselves through me—lives that have not been articulated in fiction or poetry. This is from people who are thought to be inarticulate! I'm probably the first woman in my family in two thousand years who has been able to do anything more than try to survive or try to have her children survive.

Do you have a sense of creating a personal mythology in writing?

A personal mythology? No. Very consciously, I want to communicate. Very consciously, I want my poems to flow from other people's experiences as well as mine and to flow back to other people's experiences as well as mine. You have to be able to relate to a poem in the same sense that if I carve a chair and want to call it a chair, you have to be able to sit in it. No. The poems that I write are not for myself. I don't need them after I've written them. They're for other people.

Do you think of writing as a means of exorcism?

No. I think of it as a means of working in an art. It's a means of creating artifacts which are not me, which are real, which go out in the world, which lead their own life in the world, which other people can use, which other people can relate to and will relate to if they are true. In this context, they experience the artifacts in a way which is moving and believable to them and which frequently has nothing whatsoever to do with rational behavior because poetry is a type of knowing which is only partly rational. Knowing has to do with the grids you set down in reality—the set of grids with which you interpret reality. These grids are your own philosophical presuppositions, your own politics, your relationship with your own work. You can't always take over somebody else's because theirs come from a different place frequently. The language which poets use to speak about their own work is not always readily applicable to somebody else's body of work because they may have a totally different experience, a totally different vocabulary for talking about their work.

To me it is not a question of exorcism. I have a fairly pragmatic turn of mind. I would probably write poems in any circumstances. I certainly would not write novels if they couldn't get out somewhere because it's just too long a thing to do. You can't memorize a novel and go around saying it to people. So I'm dependent upon that particular corporate structure which works very badly for me. Still that is the only system of distribution now existing which gets to people who don't go into bookstores. I want to reach people who don't go into bookstores. So that means mass paperback is very important to me. I also want to reach people who do go into bookstores.

I don't confuse myself, however, with the things that I write. I'm here. They're there. Other people take them, use them, go off with them.

Poetry seems to me useful to people both in a public and a private sense. In a public sense, the communal rite, a poetry reading, can liberate a tremendous amount of energy. It's a way for women especially to touch images we most fear, what we most hope for, what we want to be. It is a means of re-experiencing pain in that it moves us from the individual problem to the shared issue. We are able to experience what we want to become. We are offered images of strength and beauty with which we can identify. This is especially important for women because we receive very little which heals us to what we are, very little which confirms the intuitions that we have. We can know things and know them again and again and always lose them if we don't have a framework in which to hold on to those intuitions, those flashes of knowing. Much of what feminism has done for me is to give me a framework in which I can hold on to the things which I knew at fifteen and forgot again at fifteen and a half.

Poems have many different kinds of knowing in them. It isn't just rational knowing although rational knowing is part of it, but also, in addition to the rational lobe in the brain, there is a lobe which moves through images. These are the images of dreams, the images of gestalt grasping. Poetry deals with both of those. It also deals with rhythms which we perceive from our old mammalian and reptilian brains. Poetry has to do with sensual memories, with evoking all of these different kinds of knowing. There are ways of knowing, we share with our cat or our dog, that are fully communicative types of knowing. They have nothing to do with words, but are as valid and as real.

Fiction has to do with the perception of patterns in living through time; whereas, poetry is in time like a dance is in time. Fiction, however, is about time. Time is one of the things with which fiction deals in the telling of a tale. It's "and then and then and then," "what happened next, what happened after that and then what?" "What happens if you do A rather than B?" "What happens if you marry John or Tom or John instead of Tom?" "What happens if you marry both John and Tom?" "What happens if you marry neither of them, but go and live in the woods?" "What happens if you're kind to an old lady who you meet on the road?" "What happens if you run over your father, marry your mother?" "What happens if you build your house out of sand or out of bricks?" Fiction goes back to the very first perceptions of recurring and nonrecurring patterns in the world and in human life. The heart of fiction is telling. The heart of poetry is utterance.

My poetry evolves more directly out of my life and the lives of other people. Sometimes people write to me about certain poems assuming that the poem is about me when it isn't. I write poems about other people, too. The validity or the invalidity of the poems is not dependent on whether they're about me or not, but rather whether they're about you.

Would you agree that it's impossible to write a purely autobiographical poem because memory fictionalizes?

I don't quite know what you mean. There are obviously autobiographical poems. *What* are you assuming that memory fictionalizes? That assumes that there's some real data there. If you mean people lie, certainly people lie; but, whether they lie or not is rather irrelevant to the virtues of poems unless they lie in ways that have to do with being honest or dishonest. Most lying is social lying or is simplifying. If people lie to protect themselves—and much writing is self-serving in that sense—the poem or story does end up being less true, less emotionally true, less persuasively and artistically true. But that doesn't make sense to me because what doesn't fictionalize? The observers change what they observe. The design of the experiment predicts the results. Seeing organizes the data that the nerve endings collect. It is collected in a form unlike the way you see it. What happens is that you turn all the images upside down. The body organizes the incoming rush of sensations all of the time. You leave most of it out. Your nerve endings are reporting to you from the floor, from where your thigh is resting, from where your behind is resting, from the point of your elbow sticking into your thigh there. The fact that there are earrings in your ears, the fact that your glasses are resting on your nose, the fact that your clothes are resting on your body are all accounted for. If an ant began to walk up your leg suddenly those sensors, which have all along been reporting certain stimuli, would suddenly become very active in what they were reporting: because you would pay attention. You constantly organize what you think is important from what you're constantly being told. You accept and reject.

Marge, do you keep a journal or a notebook?

I keep neither a journal nor a notebook. I have a memory annex which serves my purposes. It uses edge-notched cards. Edge-notched cards are cards which have holes around the borders as opposed to machine punch cards which are punched through the body. The cards are sorted with knitting needles. I have a nice sophisticated system which I call the "General Practitioner." I once wrote a book about it, but it was never published. The system enables me to use the cards in terms of the way I think. The advantage of the system is that nothing is filed under one heading. It's not like a journal which relies on spatial location to find information. In fact, there are as many paths to the information or ideas or images on the cards as I require. There are single hole codes which are categories very commonly used like plot, character, image. There are two hole codes which correspond to topics that are of some frequency in my writing such as sex roles, love, class. Then there are the three hole codes of which there are a vast number. I use randomly generated codes from a computer. The machine runs the codes off and then I have them—the random numbers. This prevents having to go through in sequence. We make a number of false drops because the codes overlap. The card itself is divided into the subjects on the left hand margin and the body of the card and over on the back which holds, the information—the entry. I do it for bibliography. I do it when I'm writing a novel. I generate a great many cards. I use this system the way other people would use a journal. I find it much more useful because there are things I've learned about myself from needling the deck on certain categories over time. I've made observations of patterns in my life because it isn't spatially bound or time bound. It's organized as I think. I also use it for indexing things. I use separate decks for different purposes. It's a very nice system.

Is it usually one line or a cluster of images that start a poem?

Poems start in a great variety of ways. There are poems that come entire and that's that. Some of those are good and some of those are bad. There are poems that start with an idea and the problem is to figure out how to body forth that idea in a way that will work. There are poems that start from a specific observation. There are poems that start from a line. There are poems that start from an image or a cluster of images. There are poems that start from almost anything: a dream, an observation, a conversation, a reaction.

Writing in free verse, do you find it difficult to ascertain line breaks or to punctuate?

There's no such thing as free verse. I write in organic verse which is the predominant poetic form of our time. How do you know how to phrase a song? How do you know how to phrase music? If you have such a tin ear that you have to count to find the end of a line, then you're in trouble. The use of silences in a poem is as important as the use of sound. A line break is a small rest. A stanza break is a large one. There are a number of ways in which you can indicate the sound qualities of a poem when you set it on the page. All of these ways are instructions to the readers so that they can hear the poem.

Do you write a given poem over an extended period of time: Weeks, months, years—or within the confines of a morning, afternoon, evening?

As I started to say before, there are poems that simply come. Then there are poems that take twelve years to write. Some of the poems that come are very good and some of the poems that come are not so good. Some of the poems that take twelve years to write are very good and some of the poems that take twelve years to write never really get finished. The average poem is somewhere in between that. It goes through a number of revisions. I never think of any poem as done before I've read it at a public reading because that shakes down a poem. You really hear it then. Often I'll read a poem over a period of six months and revise it constantly. Every time I read it I'll listen to it until I shake it down, really shake it down so that it's solid. Then I'm done.

Do you ever revise published poems?

Almost always. When I'm putting a book together almost all of the poems in it have already been published. I re-write at least a third of them and some of them substantially. I regard magazine publication as a halfway house. Putting a book together is the time when I go over a poem and knock any stuffing out of it. I look at it with very hard eyes.

Then you would consider revision a creative process as opposed to a desperate process?

I don't see much difference between the first draft or the fourteenth draft. Sometimes you get desperate when a poem just won't come right. You diddle and diddle and diddle and diddle and diddle with it. I'm always trying to shape the artifact a little bit clearer, a little more radiantly, a little more into what I want it to be.

You've mentioned two manuscripts I believe. A poetry manuscript and a novel?

The novel is titled *The High Cost of Living*. It's set in Detroit. It's about three young people: a triangle. It's also about labeling. It's about the cost that attends moving from the traditional working class to the college-educated working class. It has to do with confusing morality and politics.

Would you like to speak about your new volume of poems?

The Twelve-Spoked Wheel Flashing is built on the rhythms of a year. In the past I've set my poetry off in neat categories. In *Living in the Open* the nature poems, about relationship to place, are all in one part; poems about human relationships are in another part, and then poems about politics and society are in a third part. Thematically, the different parts of the book fall into neat categories. In *To Be of Use* the first part deals with the evolution of a woman's political consciousness. The second part is the use of that consciousness: trying to return to the world after a zap experience. It centers on rebuilding ourselves after such an experience and the impact we can have in those circumstances. The third part is a political history of the New Left in the Tarot poems. The poetry explicates history through the cards. *Hard Loving* has the same divisions. In this volume there are the political poems, the poems of one particular matrix of people, and the poems of another relationship. Each set of poems are separated from another. Everything is set off in that way.

In *The Twelve-Spoked Wheel Flashing* I made everything more organic, more true to my own life experience. There are categories, but they don't come from the outside. I don't really perceive my political activities as being less personal than anything else. That's a label that society leads us to expect. Frequently my political fighting is within relationships. Sometimes it's external and sometimes I get support from those relationships. Sometimes I don't. In this book, everything is mixed together as it really happens in my life. What I decided to do here was to base it on the rhythms of a year. I took Winter, Spring, Summer, Fall, and the poems of the seasons tied into each other. In fact, they do ricochet off each other and they do interrelate. The four seasons are partly symbolic of the experience of moving from certain kinds of pain through other kinds of pain and through certain kinds of fruition to other kinds of fruition. I've set them up in the form of a wheel as the wheel of a year is. A year isn't a circle. It is a wheel, a rolling wheel.

I mean a year goes through a complete cycle, but it doesn't bring us back to the same place. I don't think of progress forward (in time) as linear. The journey forward is that of a wheel's turn where we cannot avoid recapitulation. Yet, we don't end up in the same place. We aren't turning in a vacuum. We go forward in this very organic repetitive movement. It has to do with the things that recur and the things that don't recur. So the book has the year structure and everything is knotted together inside this structure without being neatly sorted out. Such a structure has enabled me to place poems in juxtapositions that are more interesting than those of earlier books.

The structure of a book is tremendously important to me. A book is an artifact in itself. This may be one of the reasons for my continual revision: the poems have to fit the book as well. A book of poetry is not a collection. It's an entity and there are poems as good as those appearing in the book which I don't include because they don't belong there. It's important to me that a book has the proper shape and feel to it.

Marge, have you written any drama?

Yes. I wrote my first play this year with Ira Wood. It's called *The Last White Class.*

To return to poetry, in writing poems, do you have a sense throughout of recurring images?

When I become aware that I've used a line or an image I try to take it out. Sometimes I catch myself using the same thing again. Certainly there are categories of images that recur. There's a great deal of food imagery in my poems. There's a lot of Cape imagery, from this landscape.

What are ideal conditions for writing? Being here at home in Wellfleet?

Certainly, yes. I also work when I'm in Boston though. I've been spending two days a week in Boston since 1973. I can sometimes work on planes or in airports. It depends. I can always go over things. I can edit. I can revise. I wrote part of the final draft of a novel while I was in a motel in Buffalo this summer. But I work best in Wellfleet, in my house here.

You've mentioned writing political poems and I assume this is related to feminism. When I interviewed Lisel Mueller she mentioned that she felt the term "feminist" had become a catchword—ambiguous in meaning. I wonder if you'd define it for me as it finds expression in your work and in your life?

"Feminism" is one particular branch of radical thinking: the other two being anarchism and communism-socialism. All of these I relate to and all of these are important to me. "Feminism" says that the first property was women and children, that the sexual contradictions are fundamental contradictions and antedate capitalism, that unless the sexual contradictions are dealt with and unless women achieve full equality, we cannot have a good society. This cannot be done secondarily, but must be incorporated in any political struggle from the beginning. Feminism also has developed a sound respect for ourselves as part of nature, not its masters.

When Auden was asked if poets should be engaged in "social or philosophical or political issues," he agreed but added that he didn't feel "that writing poems will change anything." Would you agree?

I think that poets have the same social duties as any other human being—that you are part of a society, that you use up resources. If you're American you use up a hell of a lot of resources. You have the same obligations, responsibilities, you're part of the same economic web, as everybody else in the society. Artistic production is true production so anyone who is engaged in it is putting things back, but they are not excused from having to pay attention to everything else that as a human being they should pay attention to. Now you have to differentiate the impact factor into two parts. As a political person, whether you have impact or not largely depends on where you apply yourself, how much you're willing to apply yourself, how much energy you've put into whatever you're engaged in. Much of my time has been spend in political activism. I think that I have a pretty good sense of what you can get done that way. To me it's very important to fight. I also have an impact through my writing. Books do influence people. Very obviously they introduce new ideas, they introduce concepts, they popularize concepts, they influence how people think about themselves. Much of what people think about relationships is popular mythology—relationships between the sexes, between the classes in the society. They're affected by what they see on television as well as what they read in books.

Then social comment would really be part of that construct— what ends poetry serves or makes possible?

People tend to define "political" or "polemical" in terms of what is not congruent with their ideas. In other words, your typical white affluent male reviewer does not review a novel by Norman Mailer as if it were political the same way he would review a novel by Kate Millet. Yet, both are equally political. The defense of the status quo is as political as an attack on it. A novel which makes assumptions about men and women is just as political if they're patriarchal assumptions as if they're feminist assumptions. Both have a political dimension. Both have to do with who wins and who loses, who gets what piece of the pie, who gets to survive and who doesn't, who gets rewarded, who gets punished, who goes to jail, who goes to mental institutions, who goes to the White House.

In an interview Olga Broumas had with the Willamette Valley Observer *she remarked: "My feeling, . . . is that language has been used to keep us out. Men have made and published complex language, while women have been closed into the colloquial— speaking to their children. What I would like to do is make a complex language that does include women, rather than use the limited vocabulary which has been considered 'our place.' I think the more complex words you know, the more deeply you can understand experience." What is your feeling concerning this?*

You're asking me whether I think that the use of complex

words enables one to more deeply understand experience? No. Often the complex words are Latinate words and they're words that by their nature are less emotionally evocative and stirring. I don't like to censor any of the concerns that I have. I prefer richer poems which share the concerns. If there is a precise word, like the name of that little covering to the snail's shell "the operculum," then that's the name for it. Fine! I try to make clear what it is. I will use a precise word. On the other hand, I try to be careful with the number of Latinate words I use in my poetry. I want my poetry to be emotionally coherent. I think that you can carry a rather complicated freight of images in a poem if the poem is emotionally coherent and is always clear about how it's feeling, how it wants you to feel, and how it's moving. I certainly try to make my language as clear as possible. Sometimes that's fairly complex and sometimes it isn't. It's difficult to write poems in simple language. I do it fairly frequently and it's exceedingly difficult. I find that it's much easier to write a much richer language, but frequently the discipline of trying to write as clearly as possible, is part of the creation of the successful artifact. It's a process of paring down, and paring down, and paring down.

Do you think that women have been locked into the colloquial because of domestic concerns and their involvement with small children?

Well, the women who have been writing haven't by and large. So there's a little problem there. Women who have to take care of their own children are just beginning to do some proportion of the writing. That hasn't been characteristically who women writers have been up to the last five years. Mostly, women writers have either been people who could pay somebody else to take care of their children or who didn't have children. So I don't think that that relates particularly.

Perhaps it will have more validity as a question in ten or fifteen years?

Yes. I mean there are beginning to be more women like Alta who have children and write, or Tillie Olsen who came back to writing after having her children.

"The woman who needs to create works of art is born with a kind of psychic tension in her which drives her unmercifully to find a way to balance, to make herself whole. Every human being has this need: in the artist it is mandatory. Unable to fulfill it, he goes mad. But when the artist is a woman she fulfills it at the expense of herself as a woman" (Mrs. Stevens Hears the Mermaids Singing—May Sarton). *Would you agree?*

I respect May Sarton, but that's a silly statement. If you manage to make a living in the arts you do it at much less psychic cost than almost any other way. It's like a bad joke. You know, working in a factory you pay a psychic cost for making a living. Writing? No! No! Come on! That's a lot of bullshit. It's hard work and all that, but, boy, to be paid to write, that's ten times better than 99 percent of the ways people make a living in this society. If you put "secretary" in there, the statement would make more sense. I've worked as a secretary and there's an enormous psychic cost in being a secretary. I think that Jackie suffers in having to deal with me. I think that when you work for anybody else in that way it's always difficult. There's always a psychic cost. If you work in a traditional office situation, there's a great psychic cost involved. Being a cocktail waitress where men really give you a hard time. Much less psychic cost to being a writer. I mean you get to do what you want to do and if you're lucky you get paid for it.

Is prose, for you, a more effective means of documenting and authenticating female experience than poetry?

No, I guess that I don't think of it in that way. I assume a book like *Women Working* (edited by Rosalyn Boxandall, Linda Gordon, and Susan Reverby) does document female experience. That documents women's experiences over a hundred year period. It's a remarkably interesting collection of original articles. I've never done anything like that. The only kind of prose I tend to write besides fiction is reviews, kind of like "duty" work. I feel that it's important to do that, but it's like writing papers for school. I do it because I want to help. Sometimes I want to attack; but, mostly—99 percent of the time—I want to call attention to the work a woman has done.

Do you find that you're asked to review women's work more frequently than men's?

I choose to do that. Sometimes when I'm asked to review a man's work, I know the work is going to get reviewed and that it will get a sympathetic hearing. There isn't really a problem. Once in a while when I think that there is a problem, then I get interested. I feel that we're in a very different situation with women's work. There's so much women's work that doesn't get reviewed at all. It's being squashed again and fought back on in these enormous reprisals against women. Reviewing is something that I just have to do. As I said, it's "duty" work, like taking out the garbage or going to town and getting the groceries or doing the laundry. It's that type of thing—something that you must do so that life goes on for other people as well as for yourself. Therefore, I try to pick and choose what I think needs help, that I feel good about giving. I have to choose because I don't have very much time.

What are your feelings about teaching?

In the last fifteen years I've only taught twice at universities and I don't particularly like it. I wouldn't say that I'd never do it again because if I go broke, of course, I'll do it again. It's one means of supporting yourself if you run out of money. Teaching doesn't combine well with my writing and it isn't something that I particularly enjoy doing. I don't like being away from home and the people with whom I live. I don't like being away from my own life that long. I travel frequently giving readings. Readings are very important to me. I'm a performer. I take that seriously. I'm a very good performer. I want to turn people on to poetry, to move them, to make it a very energizing experience for them.

I like workshop situations, like the Bloomington's Writers' Conference. I was at Purdue, recently, for a week working with gifted high school students. In both of those cases you're there for a week, eight days, in a very intense situation. I believe that I can help in those situations. I can give a lot, teach a lot, just try to be very open to what people are trying to do and show them how to do it. Then I get to go home and be fed myself. So that works out very well. I don't really like to be away from home for longer than a week. Three weeks seems about the maximum that I can go without starting to feel in exile.

So the same would be true when you are on poetry circuits, for example?

I don't do poetry circuits, no. I learned not to do that. It's really deadly. I'll do up to three readings, but no more than that before I go home again. You don't know where you are. You don't know who you are. You don't know what you're doing. You don't know to whom you're talking. You get numb.

When I interviewed Maura Stanton, she stressed character and discipline being more important than talent. In concluding, what's your response to this?

Well, talent is always a judgment after the fact. People show talent by writing well. So I don't see how you can particularly separate them out. I think that the kind of very early maturing talent that often gets admired in schools doesn't mean anything. Often people who are good writers write rather dreadfully when they're younger, but they write a lot. Perhaps, in some sense, that's what she's saying. If you're looking at student writing, sometimes the willingness to try things that can't be pulled off is more important than the attitude of the student who learns to do something rather well early and keeps repeating that. That's a bad sign. Anyone who doesn't have to write—isn't really driven to write—isn't going to stay at it because it takes so long to get established as a writer now and the rewards are minimal for a long time. So if you don't absolutely have to do it, if you can derive satisfaction some other way and it's not the writing itself that you have to do, likely you'll stop writing or only do it as a Sunday painter. This is fine. I like all that amateur substratum in the arts. I think that a society in which a whole lot of people sing is a society that really understands a great singer. I think that a society in which a lot of people play musical instruments is the one that appreciates what a virtuoso is. A society in which a great number of people write poems for each other—with perfect assurance that what they're doing is nice—is also the one in which people appreciate writing!

Shaping Our Choices

An Interview with Richard Jackson

Let's begin by talking about the problematics of language. In your poem, "Lies," you say: "I give too much importance to words / and my words define me. / I am always becoming words / that walk off as strangers." And there are a number of other poems where the possible duplicity of language is encountered. In "Some collisions bring luck" the relationship seems in trouble at one point because "We coalesced in the false chemistry of words / rather than truly touching." And in "Doing it differently" you have the lines: "a mistrust of the rhetoric of tenderness / thickens your tongue." Perhaps we could talk about your consciousness of the difficulties of saying things right in language, and of the poet's role in this context.

I think that probably anyone who works with language is very conscious of the state of it. In one poem I say: "Words live, words die in the mouths of everybody." We all make language; we all use language, and we live in a society in which the language is constantly debased by the power system that attempts to control us and by the commercial uses to which it is put. Now in a lot of poems I'm not talking about the deliberate debasing of language, as in the lies a government will tell, but about more specific and everyday experiences—the false chemistry of words, the social lies people say when they think they agree but don't. These are personal

---

First published in *Poetry Miscellany*, no. 10 (1980).

relationships where the other person fails to recognize conflicting wishes, wills, and so forth. Sometimes people just aren't aware of what this or that word or expression might mean to someone else. The more the language becomes debased generally, the tougher all these problems become.

As a writer I entrust my life's work to language. It is my tool, and as with any tool you have to be constantly aware where it fails you, and where you fail it. This doesn't mean that the poet should "purify" the language as some people suggest. There's been an argument going on in poetry for a couple of hundred years at least between those poets who want to refine the language of poetry, take it out of the daily ferment it undergoes, take it towards a level of greater artifice, and the poets, with whom I would align myself, that want to use the language of everyday in a heightened, intensified way. You can use the language of the everyday without using a debased language; it requires care and an awareness of how language works.

Some of your poems are written in a different voice such as "Postcard from the garden"— "I sit on a rock on the border and call and call / in voice of cricket and coyote, of fox and mouse, / in my voice rocks smash back on me. / The wings of the hawk beat overhead as he hovers, / baffled by waiting, on the warm reek of my flesh." In other poems, it's more of a modulation of voice, sometimes a metamorphic change of tone, that produces the great range which characterizes your best work.

Occasionally there are poems in a different voice or persona, but there are relatively few. There's "Another country" where the character goes down and swims with the dolphins, a fictional character. In terms of what we were just saying, the character says: "All conversation is a singing, / all telling alludes to and embodies / minute displacements." And there is a way in which voice provides a sense of range but I would talk about range more in the sense of subject matter, type of lens. For example, I write very imagistic poems; I write very lush poems; I write very simple, stark poems; I write with long lines, short lines, poems with stanzas, poems without stanzas.

Many of the poems are written in sections, and there will be shifts of the type you're talking about within a single poem. These poems have a more encompassing gesture, as do the various sequences you've written. The movement is described in a poem like "The perpetual migration" where you say, "We remember / backwards a little and sometimes forwards, / but mostly we think in the ebbing circles / a rock makes on the water." It puts you in the school of Whitman and Rukeyser. But there is also a poem like "Season of hard wind" which is much smaller, but is a kind of quest poem ranging from a phone to Antartica in its references.

Well, I'm not really conscious of that sort of encompassing gesture. In fact, I think of "Season of hard wind" as a very tight poem; I think I could argue why the images are appropriate to the poem. The telephone, for example, appears in several poems to represent the difficulty of communication. In other words, there is always an underlying argument and I try to censor out images that divert too much, that are too bizarre. On the other hand there are shifts in the poems—a longer poem, especially, might shift from comic to tragic, not to denigrate the emotions, but to show their complexity in these turns. These are shifts in tone; I associate them with some techniques in modern art. What is really important to me is that the poems have an emotional context.there should be a strong emotional coherence that can carry a lot of jumps of meaning and images. If there is not that emotional coherence, the poem will fall apart. Sometimes a poem will, in a sense, say more than I know, take me *past* what I know, expecially in a long sequence. The images take me to a different level, but the controlling emotion keeps it coherent.

I think of Susan Sontag who, in "Against Interpretation," wrote that what we need is an "erotics of art." She says: "Real art has the capacity to make us nervous. By reducing the work of art to its context and then interpreting that, one tames the work of art."

It's difficult to learn how poems work because of how they're taught in school. There's not enough emphasis on feeling and emotion. When I went to college at Michigan the emphasis was very much on criticism, as much at least as on the primary works. It seemed that the point of writing a poem was to fit it into a vast critical superstructure. Later, at another school, the approach I encountered was more biographical. It was refreshing to hear about someone's life because that seemed more human and poetry, after all, is a human activity. Perhaps the best thing a literature teacher could do is not teach interpretation. What you have to do is teach a passion for literature. Literature has to speak to you when you're in trouble or in pain, when you're happy. It gives you images of what you feel and what you want to feel, what you are and what you want to be, gives you strength and courage. People seem to need poems. There is a rise in amateurism. Many people, many who occasionally write poems know one book of poetry; they have one book of poetry which they read and it becomes their book of poetry which they'll wear out.

Tess Gallagher, in a recent issue of APR, *talks about "woman-time." She worries that women haven't written enough poems that are more open, longer, take more into account a woman's sense of rhythm. I think you do so in your longer poems and sequences which we talked about. "The Lunar Cycle," for example, does this. In "Cutting the grapes free" you say: "I do not seek to leap free from the wheel / of change but to dance in that turning." And in "Twelve-spoked wheel" you measure time by "the turn of the wheel" and say: "I have tried to forge my life whole, / round, integral as the earth spinning." Seasonal structures are important in* Twelve-Spoked Wheel *generally, and other poems. Could you sketch out your sense of the way you sense time?*

There are three kinds of time. The first is clock time, the everyday world of deadlines. The second involves being conscious of yourself in history, a political sense of time. For example, I am conscious of myself as a creature upon whom certain historical forces act. This is a sense of history as process, but it is a process which the individual can participate in and help create, in which you can affect other people. That is, you recreate the past and try to sense implications for the future. The third kind of time is a presence as opposed to this process. There's that poem, for example, where I am like my grandmother who's like my mother; there is a sense of continuity established here. This third kind involves cycles, too, and this perhaps relates to the way we were talking about how poems move, gather their images, talk about them, come back to them.

"Tumbling and with tangled mane" describes a kind of immersion in a physical, dynamic world, but also searches for moments of clarity. The world for the poem becomes "as in the eye of a hurricane / when the waves roll cascading in undiminshed / but for a moment and in that place the air / is still, the moment of clarity out / of time at the center of an act." These moments seem very important for your poetry, sometimes almost prophetic as in "September afternoon at four o'clock"—"In the perfect / moment the future coils, / a tree inside a pit." They are moments of stillness and recognition that give an act direction, that is, do not actually take it out of the flow of time.

I guess that what I would add is that there's no way of holding on to those moments. The perspective changes. Even though there's a sense of repetition and cycles, there's also a uniqueness and difference. And yet, unless you can apply the knowledge of that whole structure back into your life, then things will remain merely discreet, discontinuous. Feminism has provided such a structure for me, for it provides a way of holding on to and assimilating insights.

The moments bring into focus questions of will, perhaps. In "For Shoshana-Pat Swinton" you say: "No, I am not a soldier in your / history, I live in my own tale / with others I choose." In the introduction to "Laying Down the Tower" in To Be of Use *you talk about the need to break through the old roles to encounter our own meanings in the symbols we experience in dreams, in songs, in vision, in meditation." You go on to say that "The myths we imagine*

*we are living . . . shape our choices." The sequence attempts to
"reconcile" you to the various histories around you, including the
women's movement.*

Yes, that's one of a series of poems in which I've been con-
cerned about the nature of choice, what it means as a woman
to be able to choose. These are difficult issues today in
general, and especially for women on a political and social
level. Feminism provides a point of view through which to
understand problems, but I wouldn't say everything should
be reduced to that. Racism is very real; the class struggle is
very real. Feminism involves a strong sense of history, a
strong sense of ourselves in nature, in natural cycles, and a
sense of responsibility to each other whenever we need aid.

*The question of political and sociological poetry is arising once
again and its defenders have become more articulate and their
poetry better perhaps than a few years ago. I'm thinking of Philip
Levine and Ai in particular. And yet there really aren't that many
good political poets today. This, of course, is an important dimension
of your own poetry, say the poem about radiation in* The Moon Is
Always Female *or the poems against the military establishment in*
Hard Loving. *I think, too, of "Heavy as in being squashed" where
you combat "The vast incomprehensible / inertia of what is" which
summarizes a stance against injustices.*

First of all, on a personal level, we are all social beings. There
are social dimensions to poetry, political dimensions, as well
as all the other rational and irrational meanings and struc-
tures that poetry, like any human activity, participates in. It is
as absurd, though, to reduce poems to political statements as
it is to deny they have a political dimension. Any attempt to
reduce poetry to one thing is always doomed to fail. Poets in
the past have always understood this; poets like Chaucer,
Pope, Dryden, Byron, Shelley, and Wordsworth understood
it. But there is an attitude that has developed since about the
1890s that attempts to cast all politics and sociology out of
poetry. I don't understand how anyone can seriously main-

tain this attitude. Actually, the attitude is itself political. Art which embodies the ideals of the ruling class in society isn't conceived of as being political, and is simply judged by how well it is done. Art which contains ideas which threaten the position of that ruling class is silenced by critics: it is political, they say, and not art. This is what happens, for example, to feminist poetry. It's absurd.

Midgame

Making It Better, Truer, Clearer, More Gorgeous

Many decisions about a poem are made unconsciously, but each of these can be hauled into consciousness. If a poem is not coming out right, if it is stuck or if it is written through one or ten drafts and still not right, one remedy is to retrace decisions and reconsider them.

In poetry workshops, I standardly use an exercise where I destroy some quite nice poems by turning long line poems into short line poems and vice versa. I ask workshop participants to write the "same poem" in long and short lines: to start with the same impulse and work in long lines and work in short lines. I have them look at the results and with each pair of poems, decide together which works better. I ask them to fiddle around with poems so that the choice of line length can become conscious, if necessary, and if wrongly made, be corrected.

Similarly the choice of whether to write a poem that stands as a column of words, is broken into verse paragraphs, or is built in stanzas is another of those conscious/unconscious choices I sometimes make in first draft and sometimes change my mind about further down the line. If you do find yourself working in stanzas or decide to work in stanzas, that does not say whether you pick two line, three line, four line, five, six, seven, eight, nine or ten line stanzas—all quite common—or whether you use a mixture of stanza lengths. In "The perpetual migration" I alternate six and seven line stanzas. In "May apple", from the same *The Lunar Cycle*, I alternate four and five line stanzas.

I have spent some time trying to figure out why I work in verse paragraphs or a single column of words or in regular stanzas, but I cannot say I have come to much in the way of stateable conclusions. Sometimes a poem shapes itself roughly into a statement and response form, alternating voices, thrust and parry, wish and reality; some dichotomy that the form can embody. Sometimes when I am pushing hard through powerful material that frightens, disgusts, threatens me, I find I work best in regular stanzas, as I did in the poem to/about my mother "Crescent moon like a canoe." It became apparent very early in the attempt to start that poem, which had lain in me for years without my doing more than accumulating imagery toward the desire to write it, that it was going to be in stanzas. I had written a bit of it before I realized that I didn't like the stanza length I was using and wanted shorter stanzas. The five-fingered line for the birth month poem was right.

On the other hand "At the well," the poem for the hinge of the year, the month of Beth, the poem which is also the hinge of *The Lunar Cycle*, is written in verse paragraphs, corresponding to the action and to the speakers. The poem has two speakers, the angel and the old woman. It is a vision poem, and I find those kind generally resist stanzas.

I have been looking at *The Lunar Cycle* and trying to understand why I wrote some of the poems in strict stanzas and some in verse paragraphs. I can only say that it is an integral decision to the rhythm and shape of the poem. "Shadows of the burning," a highly rhetorical poem—in the sense of calling upon many rhetorical effects—has a flow I wanted to push rather than slow. On the other hand "Cutting the grapes free" turns on the basic equation of blood is to grape as poetry is to wine, or blood is to poetry as grape is to wine, and each stanza is a new take, a new shot.

Sometimes when I have had trouble with a poem, I find that taking it into stanzas will force me to be terser and more epigrammatic. "Of hidden taxes" was a poem that stayed flaccid until I decided on a seven line stanza. That got rid of the excessive talkiness. On the other hand I remember that "Walking into love" started in stanzas and simply would not move. It wouldn't walk anyplace but felt too tight, too constipated. To encounter the emotions I was tyring to deal with (an older woman succumbing to the pursuit of a younger man; two people who are both lovers and political organizers trying to work out those commitments together; a relationship that was not my marriage but just as serious and very strong) I had to loosen the line, loosen the stanza structure.

Thus, sometimes I find I go into stanzas to deal with rough material emotionally and sometimes I have to loosen up the structure to deal with equally tough sources. You play it by ear, finally. The important thing is if you have guessed wrong, that you be ready to change.

Breaking the line and breaking the poem into clumps that end-stop or leaving it run-on are supple means of enforcing rhythms or undermining them, lightening the pace, moving the poem faster or slower, giving emphasis. Like Denise Levertov, I believe strongly in organic form, in finding the right shape, the right measure, the right form for a particular poem.

I recently had the experience of reading a column about my poetry, largely praising it. However, the author, Judson Jerome, thought I just didn't understand how to write and he proceeded to rewrite some of my lines into da-*dum* da-*dum* da-*dum* iambic pentameter. When I read what he had done to my lines, a sort of absolute rage took me. The hard thing is, he meant well. He actually thought in messing those lines up he was making them nice. He certainly was making them regular. In an exchange of letters after the fact, he asked me what I am doing poetically.

Mostly I like nonrepetitive rhythms. I may have a poem that hovers around trimeter, hexameter, or I may have a much more irregular rhythm going. I find a regular repetitive rhythm soporiphic. Marilyn Hacker can work in repetitive meters extremely conversationally and so can Robert Penn Warren, but with most contemporary metric writers I can hear the metronome ticking gracelessly, the rocking horse rhythm thumping. One of the aspects of craft I admire most is phrasing, knowing where to break the line, the use of the line in harmony or counterpoint with the rhythms of spoken American.

I tend to be aware of how many accented syllables are in a line whether or not I am working in a relatively regular meter, and also aware of the proportion of unaccented to accented syllables and whether the line is ending on an accented or an unaccented syllable or word. I do not choose to do one or the other because of a scheme that stands aside from the poem, but because of the poem itself, the sound bearing up the meaning, everything working for the effect and affect the poem means to create. I don't want to pour the poem into a mold but to create a form that grows from the inside of the poem like a skeleton.

Denise Levertov on organic form always made a lot of sense to me. Like her, I find analogies between dance and poetry useful. The artists in the previous two generations at least of my mother's family were dancers, and I've always felt close to dance, as if that would have been a possible choice with another upbringing. When I am working, sometimes I have a sense of the poem carving itself on space like a dance, one step at a time, one gesture at a time.

But all analogies between the different and separate arts are only that; even the different uses you can make of words in writing poetry or fiction or drama feel extraordinarily different in their intent and their requirements. There's nothing like actually working with a dancer or a musician to make you realize how distinct are the problems of the different arts.

Breaking the line is something I expect still to be learning about when I am ninety, if I live that long. I cannot imagine ever feeling I have learned more than a little of what is to be done with line breaks. For me breaks indicate a little pause, not so large as a period or a stanza break, but a pause. Sometimes the line break marks a silence, a little catch for instance in the middle of a word so that instead of reading "battlement" you would hear it "battle . . . ment" if you broke the line

> standing on the wind blasted broken battle-
> ment over the skulls of sheep in the grass

I suppose line breaks are an aspect of a poem I fiddle with the most when I am revising or polishing, along with the words themselves.

Sometimes, as in the poem I mentioned "At the well," the poem came out first in long lines, and it wasn't working. Actually I made two changes that saved that poem, but that's the only one relevant here. It wasn't until I began working with a shorter line, one hovering near tetrameter rather than pentameter or hexameter, that the poem began to gather its energy. It had a tendency to come with too much wordiness in the longer line allowing the angel and the old woman to lecture each other. They justified too much in the longer line. They had to be reined in, shut up in a shorter line and made to be sententious.

Revision is also the point where you draw back, look at your repetitions, and decide if they are incremental or detrimental. That's the opportunity to find you used the word "love" six times in a poem or "palimpsest" twice. A common word can usually bear more repetition than an exotic. You find then that you have too many "like"s and turn some of them from simile into metaphor. You do a yard clean-up, clearing out the debris of the poem, the first two lines that belong to some other poem. They got you started but now they're irrelevant. You pull out the too-gross metaphor, the too-trite one, the decorative touches that impede the pace, or you work to enrich some bleak lines. You put in, you take out, you change. You look critically at your verbs and find too many forms of "to be" and too few verbs doing work for you. You take the blander, duller verbs and gear them up. You knock out modifiers. You prune some of the little dead words and phrases.

For me part of the revision process is reciting the poem to an audience. I find nothing shakes a poem down as hard.

That's when I hear the patches that can still be cut; and most importantly I hear where my nerve failed me or my inventiveness or my inner ear. These are parts of the poem that are not there yet, that I must push harder to get right. Extra words that my eye will glide over stand out when I recite the poem. This is odd because writing for the eye is often extremely compressed to the point where it doesn't play aloud at all—the signs are pure ideogram and you are not supposed to hear the sounds. When you write for recital, you must be aware of rhythms and you are more apt to use (although you may entirely eschew) oral devices such as refrains, incremental repetition, answer and response, oral forms like the litany. Often your poem will be less compressed than the poem for the eye. At the same time, extra words do stand out when you recite a poem, those mouthfuls of unaccented syllables that can make the line tumble out sounding like a pearl necklace broken, scattering.

In the intermediate drafts too you usually decide whether to tighten or loosen the rhythm of a poem. That has to depend on your ear and on the requirements of the individual work. I do not generally like a regular meter. Although I've worked in regular meters and think some apprenticeship in their use has to be part of the education of poets, I tire of them easily, especially when combined with rhyme. A couple of times a year I'll have an idea that seems to me to require rhyme (like the sonnet "A kid on her way" or the prayer "On New Year's Day"), but normally I avoid it. If I use it at all, it tends to be in the middle of lines and not at the ends.

I pay attention to vowels and consonants and sound qualities to the point of sometimes being so enamored by the sonorous music of the line that I will notice suddenly I have written nonsense. Then I go back and clean up my act. But it happens. Mostly however I try to notice what I'm saying or not saying, notice the implications and mental resonances as well as resonances for the ear.

What happens to me with rhyme is that I go on automatic pilot and can churn out a kind of literary mush by the yard.

Something about rhyme seems to inhibit me from pushing myself hard, from going deep, from seizing the image or metaphor that is harsh and exact, that compels me into new territory. The flow I get to in regular meter and in rhyme is a flow exclusively from the verbal lobe of the brain—it is all words, in short, with the imagery used merely decoratively. I am not suggesting all poets have this problem. I know from reading Maxine Kumin's essays that rhyme seems to free her imagination, whereas it stifles mine.

I mentioned that one of the virtues of reciting a poem in public is locating failures of nerve. We all have many inner and outer censors, but here I am concerned with the censors inside. They may be conscious. You may write something and then think, whoa! That isn't necessarily bad. If the checks you put on what you have just written are whether you really mean what you are saying and implying, or whether you are simply repeating something received that you don't stand behind (such as equating in imagery or content good with white and bad with black), then that self-checking can be healthy for your work.

But often what inhibits us is fear of what others around us may say or may feel about what we have written. Such fears may affect us after we have written the poem, so that we will change the pronouns in a poem from "she" to "he" to make the poem apparently heterosexual rather than lesbian in its reference. As Louise Bernikow points out in *The World Split Open*, editors frequently made those changes in women's poems—to protect them, we are told.

In the essay "Introduction to My Selected Poems," included in this volume, I discuss two cases where patriarchal imperatives got in my way. In one case I changed those mentioned in a poem from three men to one man, when I was putting it in the collection *Hard Loving*. In the other case, the patriarchal assumption that it is the man, the husband, who leads undermined the poem and made me coy when I was trying to be bold.

In a third case, I wrote "At the well" through all the early versions with a male protagonist—because it is traditionally

Jacob, not Rachel, who wrestles the angel, even though in my own experience it was me. I had put that poem aside for eighteen years. When I began itching for it again, the poem I wrote was more honest and even though it is written with a persona, it is a female persona. As it was. I remember seeing poems written by women (and essays) in which they go on, The Poet, He. I can remember a sequence some years ago by Nancy Willard in which the Poet had a wife—but she was the poet and she had a husband, not a wife—rather a different matter.

I remember seeing a poem that a young man in a poetry workshop wrote that was revised from tenderness to pornography, because he was afraid to express publicly the love he felt for a woman; having to present the poem in workshop to an audience that included several other men was, I think, a factor in the evolution of the poem toward tits and ass.

Women have been trained to deny our anger, and when it emerges in a poem, often we are ashamed. Poems are never total statements. In one day you can write two equally truthful poems of complete hostility and overwhelming love for one person. Sometimes if you can express the anger, you can better express the love.

Shame gets in creation's way. We all have notions of what we should be. A writer had better have considerable tolerance for the gap between what we would like to be and what we are in a daily way; at the same time, I think it helps to have experience of how extraordinary people can be in situations that stretch them utterly. Sometimes we are ashamed of what moves us or how much we are moved; sometimes we feel we ought to have been moved and we try to pretend. Women don't only fake orgasms; people have faked orgiastic appreciation of many things that bored them, from the Grand Canyon to Rembrandt.

I see an awful lot of poems in quarterlies that prefer boredom to risk. Writing a well-wrought poem of careful irony and shades of alienated indifference or mild self-pity comes as easily now as rimed quatrains about meadowlarks and nightingales to an earlier generation who looked out the window and like us, saw pigeons. They thought night-ingales were poetic; every age has subjects it thinks nifty which turns out to be the cliches that succeeding generations prefer to forget.

Oftentimes when I am dealing with something that makes me nervous, I have the sensation of pushing myself off a cliff. Once again I think total absorption in the process and the product inhibits shame. There is a sense I have of forcing myself open. Sometimes I am not prepared to take that risk yet and must let the poem wait till I am psyched up to march onto whatever particular quaking ground I am contemplating. I am familiar too with the sense of not being able to resist a subject I know may get me into trouble, but the idea is just too good. I can't keep my mind from playing around with it till I'm hooked. I'm working on it before I've agreed to let myself do it. Then I lull myself by thinking I'll just run it through a bit and see how it goes. I can't really proceed with it; I won't send it out anyplace. It's just a lark. But I secretly and simultaneously know better. That's a propaganda technique for turning off my fear of consequences.

I think some poets who have the habit of writing drunk or stoned may be turning off that inner censor, but I can't work other than clear. The censor says, You can't say that, it will hurt your mother/father/brother/sister/husband/wife/lover/child/ friend. The censor says, Write that and you'll lose that promotion or even your job. Or you'll lose custody of your kids. The censor says, What will your comrades say about that one? Is that politically correct according to the Slogan-of-the-Month Club? The censor says, Are you going to admit that in public? Nobody will want to sleep with you. Nobody will like you any more. They'll laugh at you behind your back. The censor says, That sounds crazy.

The poem in which you are finding out what you mean as you go may lead you to an insight that you might have preferred to forego. I have in fact figured things out in poems that I then had to apply to my life, to act on. I have more than once, for instance, found out how reprehensible I thought something a friend had done when I finished a poem I realized was about them. I could refuse to be judgmental in my daily self, but underneath, acquiescence was poisonous. I have discovered the same thing about myself, that something I have done that I felt good about had turned sour in me and I regretted it or felt guilty, and had not let myself know. Partway through such a poetic process, you may find yourself suddenly blocked, suddenly weary, desirous of doing anything else whatsoever: the laundry, balancing your checkbook, taking a swim, calling your mother. That is one of the times you must flog yourself forward if you want to get the poem.

And I guess I think you have to get the hard poems. You have to pay your dues by writing the ones that cost the most. I think the others get better then, but that may be superstition.

I noticed recently that when I was an unpublished or largely unpublished writer, I had certain correspondences with friends in the same predicament that were entirely or almost entirely about writing. I was recently given the letters I had written to a friend in my twenties, a period in which I married a French physicist, the marriage endured a bit and turned bad. I was divorced. I took an M.A. I was involved in electoral politics, in civil rights activities in Chicago, in protest against urban renewal, in helping women get illegal abortions. One of my best friends died—that at least received a paragraph. Yet in the whole correspondence I talked only about writing. I shared everything I wrote and read everything the friend wrote. Entire letters are detailed criticism. We also exchanged some critiques of books we read.

I think that forming a support group near you or through the mail is not the worst way of getting support. I showed my friend poems and stories I certainly did not dare show my husband and material I didn't share later with a boyfriend who wrote. It was safer to be open with my friend. In fact, it occurs to me that now when I hardly have time to write letters at all but dictate all my business correspondence, that I still have such literary correspondences, with Joanna Russ, for instance, and with Suzy McKee Charnas.

A few poems I have written make me feel simply too vulnerable to perform them, ever. "You ask why sometimes I say stop" is in that category. For a while I felt that way about "Crescent moon like a canoe" but I tried it and so many people spoke to me about that poem after the reading, I often end readings with it now. Seeing people in the audience cry made me realize it may be a poem that issues from my feelings for my mother but it speaks for many women. When I realize that about a poem, I stop feeling naked about it. It belongs to other people too and I am saying it for them. Sometimes the poems you may feel queasiest about are those that others will respond to most strongly and will most cherish. You also clear the road. If June Jordan had not written "Getting down to get over" I don't think I would have tackled "Crescent moon like a canoe" for another five or ten years. Certainly I had been turning the poem over in my mind for a long time without sitting down to it. Her poem gave me the courage to write mine. Other women have told me my poem opened the way for their's. We enable and empower each other.

In another essay that I included in this volume I talk about starting support groups, a device I think extremely useful to young writers. One of the most important skills a workshop can teach you and support groups can show you is the kind of questions you want to ask yourself as you are finishing a poem. Sometimes it is a matter of cutting the umbilical cord. Seeing the poem as "it" rather than as "me." Seeing what I have really got down on paper, as opposed to the vision I began with or what I imagined I was capturing: It is a matter of taking a cold look.

Once in a while I write a poem and send it off, and a little oftener I will work on it through a number of drafts in a day and then send it off. Ninety-five percent of the time, however, I put the poem aside in draft two or ten and then pick it up again to give it that cold eye when the immediate involvement has receded. Sometimes I put a poem aside for months and decide not to deal with it again until I am entirely free from the circumstances, to see what I have really wrought that stands and what is just froth that has subsided. I did that with "A tangential death." It was an occasional poem that I felt could be improved if the occasion departed a bit. So I put it in a drawer for six months. Naturally I'm not going to do that if I think there's an immediate need for the poem, if it's promised for a special event.

Basically I diddle and sweat over the poem because I don't think of it as primarily self-expression. I imagine the poem has a right to exist apart from me. Once I have conceived of the poem, I feel I ought to try to make it as strong and as clear and as beautiful as I am able. I revise endlessly. I write, usually, a number of drafts, although of course there are poems that come entire and that's that. What I'm concerned with here is the vast majority of poems that are built bit by bit and rebuilt and taken down and erected again. I revise when a poem comes back rejected. I revise after my first and sometimes after my second or third public reading of that work. I revise when I choose a poem to be included in a book of poetry every couple of years. When I brought together my selected poems, I revised some of those poems again.

I suppose on my deathbed, I'll still be working on a pile of poems I don't yet consider complete—some of which I probably started when I was sixteen.

The Lunar Cycle

The basic structure of this cycle is simple: a poem for each of the thirteen lunar months, an introductory poem bearing the title of the book, "The moon is always female" and a short epilogue poem. As jacket copy I wrote the following explanation:

I first heard of the lunar calendar in childhood, when I asked why Passover falls on a different date every year and was answered that it falls on Nisan 14—the fourteenth day of the lunar month of Nisan. The next time I came across the moon-month was in reading Robert Graves in 1959 in search of the old goddess religions.

But the lunar calendar has really only been an intimate part of my life since I moved between the ocean and the bay and had to become conscious of the tides; for one thing, to get the sweet Wellfleet oysters. For more precise understanding I owe a lot to Nancy F. W. Passmore and the other women of the Luna Press, who every year produce *The Lunar Calendar* with thirteen months, their old Celtic names, associations from around the world, time of moon rise and set and all the phases. It tells me at a glance when my period will come and when I can expect to ovulate, and it is the most beautiful calendar I have ever seen, with the months in the form of spirals rather than grids.

Not being constrained by commerce to produce a calendar to sell by January first, Roman time, I begin when my year opens, in the spring, with Nisan, the first month of the old Jewish religious year—although I have used the Celtic names, as does *The Lunar Calendar*, in homage to that labor of love. Rediscovering the lunar calendar has been a part of rediscovering women's past, but it has also meant for me a series of doorways to some of the nonrational aspects of being a living woman: Thus *The Lunar Cycle*, explorations of my last two years.

Mary Oliver has a book *Twelve Moons* in which she uses the Algonquin names, translated, for the lunar months. I like those poems and those names. They are more appropriate to our Northeastern seasons than the Celtic names, but they carry a web of other associations. Mary Oliver is a fine poet not yet widely enough known, and I recommend her work.

The poems of my cycle were not written in the order they are placed. Indeed, the first poem "The moon is always female" was the last written. I had completed the whole cycle before I felt that I needed a poem to stand before the year, outside it. This poem began with the experience described in the lines of the second verse paragraph:

> I wake in a strange slack empty bed
> of a motel, shaking like dry leaves. . . .

I did hear the girl crying as her clitoris was cut out at the same time that I became her and felt the searing pain. What I was using in the poem to begin the cycle is the situation of women we are told is immutable. I am placing our legislated and enforced bondage, mutilation, second-class citizenship described as biological destiny, within a context reaching back to prehistory when women were more nearly equal and held considerable social and religious power in our hands.

I was relieved when I read in an interview in Phil Levine's *Don't Ask* collection in this series about his waking experience of possession and seizure in Spain that he embodied in a poem. It was moving and reassuring to me to read that about another poet because both "At the well" in *The Lunar Cycle* and this poem began in experiences of waking into a vision that was also a bodily experience. I am a pragmatist through and through and require no metaphysics to sanction my experience. As I go through the world I encounter places, times, objects, experiences that are numinous sometimes in themselves and sometimes because of some human event that has happened there.

As the gatherers, women knew the herbs and roots and seeds. Gathering people tend to know their land and the uses of all the plants thereon the way later people never again know it. Thus women were the first healers, and for long long centuries the only real ones, the nurses and midwives and witches who cured with the herbs that still form the backbone of much of our pharmacopia today (foxglove, thyme, valerian, poppy) while doctors were using leaches and bleeding the strength from their patients. The first and kindest teachers were women teaching children what to do and what not to do to survive and flourish. We celebrated the simplest blood mysteries and when we are in touch with ourselves, we still do.

Two shore landscapes are imposed upon each other in the second half of the poem, from the lines, "I want to say over the names of my mothers" on.

> I am waiting for the moon to rise. Here
> I squat, the whole country with its steel
> mills and its coal mines and its prisons
> at my back and the continent tilting
> up into mountains and torn by shining lakes
> all behind me on this scythe of straw,
> a sand bar cast on the ocean waves, and I. . . .

This, of course, is Cape Cod, the great beach. The "scythe of straw" image comes from flying over the Cape. I am facing east and the beach is Newcomb Hollow to the left, actually the area across the dune from Fox Bottom, just short of the highest point (Pamet Hill) on the great beach. But:

> . . . I am all the time
> climbing slippery rocks in a mist while

> far below the waves crash in the sea caves;
> I am descending a stairway under the groaning
> sea while the black waters buffet me
> like rockweed to and fro. . . .

This is the coast of Cornwall. I was there in May, off-season, in rain and heavy fog. Cornwall and Devon moved me. I found some of the ruins on the moors to radiate enormous energy, as powerful as certain places on the Cape and certain Native American sites. I found it amazing that the British, who spent so much time, money and effort digging up other people's pasts in Egypt, Mesopotamia, Greece and Crete, should have these magnificent ruins and ignore them. In Devon and Cornwall, some place names are the same as in my home: Truro, Falmouth, Plymouth, Barnstable, but the landscape is starkly different.

Anyhow, I start the cycle with women's current situation and past history, then place myself where I can resonate best, lying naked under the moon as I would do to regulate my period, and catalogue all the ways of knowing that we have:

> . . . There is knowing
> with the teeth as well as knowing with
> the tongue and knowing with the fingertips
> as well as knowing with words and with all
> the fine flickering hungers of the brain.

The first lunar month in the sequence is Saille—willow—and the poem is called "Right to life" after a phrase I am reclaiming. The poem concerns women's most basic right, the right to control our bodies, the right to control the life within us, to choose when and whether to give birth—not to be used as field or factory. That is the most basic choice a woman makes, and without it there is no other freedom.

The pear tree in the first stanza, "gone wild," is local. I have a couple of wild pear trees on my land that bear biennially. They bristle with long thorns and bear small exceptionally sweet pears I usually can, something like seckels.

Friends of mine live in an old Cape house surrounded by black locusts (Gloria Nardin Watts to whom the poem "Morning athletes" is dedicated, and Peter Watts, whose poem "Out of the hospital Peter" will be in *Stone, Paper, Knife*) and they too have a wild pear. Theirs is immense and does stand at least forty feet tall.

The reference in the fifth stanza is to Rosie Jimenez, the first woman I know about to die of a backstreet abortion because she could no longer get Medicaid for a hospital abortion. Her story is told in Ellen Frankfort's moving book *Rosie (Rosie: An Investigation of a Wrongful Death*, by Ellen Frankfort with Frances Kissling [New York: Dial Press, 1978]). The pinsticking reference came from a social worker friend. I rewrote the last stanza at least twelve times before I finally got what I wanted. This poem is one of those passionate and didactic poems I am proud of.

"May apple" for Uath, the month of hawthorn blooming, is a meditative poem. After the basic freedom to control one's body, not to be a chattel or a domestic animal, comes the freedom to be alone. "May apple" is concerned with virginity in the old sense, not whether or not a woman has a hymen but a virgin as a woman unmated at a particular time, a woman in her own company and her own keeping.

I date my beginnings as a writer to the time I was fifteen when my family moved from a tiny house to a far more spacious one. My parent's bedroom was downstairs but mine was a small room in a gable, across the hall from the two bedrooms that were rented out to roomers. For the first time in my life I had real privacy, a door that shut, a room entirely my own. Since I was the youngest in my family and since I was working, I often got to stay home when the house was empty. I liked being alone and from fifteen on, I had the privacy I craved.

Many women never have the solitude they need, while others feel isolated, boxed up alone in a house or alone with small children. I remember when I was in Greece in 1964 meeting a Greek actress about twenty-six or twenty-seven. A strikingly beautiful woman, she lived at home with her mother and her brother, an engineer, and all her activities in film making or on the stage were strictly chaperoned. She told me that the most wonderful experience of her life occurred when she was acting in a production in Thessaloniki and something had forced a delay. A friend turned over to her a cabin way out on the peninsula that Sikia is on, on the Gulf of Kassandra. For three days while waiting for the production to resume, she had stayed there alone. Alone, she kept saying, for three days no one looked at me! There wasn't even a mirror! I was myself. For her it had been almost a mystical experience.

This being a meditative poem, it is in a fixed stanza form, alternating four lines and five lines. You might contrast this poem with another on solitude, "Going in" from *The Twelve-Spoked Wheel Flashing*. In that earlier poem I am concerned with a forced solitude in exile, in which all the things and people I depend on, all that gives me a sense of myself, fall away and leave me feeling the insecurities of adolescence, the fears of childhood, intact after all this time, revived in a situation of deprivation and isolation. Then penetrating further, the basic strength of consciousness, the resources that power us past the flimsy structures of the self, emerge at last.

In "May apple" I am concerned more with a woman alone in a daily sense, not in some kind of sensory deprivation, imprisonment, exile or state of outcast, but simply choosing to be alone. I have by the way extreme respect for hawthorn, since I conduct a running battle with it, one I have scars to document. Nevertheless I admire it. Only someone who has dug out a wild hawthorn tree knows what tenacity they exhibit.

"Shadows of the burning" marks the month of Duir—oak—but is also a poem for Midsummer's Eve, the longest day and shortest night of the year. Just as summer is truly coming into its own, the year secretly shifts and the days begin to shorten and the nights to lengthen. The fire is traditional, of course, and has been with me as a powerful symbol and often an actual observance of the solstices since I read *The Golden Bough* at age sixteen. After I had taken it out of the library and read it through, I went and bought it in hard cover. I remember I was working in a department store in downtown Detroit and it took me a while to find a bookstore that had it. Then I discovered Jane Harrison's *Prolegomena to the Study of Greek Religion*, another early and even more important influence.

Actually when I was sixteen, seventeen, I had a vast hunger for theory and analysis. I read the anthropologists of myth for the same reasons I read Marx and Freud. Myth was important to me. I had grown up with a lot of it. My mother, who loved yard sales and stuff people got rid of when they moved, had in my early childhood picked up a set of twenty-odd volumes of some set I wish I could identify. They told, quite decently, I think, a number of fairy tales, versions of the Nebelungleid, Native American mythology, Greek, Roman, Norse, the Arthurian legends. I would give a lot to lay my hands on those books, but as soon as I left home, my mother cleared my room out, and nobody in the family seems to have any idea what they were. I read, reread them, and they did a lot to form my imagination and give me a basic culture of stories to set with the amazing storytelling of my grandmother and my mother.

"Shadows of the burning" is about sexual passion conjoined with love, its dangers, how destructive it can be to women, my own difficulties in assimilating it into my life without giving up my direction, my faith. The poem starts on the same beach where I watched the moon rise in "The moon is always female," this time with the man I live with, Woody. We do in fact have parties there sometimes at the full moon. After the initial celebration, I retreat into a recapitulation of how often love has been a damaging obsession that has killed women, quite literally. I quite believe with Shakespeare in *As You Like It* that few men have died for love, but I see that a great many women do.

The midsection of the poem is autobiographical. The girl in stanza seven is a young version of the women alone in "May apple." The maenads tore Orpheus, but it is my own senses that dismember me. Then there's the messiness of trying to live through my twenties and thirties in a variety of relationships. The reconstruction of stanza ten is a process I found through the values of feminism. By giving up trying to find one good relationship as a priority, I made myself stronger and clearer politically and in my own thinking, writing, acting, as my own person. Then I could try again with a lover whom I could dare admit to the center of my life. You might consider "The homely war" in *Living in the Open* along with this poem. Basically there I'm concerned with why I'm predominantly in my adult life heterosexual, when so many feminists have decided to be lesbians. Both poems deal with the power and centrality of sexuality to my creativity and my sense of self.

> My strength and my weakness are twins
> in the same womb, mirrored dancers under
> water, the dark and light side of the moon.
> I know how truly my seasons have turned
> cold and hot
> around that lion-bodied sun.

The sun is a lion not only because of the color, because of the old associations of lion mane and sun shield (Edith Sitwell has I think a number of poems with similar associations), but because the sun here is both my own sexuality and the core energy as in "Going in" and the lure of the beauty of the male body.

The imagery of the last stanza is that of my own peculiar earth kinship and worship, that in sexuality we align ourselves with the place we are and the other beings occupying it with us. It may seem a lot to build on a fuck, as in D. H. Lawrence, but it is not really one sexual act but a sexual relationship I am talking about. Diane di Prima has similar poems, I believe, especially in the marvelous and brilliant *Loba*. Sometimes in making love with someone we do truly love and are loved by strongly in return, we touch very powerful forces within and without.

"The sabbath of mutual respect" is for the month of Tinne—holly—the celebration of the old Thanksgiving.

> In the natural year come two thanksgivings,
> the harvest of summer and the harvest of fall. . . .

I like harvest celebrations and like to make a fuss of the traditional fall Thanksgiving. This poem begins with a paean to the grasses that sustain us, the daily humble base of life on land that feed us directly as grain and indirectly through other mammals as fodder for their meat or their milk and cheese. It's about abundance and choice, the thanksgiving in full summer that does not, like the fall thanksgiving, come as the last harvest is in and the winter battening down, but in the midst of full plenty.

Whatever you plant you must weed and tend and harvest. Whatever you start makes more work for you and more responsibility. Every choice brings not only potential advantages but lots of care. The more abundance you desire, the more responsibility you must assume. Then I catalog the love choices of women and praise them all, insisting that we respect each other's choices. When I read this poem recently at a women's festival, a young lesbian separatist challenged me, insisting I could not mean that choosing a man was as good a choice for a feminist as choosing a woman. I told her that my basic value is freedom, not purity, and that I respect all choices equally as free choices, providing they are free and do not involve injuring others (choosing to prevent other people from doing what they want to do, for instance, such as passing laws forbidding women to love each other).

The catalogue of goddesses belongs in the poem partly because it is a thanksgiving poem and partly because goddesses embody forces, powers, histories, states: they are the choices we may or may not make—we certainly will make some of them and certainly will not make others. But all are holy and all the choices we make freely—the love of other women, the love of one woman or one man, the love of a number of people of whatever sex, the love of solitude, the maternal love—all are precious and holy and must be honored by us whatever we choose.

It is, I guess, an ecumenical poem for the women's movement. "Freedom / is our real abundance." It ends with the image of the doorway as sacred to women, who are the doorways of life.

For the month of Coll—the hazel, tree of inspiration—the poem is "Tumbling and with tangled mane," a meditation in four parts on the ocean and on creativity, which to me is exemplified by the ocean, where life began. You might want to look at some of my other ocean poems along with this, for instance, the eighth section of "Sand roads" from *Living in the Open*. The ocean in the poem is immense unknowable power, a god, but also mortal. People can kill it with greed and garbage. There is a kind of airiness of mind I only experience at the ocean, a different kind of alignment.

The first three parts concentrate on different experiences of the sea in itself, in fog, in sunshine, in storm—a summer storm, for the aspects of the shore depicted in the first three parts of the poem are all of the month Coll.

In the fourth stanza I am dealing with the sea as metaphor. "Tumbling and with tangled mane" is about the irrational aspects of creativity, the power and energy it issues from and the sense of guilt that sometimes attaches to creation—both the marvelous delight in that energy and the fear of it. The dream is one I have often had, as I described it. I think it represents my own ambiguous feelings about what I do—what it issues from.

The image that ends the poem actually came from a snow hurricane, but it is appropriate to the eye of a regular hurricane as well.

The horse imagery of the first stanza of the last part, of course, dates back in my reading to the Greeks, and makes me remember, also, Robinson Jeffers, who wrote so well about the sea. I am one of those people who dreamed about the sea constantly when I lived inland and had to come to live within a mile or so of it, eventually. There are poets who write of the sea from being on it (I think of Homer) and poets who write of the sea from the shore. I am one of those.

The moment celebrated at the poem's end is the moment when something is commenced—not stumbled into but commenced with a knowledge of its length and breadth and difficulty: the moment when a poem is conceived with the vision that it may take forty drafts to build right; the moment when the novel is imagined that will occupy the next three years. It is the moment to which the labor of art strives to be true.

"Cutting the grapes free," the poem for the month of Muin—the vine—celebrates art also, but from a more deliberate point of view. "Cutting the grapes free" is in a six line stanza that forms an extended comparison of blood is to poetry as the vine is to wine: what we make carefully and with great work out of the guts of our lives. The blood we spill—our accidents, our losses, our excitements—we make with all the skill we have into poetry, as the blood of the grape is made with all the skill and knowledge and hard work of the vintner into fine wine.

The reference in stanza seven is to an actual event: when the vines of its native river valley are in bloom, the Mosel wherever in the world undergoes a brief secondary fermentation that makes it slightly effervescent.

The poem also celebrates the connection of art back to life, that it issues from our contingencies, and the requirement that art must be preserved by others to survive. Others take it, use it, or it perishes.

> Like wine I must finally trust myself
> to other tongues or turn to vinegar.

You might compare that closing with the ending of "Athena in the front lines" from *The Twelve-Spoked Wheel Flashing*:

> Making is an act, but survival
> is luck, caught in history
> like a moth trapped in the subway.

> There is nothing to do but make well,
> finish, and let go. Words
> live, words die
> in the mouths of everybody.

Thus from the poems about basic female choices in the realm of blood—the biological choices of love, sex, child-birth—I have moved into two poems about creativity, one concerned with the unconscious and the creative power, the other concerned with conscious art.

The next poem deals with our social being, with our larger evolution, with political choice. It is "The perpetual migration" for the month of Gort—the ivy—the month of the great migrations. Influenced by Elizabeth Fisher and her epochal work *Woman's Creation* and also by Richard Leakey, I see human beings as social animals—forced to be social because our young depend on us so long a time. We are the animal that must share food, that must cooperate. You might compare the view of evolution in this poem with that in "For Shoshana-Pat Swinton" from *The Twelve-Spoked Wheel Flashing*:

> a history flows of rivers and amoebas,
> of the first creeping thing
> that shuddered onto the land,
> a history of the woman who
> tamed corn, a history
> of learning and losing, a history
> of making good and being had,
> of some great green organism
> gasping to be free.

Basically I argue that our biology is on the side of our continued evolution toward a more decent, more equal society and a sharing of what we all would like to have to make life comfortable and pleasant—that social change is programmed into us as a species, and must be achieved if we are to survive. The poem is written in six and seven line stanzas.

The next poem, "The great horned owl" is for the month of Ngetal—the reed, the hollow creature you blow on. It was the first poem I wrote of the series and one of the least programmatic. I finished it and then right afterward, I had the idea of a lunar cycle, which I was to work on for the next year and ten months. The next one I wrote was "Another country"; then "At the well," and then "White on black." I did almost all the winter poems first. I can't be as clear about the order of the others because a number of them I worked on alternately over a year. I know that "Tumbling and with tangled mane," "The sabbath of mutual respect," "O!," and "The moon is always female" were the last I wrote, in that order.

"The great horned owl" is a simple poem about the mingled fear and respect and admiration I feel for that marvelously successful predator who rules the winter night here. I feel awe when I hear her hunting, as in the poem. I have seen her, but usually I hear her. The kernel of the poem is the sensual experience of lying in a warm bed next to the man I love and feeling the cold night about us just outside the membrane of wall and ceiling, hearing through that thin membrane the predator at work. With predators as with poets, there is no distinction between work and pleasure and play.

That great white oak that grows at the corner of my land where it slopes down into the marsh occurs in many of my poems, here as in "Crows," another bird I have great respect for. It is a tree with very strong presence and is the oldest on my land. Because it grew on the slope to the marsh, it was not chopped down when this land was farmed, and it did not burn in the fire that I can find the scars of still, that happened many decades ago.

"The longest night" is as it says for the winter solstice and the month of Ruis, the elder. The moon is in the dark of the moon:

> New moon, no moon, old moon dying,
> moon that gives no light, stub

of a candle, dark lantern, face
without features, the zone of zero:

As feels appropriate to the winter solstice—an occasion
for which I have written poems now and then since I was
eighteen—the poem concerns despair. As a political person,
as a feminist, as an active woman, as a human being getting at
least the usual number of lumps, despair is something I have
to acknowledge and face down, assimilate, to survive.

Except for the catalog of names in the poem for Tinne
and the last poem, "O!," this is the only poem in the lunar
cycle which addresses the triple goddess directly, in this case
as Hecate, her appropriate form at the winter solstice on the
new moon at a crossroads. It concerns defeat, repression,
fatigue, loneliness, my experience of my own mortality when
I almost died in New York. If "Shadows of the burning" and
"Tumbling and with tangled mane" celebrate various aspects
of the energy of the life force that flows through us, this deals
with the termination of my particular role in that life force,
my own death, my limits, the end of my own energy and
ability and health.

Here too at the center is strength but the strength that
comes from confronting one's own despair and one's own
mortality:

> . . . The dark of the mind.
> In terror begins vision. In silence
> I learn my song, here at the stone
> nipple, the black moon bleeding,
> the egg anonymous as water,
> the night that goes on and on,
> a tunnel through the earth.

"At the well" is the hinge poem. In other essays in this
volume I have talked about some of its technical aspects,
which I'll skip here. Beth is the month in which the conven-
tional calendar now in use begins, the month of the birch.
This poem issues from an experience I had, or which had

me, when I was twenty-three. I was trying to decide whether to leave a conventional marriage to a physicist. He and everybody else around us told me he loved me, but he did not respect my writing or my independence and he tried ceaselessly to grind me down to what a wife should be. As a Frenchman, he had a finely honed sense of "comme il faut." "On ne dit pas çela." "On ne fait pas çela."

That summer while he was on a cyclotron run one afternoon, a force, a goddess, an angel wrestled me. I had no language with which to deal with what I experienced but I knew I had to go. Whatever it was that came and struck me and fought me, it was surely my Muse. It was that force in whose service I labor and I was about to kill myself by inches and my art inside me in order to fulfill a conventional wife role.

I tried to write the poem then and I could not bring it off. One thing I did without thinking was make the protagonist male. That changed everything. The force too became a He. I had tried and failed with the poem for a couple of years before I put it aside, but I retained a sense of the power of what was in it.

When I began the lunar cycle in earnest, I dreamed of that old experience and I found the old notes. I finally wrote the poem, but immediately when I launched into it, I corrected the sexes. Women are not supposed to wrestle angels, but then women are not supposed to write poems either.

In the poem the woman refuses the gamble. In other words, she succumbs to the conventional cynicism which says:

"Now I clutch a crust and I hold on."

The confusion, the blurring of sex in the apparition is intentional: it/he/she. In fact, despair blinds. Cynicism blinds. Nothing blinds a writer faster than refusing to make changes, to grow, to push on. When I walked out of that marriage, I walked out on the little security I had known but I walked back into my own life. Each tub on its own bottom.

Or, to repeat a quotation from the Talmud that hangs over my desk, "It is not incumbent upon thee to complete the task but neither are thou free to desist from thy part." I grew up, of course, with all the rich Jewish tradition my grandmother and my mother imparted to me, Biblical, Talmudic, Hasidic, folklore, history, all stewed together.

"White on black" comes after the crisis. Although the old woman in the poem refuses the angel and is blinded, we, the readers, and I, the writer, take what is offered us and rush ahead if blindly too in our way, as clearly as we can. This is a celebration of nature in its less grim aspects, the little comical skunk who defends herself so uniquely. It is a poem in praise of the small pieces of nature that manage to survive among our houses, our cars, our dumps, our highways, and the pleasures of everyday living.

It is true that in the middle of the winter few things seem to vibrate such intense life as chickadees and skunks, and of the two, the skunks seem the more independent and secure. After all, we don't feed them—intentionally. Luis—the mountain ash or the rowan—is the tree. Although winter rules, the year is rekindled and there is often a serious thaw and the very first signs that winter may end eventually.

"Another country" is the poem for Nion—the ash, a tree associated with the sea and with water. Like "At the well," "Another country" uses a persona or mask—a person unidentified as to sex who enters the ocean to visit the porpoises, those intelligent warm-blooded mammals I have often watched and am fascinated by. In a poem from *Hard Loving*, called "In praise of salt and water," dolphins are contrasted with human beings—unfavorably for us—because of their cooperative nature and their wisdom in returning to the ocean where the living is a lot easier.

This anthropologist apparently can speak the language of the natives being studied, and reports on their art forms. What I am basically dealing with is that scarcity does not improve our tenderness toward each other.

> Greed has no meaning when no one
> is hungry.

I admire porpoises very much and I think we commit murder when we kill the porpoises or the great whales, murder being the killing of any intelligent life form, however different from ourselves it may appear.

I also think we could learn much from them and wish we would learn it fast—things we used to know when we were technologically more primitive but sociologically more sophisticated, about caring for each other, about socializing each child to cooperate with other children and adults, about promoting the general good.

Both "White on black" and "Another country" deal with re-education through the realization of ourselves as part of nature, however hard it may be to get back in touch—"clattering with gadgets."

The last month of the lunar cycle is Fearn—month of the alder—my birth month, the month when winter begins to give way in earnest to spring. It is the time when the mysteries commemorated the return of Persephone from the underworld to reunite with her mother Demeter, as the first stanza in the poem mentions. It is also the time of the vernal equinox, when the light and darkness are balanced and light and warmth begin to return (in the Northern hemisphere of course, where I live and my associations were formed).

The direction of the last three poems has been outward, through the use of masks or persona, through the medium of other animals, the natural world, the social web—in "Another country." I chose for the last poem—except for the little lyric "O!"—and for my birth month the poem "Crescent moon like a canoe," a poem about the mother/daughter relationship and particularly my own mother and myself. It is written in five line stanzas. The crescent moon is the waxing moon, and I have chosen it although in the last stanza I identify my mother well into her eighties as my waning moon, because the poem is concerned primarily with our relationship when I was a child—and because it is my birth month. It begins with her pregnancy and final late delivery, for I was a ten-month baby.

What I am dealing with is the double message that a great many mothers give their daughters, who go on to do the things the mothers only dreamed of: that you'll be killed if you do, but that only daring is worth anything.

> . . . yet you wanted too
> to birth a witch, a revenger, a sword
>
> of hearts who would do all the things
> you feared. Don't do it, they'll kill
> you, you're bad, you said, slapping me down
> hard but always you whispered, I could have!
> Only rebellion flashes like lightning.

I had wanted to write a poem about my mother for many years. I remember taking a stab at it back in 1961. I was inhibited. I think before feminism, I lacked a theoretical framework to enable me to approach the subject. The writing of several Black women about their mothers, especially June Jordan's "Getting Down to Get Over" and the many poems Audre Lorde has written about her mother enabled me finally. I seemed to myself to feel very differently about my mother than many women from middle-class backgrounds who were beginning to write about their mothers. I had a strong sense that my mother had formed me as a poet early and a strong sense of how first poverty, and then the iron sex roles of working-class life, had confined her, warped her: and yet the gifts she gave were precious and radiant with energy.

The title and the third from last stanza refer to a lullaby my mother used to sing me when I was a little girl. I have no idea where it comes from, and have never found anyone else who knew it:

> Oh, mother, how pretty the moon looks tonight.
> It was never so cunning before.
> With two little horns so sharp and so bright.
> I hope they don't grow any more.
>
> If we were up there in the beautiful sky
> Oh, how nicely we'd roam.

We'd sit in the middle and hold on both ends
and on the next rainbow come home.

We'd call on the stars to keep out of our way
lest we should rock over their toes,
and there we would stay till the dawn of the day
to see where the pretty moon goes.

Although I hardly expect you to share my childhood enthu-
siasm, this was my favorite song. I can still hear my mother's
voice singing it. Out of such odd little childhood pieces of
banality we can sometimes generate considerable power.

I believe a woman must reconcile herself to her mother
and to her mother within her, if she is not to become her. Few
of us can feel anything but fear, disgust, or contempt at the
idea of becoming our mothers: powerless women, unhappy
women, women in whom the wine of life has soured. But
what I believe important in the project of this poem and the
reason I suspect many women are moved by it, is that we
must manage that reconciliation, in life if possible, and in art
at least.

The last poem, "O!," is an evocation of the moon, a lyrical
summing up: the moon as reflection of our womanhood, our
roundness, the moon as controller of our menstrual cycle
and the tides, the moon as patron of what is left of the wild
and of the wild within us, ourselves as one among many
furry mammals and part of the food chain on land and in the
sea, and the moon as the triple goddess we turn to as to a
magnifying mirror to trace our lineaments, the powers
within us, the powers we hope to touch in freedom and full
lives:

> . . . the island
> in the sea where love rules and women
> are free to wax and wane and wander
> in the sweet strict seasons
> of our desires and needs.

Why write a lunar cycle? Occasionally the idea for a cycle of poems occurs to me, such as the Tarot card poems "Laying Down the Tower" from *To Be of Use*, and now included in the selected poems *Circles on the Water*. I think these schemes combine some kind of structure (the lunar calendar, the eleven cards of a traditional divinatory reading) with a great richness of symbols. The "Elementary Odes" in *Stone, Paper, Knife* are another example.

In the case of the lunar months and the poems, I could have written on about the mythologies and associations each lunar month trails behind it, but writing at even greater length about a set of my own poems strikes me as somewhat overblown. I have tried to suggest the rich lode of material I was working. I find these cycles stretch me. I have to work extremely hard on them and do more than I can, always with the feeling how much more could be done, if I were able. Art is infinite.

Revision in Action
Chipping and Building

I have put together three accounts of the process of writing through various drafts toward the finished poems. Each of these brief descriptions includes the various drafts of the poem I was working on. Each process offers a somewhat different route between onslaught and finished product, with differing problems to solve en route.

How "Becoming new" Became

"Becoming new" started as a rambling love lyric of no particular distinction in first draft. Not atypically, however, for the type of poem revised by cutting as much as by rewriting, most of the imagery of which the later poem would be built was present in the wordy original. Some poems I work on from a stark beginning into more elaboration and development. Some poems, like this one, need pruning to reach a shape.

How it feels to be touching you

An Io moth, orange
and yellow as butter
winging through the night
miles to mate
crumbling in the hand to dust
hardly smearing the wall.

It feels like a brick
square and sturdy and pleasing
to the eye and hand
ready to be used
to build something
I can keep warm in
keep tools in
walk on.
Hardy as an onion and layered.
Going into the blood like garlic
secretly antibiotic.
Sour as rose hips.
Gritty as whole grains.
Sweet and fragrant as thyme honey.
Scarce as love,
my dear, what we have started.
Its substance goes out between us
like a hair
that any weight could break,
like a morning web shining.
It flares into pockets of meeting,
dark pools of touch.
What does it mean to me?
What does it mean to you?
We are meaning together.
We become new selves in private.
When I am turning slowly
in our woven hammocks of talk
when I am melting like chocolate
our bodies glued together
I taste myself quite new
I smell like a book
just off the press
You smell like hot bread.
Though I seem to be standing still
I am flying flying flying
in the trees of your eyes.

By the next version, still with the same title, the poem
begins to assume a little shape. It is in paragraphs now,
centered each around the imagery. I cut some of the wordier

sections but I am still adrift, not yet focussed on what in the experience or the blob of the poem is interesting. The ending is the one that will stay through all versions of the poem. These first two versions were done in rapid succession.

How it feels to be touching you

An Io moth, orange
and yellow as butter
wings through the night
miles to mate,
crumbles in the hand to dust
hardly smearing the wall.

We feel like a brick
square and sturdy and pleasing
to the eye and hand
ready to be used
to build something
I can keep warm in
keep tools in
walk on.

Hardy as an onion and layered.
Going into the blood like garlic
pungent and antibiotic.
Sour as rose hips.
Gritty as whole grains.
Sweet and fragrant as thyme honey.
Its substance goes out between us
like a hair
that any weight could break,
like a morning web shining.
It flares into pockets of meeting,
dark pools of touch.

We are meaning together.
When I am turning slowly
in the woven hammocks of our talk
when I am melting like chocolate
our bodies glued together

I taste myself quite new
I smell like a book
just off the press
You smell like hot bread.
Though I seem to be standing still
I am flying flying flying
in the trees of your eyes.

At that point I put the poem aside for a while. When I took it out again, I decided that what is interesting is that the two people were friends who have become lovers while still being friends. The wonder of the friend developing the charisma and magic that a lover possesses while still being the same friend is the focus of the poem. The imagery that stresses the strength and dailiness in terms of bricks, buildings, tools disappears, as being irrelevant to the revelation of sensuous pleasure. I realized as I returned to the poem and began to shape it, to focus it, that the sensuality was important to the poem and equally important was leaving the sexes ambiguous. The poem had begun as one about a man with whom in the course of a long friendship, I had a three-week sexual involvement; but by the time I returned to work on it, the piece seemed to me more about friendships between women that become love relationships. Then I realized I wanted to make the poem truly and carefully androgynous (a word I am not fond of) because friendship is.

The hair imagery disappeared when I realized I was using the same metaphor in another poem of about the same vintage—"Bridging," also contained in *To Be of Use*—where the imagery is far more relevant to a completely different theme. The associations of smelling like a book just off the press seemed inappropriate to the new focus, and the hot bread image seemed trite, so they were lopped off, replaced by a simple statement of the theme. The first stanza remained the same.

Something borrowed

How it feels to be touching
you: an Io moth, orange

and yellow as butter
wings through the night
miles to mate,
crumbles in the hand
hardly smears the wall.

Yet our meaning together
is hardy as an onion
and layered.
Going into the blood like garlic,
pungent and antibiotic.
Sour as rose hips.
Gritty as whole grain.
Sweet and fragrant as thyme honey:
this substance goes out between us
a morning web shining.

When I am turning slowly
in the woven hammocks of our talk,
when I am melting like chocolate
our bodies glued together
I taste myself quite new
in your mouth.

You are not my old friend.
How did I used to sit
and look at you?
Though I seem to be standing still
I am flying flying flying
in the trees of your eyes.

In the next version, published in *To Be of Use* and anthologized, the title settled into "We become new." In fact there is an anthology named for this poem: *We Become New*, edited by Lucille Iverson and Kathryn Ruby (New York: Bantam Books, 1975). This title emphasized what I had fixed on as the core of the poem. There are many routes into poems. Sometimes when I launch into a poem, I know exactly where I'm going, although it may take me one or many drafts to fix that vision in words. Sometimes, as in this poem, the basic imagery is there but I don't know quite what

I'm getting at for a while. I have to hack away at it until I perceive what it is I'm trying to say, even in a case this simple. The discovery of the secret sensuality or the repressed sexuality in a friendship either between women or between a man and a woman is a common experience that makes this poem interesting to a number of people, who have mentioned it to me, or written me about it. We tend to see people with whom we make love as more luminous, more radiantly physical than those with whom we haven't been as intimate. In the case of someone we have known for a long time or perhaps even worked with, we had thought we knew her or him quite well. We feel dazzled with the change of perception love-making brings.

The morning web shining I liked, but somehow it didn't fit. It wasn't exactly a web I was dealing with—not a couple formation. Furthermore, I had noticed a strong oral component in the imagery, especially after the first stanza, and I like that and wished to concentrate on it. The moth smeared on the wall also disappeared. What does crushing a moth have to do with sensuality unless you're being a little weirder than I intended? I decided the image was peculiar and distracting.

The two changes I like best occur in the third stanza, where the chocolate image finally comes into its own, and where what is experienced new when the perimeters of the relationship change, is "everything" rather than "myself." In that small context, I like the large claim.

We become new

How it feels to be touching
you: an Io moth, orange
and yellow as pollen,
wings through the night
miles to mate,
could crumble in the hand.

Yet our meaning together
is hardy as an onion

and layered.
Goes into the blood like garlic.
Sour as rose hips.
Gritty as whole grain.
Fragrant as thyme honey.

When I am turning slowly
in the woven hammocks of our talk,
when I am chocolate melting into you,
I taste everything new
in your mouth.

You are not my old friend.
How did I used to sit
and look at you? Now
though I seem to be standing still
I am flying flying flying
in the trees of your eyes.

When I included this poem, finally, in my selected poems (*Circles on the Water* [Knopf, New York: 1982]), the only change I made was to move the last line of stanza two down to become the first line of stanza three. That brought the poem into regular six line stanzas. Although I talk a lot about the ear being primary, that is one of the occasional changes made primarily for the eyes. I liked the look on the page better.

The Evolution of "Rough Times"

"Rough times" is a poem that began with a rather prosy fragment:

Those who speak of good and simple
in the same mouthful
who say good and innocent
inhabit some other universe than I struggle through

I find it hard to be good
and the good hard: hard to know
hard to choose when known
and hard to accomplish when chosen:
rocky, sprace and

good makes my hands bleed,
good keeps me awake with fear, lying on broken shards
good pickles me in the vinegar of guilt
good goads me with burrs in my underwear

I have no idea whatsoever about the meaning of "rocky, sprace and." However, this note was a sufficient fragment to launch the poem, not immediately I think. The above jottings were an idea for a poem which remained dormant for a while—in this case I think a matter of weeks. The fragment arose from my irritation with the presumption that good is simple or clear, that ethics and matters of right and wrong are as automatic to decide as calling up the time by dialing N-E-R-V-O-U-S on the telephone and resetting your watch for accuracy. If you do not accept the prevailing patriarchal standards of right and wrong, then you have to hammer out your own ethics at the same time that you try to change yourself to adhere to your values.

A short time—weeks—later, I wrote a true first draft. The first stanza is one that will remain through all subsequent drafts, but after that, I had a lot more trouble. This version remains fairly prosy although some of the imagery about two thirds of the way through is strong enough to stay the route. Finally this version simply trails off. I could find no completion to my complaint.

Trying to live
as if we were an experiment
conducted by the future.

Tearing down the walls of cells
when nothing has been evolved
to replace that protection.

A prolonged vivisection
of my own tissues, carried out
under the barking muzzle of guns.

Those who speak of good and simple
in the same mouthful of tongue and teeth
inhabit some other universe
than I trundle my bag of bones through.

I find it hard to be good
and the good hard. This sierra of
of broken bottles and charred bones
I am clambering over with every soul I respect
does not exist on the maps of the state.

I find it hard to know what's good,
hard to choose when known,
hard to accomplish it when chosen,
hard to repeat it when blundered through.

Good makes my fingers and the roots of my nerves bleed.
Good keeps me awake with fear while the night's iron ceiling
comes down to crush the breath from me,
good pickles me in the vinegar of guilt.
Good robs the easy words there where they rattle between my
    teeth
and draws blood
Good makes my fingers and the roots of my nerves bleed.

Good runs the locomotive of the night over my bed/chest
good pickles me in the vinegar of guilt
good robs the easy words as they rattle over my teeth
and leave me naked as an egg.

Some love comfort and some pleasure;
perhaps of the good, the beautiful and the true
each person can crave

We are tools who carve ourselves

You can see here two of the stanzas evolving as I work. I was playing with crave/carve at the end but the playing came to nothing.

The next draft still has no title. The beginning three line stanzas are slowly taking shape. Finally, I have an ending; I see where the poem is going. Basically, the verb "evolve" in the second stanza had hidden inside it my ending.

Evolution is a concept with a marked place in my poetry, forming an important element in poems such as "For Shoshana-Pat Swinton" about taking an active role in history; "Two higher mammals" about trying to change from what I mistakenly believed then about human prehistory as predators, for I hadn't yet read Richard Leakey or Elizabeth Fisher; "For Walter and Lilian Lowenfels" about trying to grasp one's own time; "The perpetual migration" from *The Lunar Cycle*, that compares us to seabirds and views our whole prehistory and history in terms of social evolution; and the recent poem "Let us gather at the river."

The poem is still shapeless and wordy, but it begins to acquire a direction and a consciousness of its intent.

We are trying to live
as if we were an experiment
conducted by the future,

bulldozing/bombing/blasting
Blasting the walls of the cells
that nothing has yet
been evolved to replace.

A prolonged vivisection
on my own tissues, carried out
under the barking muzzle of guns.

Those who speak of the good and simple
in the same mouthful of tongue and teeth/in the same
    sandwich
inhabit some other universe
than I trundle my bag of bones through.

I find it hard to know what's good,
hard to choose when known,
hard to accomplish when chosen,
hard to repeat when blundered into.

Good draws blood from my scalp and the roots of my nerves.
Good runs the locomotive of the night over my bed.
Good pickles me in the brown vinegar of guilt.
Good robs the easy words as they rattle off my teeth
and leaves me naked as an egg.

We are tools who carve ourselves,
blind hands righting each other,
usually wrong.

Remember that pregnancy is beautiful only
to those who don't look closely
at the distended belly, waterlogged legs, squashed bladder
clumsily she lumbers and wades, who is about
to give birth.

No new idea is seldom borne on the halfshell
attended by graces.
More commonly it's modeled of baling wire and acne.
More commonly it wheezes and tips over.
Most mutants die; the minority refract
the race through the prisms of their genes.

How ugly were the first fish with air sacs
as they hauled up on the muddy flats
heaving and gasping. How clumsy we are in this huge air
we reach with such effort
and can not yet breathe.

I think the association of Venus with the lungfishes is that
they are both born from the ocean, with tremendous novelty.
And like Lucretius, I associate Venus with the energy in
nature. That's what the as yet unnamed reference to her is
doing here.

Finally comes the version printed in *Living in the Open*.
The poem now has a title taken from a periodical called

Rough Times, where the poem was first published. *Rough Times* was the second incarnation of the collectively edited periodical known, in order, as *Journal of Radical Therapy*, *Rough Times*, *Radical Therapist*, and finally *State and Mind*. I named the poem for a magazine that made a genuine and prolonged effort to connect the personal and the political with fairness to both, that recognized the problems of attempting to live in new ways, that dealt with the bruises and abrasions of living in a brutal, racist, and deeply hierarchical society but also dealt consistently with the casualties of trying to change that society. The whole collective at *Rough Times* was extremely helpful when I was researching mental institutions, psychosurgery, and electrode implantation for *Woman on the Edge of Time*.

The poem in this final version has also acquired a dedication to Nancy Henley, now head of women's studies at UCLA. At that time Nancy was living in the Boston area and we saw each other frequently. We are friends equally fascinated through our different disciplines by the personal and the political dimensions of the psychology of every day life— how men and women and people with different positions in the social hierarchy and different amounts of power address each other, touch each other, question or confront each other. When I was writing *Small Changes* and Nancy was writing *He Says/She Says*, we often exchanged observations.

Nancy Henley is a rare dear person, a passionately committed feminist with a strong sense of economic issues, a woman who deals with the theory of social change and also with the practical consequences, who has always taken on far more than her share of the daily work of change—the unglamorous equivalent of taking out the garbage in committee work—as well as writing, speaking, and always thinking clearly and well. I know how hard her life and her choices have been at times, so I dedicated the poem to her.

I had by this version decided on a combination of three line and five line stanzas. The "yard engine" was a better metaphor than in earlier versions, for I remember in childhood watching yard engines shuttle back and forth, back and forth. The extended description of the ninth month of pregnancy has been reduced to one line. The reference to Botticelli's Venus is more explicit and reduced in length.

One of the technical aspects of the poem that picked up the most as the drafts went on is the matter of line breaks. Note the difference between the rather flat:

> Most mutants die; the minority refract
> the race through the prisms of their genes.

and the less obvious, far more potent setting off of the image:

> Most mutants die; only
> a minority refract the race
> through the prisms of their genes.

The tools who carve each other have dropped out entirely, as that image didn't belong to the rest of the poem once I had found my predominant biological metaphors. The vivisection image came early and I still like it, reflecting as it does the pain attendant upon trying to live as if you were changed while trying to change the society.

One of the reasons I worked on the poem after its rather unpromising beginning was a sense that such a subject is difficult to tackle in a lyric but also important. A great many people try to live ethically with a sense of wanting to move toward a better future; but I have seen little in the poetry of our time that alludes to that not uncommon activity. I changed the parallel sentence structure in the last stanza because I wanted to emphasize our clumsiness rather than to emphasize equally the ugliness of the lungfish. I also had used the rhetorical device of initial repetitions earlier in the poem in two places: the four lines in the fifth stanza that begin with "Good" followed by a verb, and the last two lines of the sixth stanza, which both begin "More commonly it." I liked the first two instances of initial repetition much better than the third usage.

I think the final strength of the poem lies in the increasingly concrete language and images and the hard-working vivid verbs. Thus while the poem is about a fairly abstract idea, it is not an abstract poem.

Rough times

—for Nancy Henley

We are trying to live
as if we were an experiment
conducted by the future,

blasting cell walls
that no protective seal or inhibition
has evolved to replace.

I am conducting a slow vivisection
on my own tissues, carried out
under the barking muzzle of guns.

Those who speak of good and simple
in the same sandwich of tongue and teeth
inhabit some other universe.

Good draws blood from my scalp and files my nerves.
Good runs the yard engine of the night over my bed.
Good pickles me in the brown vinegar of guilt.
Good robs the easy words as they rattle off my teeth,
leaving me naked as an egg.

Remember that pregnancy is beautiful only
at a distance from the distended belly.
A new idea rarely is born like Venus attended by graces.
More commonly it's modeied of baling wire and acne.
More commonly it wheezes and tips over.

Must mutants die: only
a minority refract the race
through the prisms of their genes.

Those slimy fish with air sacs were ugly
as they hauled up on the mud flats
heaving and gasping. How clumsy we are
in this new air we reach with such effort
and cannot yet breathe.

Genesis of "The Sun"

The scheme of the Tarot poems, the eleven cards of a Tarot
reading, was worked out before I began the first of the
poems. I no longer have any memory of in what order I first
wrote the poems, but the earliest fragment of "The Sun" I
have extant dates from the scheme of the whole. On a piece
of paper I have listed the cards I planned to work with—not
even the final list, for in the notes on that piece of graph
paper, three of the cards are different from those I actually
wrote about. Next to the sun I have written:

> us into the new world
> concrete images of liberation
> from the garden outward
> naked on a horse that is not bridled
> androgynous child

The first draft of the poem I can find begins with the
image on the deck I was using created by Pamela Colman
Smith and Arthur Edward Waite, as do all subsequent ver-
sions of the poem. That description comprises about a third
of this draft.

From that point on, in the last two-thirds of the poem, I
was describing a particular vision, also the seed of *Woman on
the Edge of Time*, which did emerge from meditation on this
particular card when I was preparing to write the Tarot
poems. Some of the cards I was able to penetrate immedi-
ately and got a fast fix on what in their imagery and their
symbols I wanted to use and how I wanted to treat them;

others of the cards resisted my comprehension (beyond the obvious, I mean). "The Sun" was a resistant one until it came blindingly.

Thus the structure of this particular poem was set a priori: beginning with the card and then proceeding to an attempt to embody what I had imagined. Even the image of the sunrise that ends the poem in all versions was a given, being obvious in the card and given in the vision. The struggle with the different versions is almost entirely a struggle of cleaner, stronger language and better rhythms. I was committed to a fairly long line in all the Tarot poems.

The Total Influence or Outcome: The Sun

Androgynous child whose hair curls into flowers,
naked you ride the horse, without saddle or bridle,
naked too between your thighs, from the walled garden
    outward.
Coarse sunflowers of desire, whose seeds the birds and I eat
which they break on their beaks and I with my teeth,
nod upon your journey: child of the morning
whose sun can only be born red from us who strain to give
    birth.
Joy to the world, joy, and the daughters of the sun will dance
Grow into your horse, child: let there be no more riders and
    ridden.
Learn his strong thighs and teach him your good brain.
A horse running in a field yanks the throat open like a bell
swinging with joy, you will run too and work and till and
    make good.
Child, where are you headed, with your arms spread wide,
as a shore, have I been there, have I seen it shining
like oranges among their waxy leaves on a morning tree?
I do not know your dances, I cannot translate your tongue
into words of my own, your pleasures are strange to me
as the rites of bees: yet you are the golden flowers
of a melon vine, that grows out of my belly
up where I cannot see any more in the full strong sun.
My eyes cannot make out those shapes of children like burn-
    ing clouds

who are not what we are: they go barefoot on the land like
    savages,
they have computers as household pets, they are six or seven
    sexes
and all one sex, they do not own or lease or control:
they are of one body and they are private as shamans
learning their magic at the teats of stones.
They are all magicians and do not any more forget their
    birthright of self
dancing in and out through the gates of the body standing
    wide.
Like a bear lumbering and clumsy and speaking no tongue
they know, I waddle into the fields of their play.
We are not the future, we are stunted slaves mumbling over
the tales of dragons our masters tell us, but we will be free
and you children will be free of us and uncomprehending
as we are of those shufflers in caves who scraped for fire
and banded together at last to hunt the saber-toothed tiger,
the mastodon with its tusks, the giant cave bear,
the predators that had penned them up in the dark, cowering
    so long.
The sun is rising, look, it is the sun.
I cannot look on its face, the brightness blinds me,
but from my own shadow becoming distinct, I know
that now at last it is growing light.

In the next draft I have preserved, the poem has assumed
verse paragraphs and has been cut somewhat. There are
many small omissions and small developments, but not
enough difference for me to feel it is worth quoting in its
entirety. The image of the melon vine came out of an old
woodcut I had seen, medieval I believe, where Abraham sees
all his descendants growing up out of his prostrate body.

However, I do feel it's worth quoting the third draft.

The Total Influence or Outcome of the Matter: The Sun

Androgynous child whose hair curls into flowers,
naked you ride the horse without saddle or bridle
easy between your thighs, from the walled garden outward.

Coarse sunflowers of desire whose seeds birds crack open
nod upon your journey, child of the morning whose sun
can only be born bloody from us who strain to give birth

Joy to the world, joy, and the daughters of the sun will dance
like motes of pollen in the summer air
Grow into your horse, child: let there be no more riders and
    ridden.

Child, where are you heading with arms spread wide
as a shore, have I been there, have I seen that land shining
as oranges do among their waxy leaves on a morning tree?
I do not know your dances, I cannot translate your tongue
to words of my own, your pleasures are strange to me
as the rites of bees; yet you are the yellow flower
of a melon vine growing out of my belly
though it climbs up where I cannot see in the strong sun.

My eyes cannot decipher those shapes of children like burn-
    ing clouds
who are not what we are: they go barefoot like savages,
they have computers as household pets; they are six or seven
    sexes
and only one sex; they do not own or lease or control.
They are of one body and of tribes. They are private as
    shamans
learning each her own magic at the teats of stones.
They are all magicians and technicians
and do not any more forget their birthright of self
dancing in and out through the gates of the body standing
    wide.

A bear lumbering I waddle into the fields of their play.
We are stunted slaves mumbling over the tales
of dragons our masters tell us, but we will be free.
Our children will be free of us uncomprehending
as are we of those shufflers in caves who scraped for fire
and banded together at last to hunt the saber-toothed tiger,
the tusked mastodon, the giant cave bear,
predators that had penned them up, cowering so long.

The sun is rising, look: it is blooming new.
I cannot look in the sun's face, its brightness blinds me

but from my own shadow becoming distinct I know
that now at last it is beginning to grow light.

Here the second paragraph has become quite short. The extended development of the horse has been lopped back to one line. In the fourth paragraph the children of the future have become not merely magicians but magicians and technicians, a not particularly felicitous phrase. The "gates of the body" I associate with Blake, some amalgam of his "The doors of perception" with "Twelve gates to the City," a song I recall from civil rights days.

I am still having trouble with the image and words of the last paragraph. I am aware as I write it of Plato's cave. I am still having trouble with the line breaks and the phrasing of the words themselves.

The final version of the poem makes many small changes: in the second line, "the horse" becomes "a horse" in keeping with its diminished importance while the second paragraph has been assimilated into the first. I have finally realized that it is not the future sun that ought to be bleeding but the mother giving birth, and fixed that.

In the second verse paragraph, the replacement of "to words of my own" with "to words I use" is a matter of rhythm. The image of the oranges among their leaves on that tree has finally gone—it never quite took or worked—and been replaced by a far more appropriate image "like sun spangles on clean water rippling," a line superior in its rhythm by far. The sun entering that line meant I had to change the last line of the stanza, where to avoid repetition "strong sun" became "strong light," a more accurate word in that context.

The children have stopped being "like" burning clouds and that has become an alternate way to see them. There are many small cuts there, "seven sexes" for "six or seven sexes"— I was thinking of paramecia. "The teats of stones" has become "the teats of stones and trees" because I wanted a longer line and because that seemed to me more evocative of the kind of earth reverence I was trying to bring to mind. Finally it is "technicians and peasants" they become. "Magic" has already appeared and what I wanted was the connection to the basic means of production, agriculture, the commitment to the land insisted on, along with the full use of science. Finally instead of only a "birthright of self" it is that plus "their mane of animal pride" they do not forget. I wanted to describe a people sensual, proudly physical, connected to other living beings and the earth, who were also highly civilized in the best sense.

"The fields of their play" has become "the fields of their work games" because I wanted to emphasize their productivity and did not want them to sound trivial or infantile.

I finally got the ending together. That changing smell of the air at dawn is something I have often noticed in the country. I also got the line breaks functional at last in the ending.

> The sun is rising, feel it: the air smells fresh.
> I cannot look in the sun's face, its brightness blinds me,
> but from my own shadow becoming distinct
> I know that now at last
> it is beginning to grow light.

When I put this poem in my selected poems (*Circles on the Water* [Knopf, New York: 1982]) I made only one change. I took out the mastodon, as not properly a predator and because it was messing up the line breaks. I broke it as follows:

> and banded together at last to hunt the saber-toothed tiger,
> the giant cave bear, predators
> that had penned them up cowering so long.

An Interview with *Sandscript*

How long did it take you to write Woman on the Edge of Time?

Oh, about two years and nine months.

Were you writing other things at the same time?

I was writing poems. There's always a period of time when a novel is in production—when I don't start the next novel, but write more poems and usually other things. This year it happened to be that I coauthored my first play, but normally I write articles and a lot of poetry.

What's the name of your play?

The Last White Class.

And who's the other author?

Ira Wood.

In the Woman on the Edge of Time *would you consider the first future that Connie enters through Luciente a utopia?*

From an interview with Barbara Dunning and Jean Lunn for *Sandscript*, 1, nos. 2 and 3 (1977).

No, because it's accessible. There's almost nothing there except the brooder not accessible now. So it's hardly a utopia; it is very intentionally not a utopia because it is not strikingly new. The ideas are the ideas basically of the women's movement.

Do you see Woman on the Edge of Time *primarily as a novel about social injustice?*

It's primarily a novel about Connie. There's a lot about social injustice in it, and about how a woman stops hating herself and becomes able to love herself enough to fight for her own survival.

There's a lot in this novel.

To me, the vision of a reasonable society was one in which it might be rather nice to live.

I think so. I could fit very nicely into that society, I think.

So could I.

Now what about the cities of the society? You don't deal at all with the cities in Mattapoisett. On the other one, the future in chapter fifteen that she gets to by accident, that was a frightening one.

It was supposed to be frightening.

It was all city: the pollution, and all the bad things that are actually potential today. Both of them were potentially future societies.

Yes, depending on who wins, essentially.

Through Connie we understand that this is a serious actuality and that either of these potential futures could be our children's or our great-grandchildren's. Does the polluted society mean this is what we'll choose if we don't repent? I am immediately reminded of "I set before you life and death, therefore choose life," but that you have a choice.

I think you do always have a choice. I think you always have a choice of what you'll do and what you'll refuse to do; of what you'll choose to do and what you'll be afraid to choose to do. I've been very concerned in my work with the meaning of— particularly to a woman—saying yes and saying no. There's a number of poems in *Living in the Open* which pertain to that and in *The Twelve-Spoked Wheel Flashing.*

Now in this future society, is there a reason for each child having three mothers?

First of all, they have broken sex roles. Each child has three mothers because what use was a father? What does a child need? The only reason everyone says a child needs a father is because little boys have to be sexually imprinted to be little boys and girls have to be sexually imprinted to want daddy. What everyone needs—what the child is born needing—is mothering; that is, nurturing, loving, teaching, being held, being comforted.

Breast-feeding. . . .

Right. Biological males and biological females breast-feed in that society. It is very important for men to have a direct responsibility for children if men are ever to be loving, nurturing, giving human beings. If they're to become human they have to have a direct responsibility for biological offspring the same as women do. I think that's the only thing that's going to break down the roles where you have half the society socialized to love and half the society socialized to kill. If you want to get away from that distribution of sex roles— into those who are socialized to love or to be loved, those who are taken care of and those who take care—if you want to break that down, you have to have everybody responsible for the young. Until everyone's responsible for preserving life, you won't have a real respect for life institutionalized in the society. And that's what I was trying to talk about: a society in which everybody respects life. So to make sure the nuclear family of recent history isn't repeated, every child, in fact has three mothers, at least two of whom can breast feed the child, and maybe all three of them. So that a very young child doesn't drive anybody crazy. If you have eight-hour shifts, everybody gets a night's sleep.

That's a very valid reason for three.

Because by the time you get to four, you don't really need four. It's true with a small child—eight hours with a two-year-old is really enough. The reason for three mothers is so that nobody has to cease living, and so that the child is nurtured.

Now to me Sybil is an interesting character. But at the end it's left . . . you don't know whether she does escape.

I think you hear you're fairly sure she does escape. Whether she can make it and stay outside, you don't know.

In One Flew over the Cuckoo's Nest, *another novel about mental institutions, the character runs away. Why didn't Connie do that?*

I'm not responsible for Ken Kesey. I think our politics are exceedingly different. Are you asking me why doesn't Connie escape?

Well, I felt reading it that she had a drive, a strength which she didn't have before, and she did escape.

But she escaped from a much easier institution.

That's true. She was in a different hospital at the time.

And once you escape, you're watched much more carefully.

Was Diana a psychiatrist? In the future society?

They don't have psychiatrists. She's a healer. Sybil's twin.

Sybil's twin?

Yes. Her mirror image.

If it goes one way, it's healing; if it goes the other, witchcraft?

Midwives have much better legal status in a number of other countries—countries with much lower infant mortality than our own.

And there's also a trend in health foods. Some of the old ways are coming back, we can see that. But I was bothered by the way land is owned today and the way land was owned by the tribes. In other words, how could we go back to the way land was owned, or forward; if we wanted to change the way property was owned?

If you're talking about a transition to socialism, do you mean how do we get there? Or back to Native American ideas.

Uh-huh.

I think it's going to be a very long struggle, as I said in the book, because I think there's a lot of opposition to it.

One of the last frontiers, or first frontiers today is research into understanding ESP, clairvoyance, alpha states, and other powers of the mind.

And you notice that in my future there's a lot of respect for understanding what goes on inside you as well as what goes on outside you, which I think has a lot to do with it being truly an androgynous society—one in which women's values and what women represent are respected as much as the more traditional patriarchial ideas. People are trained to pay a lot of attention to what is going on inside themselves and be responsible for it.

Right, there is a lot of that, and just the fact that she is a sender; a catcher—the sender-catcher idea where they're both receptive to each other, and they (Luciente and Connie) can communicate through each other's minds.

Right. My mother's very psychic so I grew up just taking that for granted as one of the things that people can be, like double-jointed. It isn't a real exceptional thing; it's just something that some people can do and some people can't do.

Do you consider research like they are conducting at Duke a high priority issue? Is that important?

No, not particularly. Experimenting with ESP doesn't seem to be nearly as important as learning biofeedback, as people learning to control some of their own responses to stress. It's far more valuable to learn how *not* to develop hypertension. Oppressed people have a tendency to internalize stress, which is one of the reasons black people in our society have such a high incidence of high blood pressure. People can teach others how to take oppression and not to turn it into bodily anguish. That affects people's health and their ability to fight. Not keep the pain inside them. I know a therapist who teaches women how to go into alpha, teaches women how to begin not punishing ourselves bodily. That's just one of the tremendous uses of that kind of technology with her taking it to people and working primarily with poor women teaching them to begin not punishing themselves.

And poor men. I would think the same stresses would apply.

People are often socialized so that in families like that the man is more inclined to drink and beat the woman than to internalize it. She is working in a situation of rural poverty where the commonest problems she sees are alcoholism, wife abuse, child abuse, and incest.

She's trying to deal with that situation. O.K. Now there was a passage in the book Woman on the Edge of Time *where it was stated, or one of the characters had stated, that you could take a sabbatical and write a book.*

Well, you might write books or not. Every seven years you have a sabbatical; everybody has a sabbatical—a year in which they are released from productive labor.

Where they produce the holis?

They also have ordinary sculpture.

And the children, in the very beginning there was a place where the children and the adults displayed their art work in the dining area.

Yes. But in fact, if you remember Jackrabbit saying that they consider art productive labor as much as any other kind of production.

I had a little trouble with the way they went about studying, because they could study fairly freely, but yet our concept now of the way you study to be a musician or something like that is that it takes years of study. So would that be lost, or would they continue to, you know?

I think that probably certain kinds of things would be lost. For instance, the violin prodigy who starts at age two and practices seventeen hours a day, yes, I don't think there'd be any. Because I don't think anybody would be willing to have their life warped in that way.

Most musicians do not practice efficiently. It can be done now. It is just that tradition dies hard and it's another one of the confusions that the time put in equals the result produced. But this kind of study would not be carried on, I take it.

Well, I don't think that people would be used in that sense. If you value the sound that you get out of castrated boys enough to castrate boys to get it—if you don't, you won't. I think that that's a society in which no thing is valued enough to destroy a person to get it. I suspect that such a society would produce actually more interesting art. Almost everyone in that society practices some art, and some people do it full time.

Just about everyone does.

It doesn't mean that everyone's an amateur. There are people who do nothing but their art. . . .

There's a passage in the novel where Connie says "Oh, you're all amateurs," or something to that effect, and then there was a collaboration for a film in the sense that artistic creation needs to be judged by the population as very fine pieces of work.

The place actually is the death of Sappho. Connie is upset because Sappho, the old woman, is dying outside under a tent by the river where she's chosen to be taken and Connie doesn't see—it's not a hospital, it's not scientific, it's not clean. There Sappho is outside and she's reaching with her hand in the river and she's calling for things. . . .

And she keeps saying "I can't hear the river, put me closer I can't hear the river," that's really a nice way to go.

Anyhow, Connie is very upset because Sappho is outside in this sort of drippy tent—how can she die out there—and why isn't she in the hospital—just a bunch of amateurs, that's when Connie says that, but we're all amateurs at dying. Connie is not immediately knocked out by the future.

She isn't, she's holding on to what she's used to.

It's a very penny ante kind of future. It isn't shiny. It isn't Buck Rogers. There's not a lot of visible machinery. It's just a bunch of people running around—goats, chickens, people.

Well, no, it's a little more glamorous than that. They have flimsys.

Basically there are two types of nonwork clothing. Essentially people wear work clothing—in all colors of the rainbow but practical.

Connie put on a pair of pants, wasn't that right, and they were too loose, so she found the adjustment in the seam. She just had her hospital clothes on.

There are two types of luxurious clothing. Basically you have a certain number of luxury credits and you can spend them on anything you want to and there are some things which circulate all of the time. Beautiful art objects, luxuries— some are consumable and you spend your credits on them; others you simply take out and enjoy for awhile then put back.

And there are ceremonial garments. Or if you really want to wear a sable coat for a month. All right, if person wants something, this or that, you take it out of stores. It's a ceremonial occasion, so you sign out something really fancy to wear and keep it around for awhile—wear it a few times— and then you put it back in for somebody else. For a lot of holiday occasions there are flimsys. Flimsys are one-time-only garments which are produced by the computer according to your fantasies and they're made out of algae. Pressed. But they're made in all kinds of shapes.

They must be edible.

Yes, they would be. They may not taste very good. They're mainly made of cellulose.

They must be dyed too. That sounds like a good hangover cure. You go to a party, then eat your garment then wake up and you're fine.

Anyhow, they're instantly recycled and they're objects which are produced according to your fantasies and they're not designed to last. They have many many holidays.

Isn't that wonderful. There were fourteen main ones. . . .

And twenty-six minor ones.

Almost one a week.

Well they were big on them.

Luciente says: "We want each other to feel cherished. That's a point of emphasis, now, maybe always, some cooperation, some competing goes on. Instead of competing for a living, for scarce resources, for food we try to cooperate on all that. Competing is like decoration."

Yes. It's what they do in sports and the arts and all kinds of things which decorate life. In the flimsys too. Everyone in *Woman on the Edge of Time* wants to be in a more outrageous, more exciting, more fanciful costume than everyone else.

Also, right after that there was a part where you included jealousy in the characters.

Luciente and Bolivar are essentially competing under the surface for Jackrabbit, and they have the worming, which was everybody trying to help them to work out what they're feeling. People from each of the families are trying to help them work it out and figure out what to do, because it's beginning to get in everybody's way. In a worming, you're dealing with the things that are eating you away. In other words, people caring about each other to try to help each other. Sometimes in order to help each other they're forbidden to speak—the mother-in-law taboo.

After they come out of the wilderness, isn't there a taboo? The mother and child can't speak for a certain period of time.

Adolescence. When the child decides that person is no longer a child, but person is going to assume full responsibilities, person elects to go through the survival experience. When person returns, the mothers cannot speak to them for a period of two months and by that time the patterns are all broken.

I love the way they handle the transportation in that society. There are bikes which people just pick up and leave.

The Provos did that in Amsterdam. White bicycles are just community property.

Then they also have public transportation. Then they had floaters. But what about the old people?

You see them using the public transportation. But old people tend to be healthier because the food is better and secondly the people are physically active. Also, old people are much more successfully integrated into the culture.

Also, old people are used as far as the child care goes, although that's a separate house.

Yes, but everybody's there.

I could live in that society. Now I want to talk about the society with the multis. They apparently keep building up and up and up and up. I was unclear whether these two societies were coexisting.

No, they're alternate futures.

But there is someone the people are fighting—the they and the us. But that's not the other one.

Well, in a sense it is; it's all alternate future and it's who they're fighting. It's really both.

Connie becomes involved in the fighting.

That's a hallucination.

Well, the whole thing could be an hallucination, but to me, that doesn't really matter.

It's very carefully kept that way. The battle that she imagines is a dogfight in the floaters.

You know what it reminded me of? Star Wars. *Have you seen that movie?*

Yes, but I hadn't seen it then. The floaters are not supersonic. They've given up on all that because it costs too much.

Everything is energy-related. This is a very well thought-out book. There's a passage in it that says we have energy, and then she names it off on her fingers. . . .

. . . methane, sun, the waves, the wind.

There are certain places where they get energy, and then they have to allocate them and they decide that.

And there's a lot about that process of how it's decided. I was recently up at Goddard where there's a social-ecology program and they kept pointing out to me that I don't believe in postscarcity, which is a theory that has been very popular on parts of the left and parts of the right in the United States. It essentially says that with a technological society we shall reach a stage of "postscarcity" in which scarcity belongs only to the past and we will no longer have to allocate resources or divide up resources because technology will take us beyond that point and we will be in a society in which there will be no scarcity of anything. I don't believe that.

Now I'm concerned with the alternate future. To me it was one of the strengths of the novel. You could have written it with just the one future. But instead, you had these alternatives. How do you think men are going to react to this novel?

Well, I think different men react different ways. A lot depends on their sympathies, their politics, how they feel. I mean I don't think it's a book that men *can't* relate to because it is a society, after all.

It's not an Amazon society.

Some women were very disappointed in my future because men still exist. I think some men would find it very attractive, because it is a society in which men are human.

My next question was where do you predict your work will go from here, but since you've already written another novel. . . .

Yes. I've got the copyedited manuscript upstairs that I've got to return by Wednesday. . . .

I think your characterization is brilliant in Woman on the Edge of Time.

In my opinion, it is my best novel and may remain my best novel . . . I'm very proud of it. I like the one I just wrote, but the one I just wrote is a smaller novel, it's a triangle, it's much more encompassable. Sort of the opposite of *Woman on the Edge of Time. The High Cost of Living* is basically about three people, about the "cost" of moving from the traditional working class to the college-educated working class, about a certain type of politics based too much on morality and not enough on human considerations and not on economic enough—sort of when morality takes over and labelling and morality become the driving forces. What can happen in that.

I'll have to read it. You tend to use the word politics in broader sense than it is generally used.

Well, you see, in a society in which the left has been defined as illegitimate and politics gets defined as who you vote for of two candidates indistinguishable except who has had the opportunity to screw the voters most recently, politics tends to be a kind of spectator sport. A great amount of money has been spent in the United States to make the left illegitimate and the left always talks about economics. If you're not supposed to talk about who owns things, you end up with dull politics.

Through the Cracks

Growing Up in the Fifties

I. A Protracted Adolescence, a Foreshortened Perspective

I think I have some notion how growing up in the fifties compared with growing up in the sixties, because I arranged to have two adolescences, one at the normal age, and one again in the sixties, in SDS. Growing up in the fifties: I never could, exactly. Part of maturing is strengthening a sense of I as an identity and a strong project, and then blending that into some larger We. Being an adult involves a bonding with a community, and therefore of history and progeny, a meshing with time, a sense of struggling and yielding, shaping and being shaped in that river.

In the fifties I found myself a perennial adolescent, isolated, stuck in the alienated pose of an individual in a hostile environment. History had ended in the American apotheosis; it was only a matter of time (and struggle with the forces of evil) before the rest of the world became just like Our Town with cigarette commercials. I remember my best friend's brother-in-law yelling at her, "You aren't satisfied with anything. What do you want, to go live with savages in a cave in Italy?" Changing this country felt inconceivable. Politics was voting. The long ice age of General Motors, General

---

First published in *Partisan Review* 41, no. 2 (July, 1974).

Foods, General Eisenhower, and general miasma: the only choices were conformity or exile. I could not imagine a future. Only sci-fi freaks were into that, and mostly their future looked like the old frontier with shinier gadgets. My own actions of protest against the distribution of wealth, rights, power were doomed to be symbolic and abortive.

Survival was hard enough. It was harder to be poor then than now, I think, although of course that is a snotty judgment eased by the fact that I am no longer poor. There was no support for choosing anything other than a narrowly defined norm. There was no subculture to drop into especially, especially for women. (To an independent woman the enclaves of beat and hep were more piggish than the straight world.) Still, beyond survival or a clubby grouping of nervous politics played by Robert's Rules, the only actions I could see were gesture, bordering on prank. My anger was enormous, when I was in touch with it at all, but the isolated gestures available trivialized it: soapsuds in a fountain, a faked news story, refusing to use footnotes or keep hours, taking off my clothes. Either you got away with it because you didn't get caught so it might as well not have happened, or you did it publicly and were promptly punished.

The end of ideology produced a world in stasis. Actually the fifties represented the last gasp of WASP history as history: the history of the affluent white male Western European and latterly American presence in the world given to us as the history of humankind; Western European culture of the better-off sold us as Culture. This battle is still continuing, and most of what is taught in school is still official cult, but at least now it is being challenged. The vast rest of us were deviations from the norm. I call the fifties the end of that but what a fat squat end. What a grey smug tight world. Everything that moved me at first contact (Whitman, Dickinson) turned out to be déclassé or irrelevant to the mainstream, the tradition. It was not, of course, a mainstream that had produced me, a tradition to which I was a natural heir. I would never be a gentleman.

What a need to tidy everything, librarianlike. Everything in art was taught as fitting somewhere in a vast hierarchy. The Great Chain of Being seemed still intact. Even the lawns were Christian. Human nature was a universal constant, each of us with her heart of darkness. In this period of successful identification of ruling class interests seamlessly with the interests of "the people" (who were the images on the cover of the *Saturday Evening Post*) the concept of American class-lessness was being pushed at the same time that critics like Lionel Trilling were calling for a novel of manners: meaning literature *interior* to the world of the affluent. The defeat of Marxist literary criticism and theory meant rejection of the class struggle and somehow even of working-class experi-ence as a viable theme. Yet class was a fact of my life, some-thing I brooded over constantly in childhood every time I took the Joy Road or Tireman buses in Detroit and noted how if you went downtown there were even more blacks than in our neighborhood and housing got worse and worse, and if you went the other direction there was more space, more trees, yards, single-family brick houses, parks. If I had come to college never having thought about poverty, born out of an egg the day before, going to college was a never-ending education in the finer distinctions of class insult and bias. It kept kicking me in the teeth.

When characters who were not white, male, and affluent appeared in the literature we read, including novels of the time, they were all image and mythology, when not comic relief. When a character was black, generally she represented something in the white writer's psyche—nature, evil, death, life, fecundity. Like Indians. Like women to this day. Such beings were never assumed to have an inner reality equal and coherent to the white male writer. Now we begin to have a diversity of culture to begin to match our different realities, values, lives.

Yes, the world was a dead egg. I felt impacted. Nothing would ever move or change. All that could be imagined was slipping off somewhere special like near Sartre, where things were obviously more vital; or wriggling through the cracks, surviving in the unguarded interstices. There was no support for opting out of the rat race or domesticity. On the other hand, it was easier in some ways to get by; i.e., shoplifting was pitifully easy in the fifties, with none of the organized and increasingly mechanized war between stores and customers that goes on now, only store dicks and a few mirrors. What people conceived of as possible for them to do was small: the possible lives seemed only two or three, like the differences between men's sport jackets or suits. Marry or die! The painfully slow process of work in communities that has produced a smattering of free clinics, drop-in centers, women's centers, hot-lines, abortion referral services, pregnancy counseling, law communes, food co-ops, switchboards, alternate schools, wasn't even a gleam in an organizer's eye. If you got sick, suicidal, depressed, in trouble, pregnant, hungry, you were on your own. I remember eating flour and water for four days during vacation in the university town, trying to pry my paycheck loose. Now there would always be someplace I could get a meal. Kids take slightly, slightly more care of each other; the subculture trains folks to pretend at least to care.

There was, I think, more general sense of intellectual adventure in the fifties, for books were one of the only escapes to Otherwise. About the only perspectives available for projecting a reality alien to Plainfield U.S.A. came from steeping oneself in Alexandrian Neoplatonists or the habits of the army ant. When I was nineteen, some of the most alive people I met were university types, giving off an intellectual electricity. I would never make that judgment now. That perspective lent to purely verbal or mental adventuring a glamour it no longer has for me. For if you cannot conceive of doing anything to alter your world, you reserve your admiration for manipulating concepts about those who have done something, or even for those who manipulate concepts about others who have manipulated concepts. I was particularly fascinated by scientists (and in graduation panic married a physicist) because they seemed elected to have some effect. I would then sometimes derive a heady excitement from the distance between my intellectual labors and everything visible to me. Partly no doubt that was due to a naive working-class based zest for "real learning" which had to be esoteric to assure me that I was being truly educated. But some had to do with advanced learning in the various disciplines (that word! It conjured up for me then an almost Marquis de Sade shiver: I was crazy about that word at nineteen) representing an available exit from a crushingly repressive world. A world in which the Left was dead (or comically irrelevant: meetings of five socialists representing five factions, all competing in anti-Communist pieties) was for me a world without historical movement and a world without hope.

My existence in the English Department at Michigan was exceedingly perilous and bumpy. One of my teachers there who is now at Syracuse said, when some students wanted to invite me to read a couple of years ago, over his dead body. I was a garlic among the Anglican-convert lilies. I felt the wrong shape, size, sex, volume level, class, and emotional coloration. I fought, always with a sense of shame, for I could never define what I felt was being throttled in me. And I wanted approval. I loved working in the dim mustily fragrant stacks of the library, safe, busy. I loved the old clanking conveyor belt that delivered books up to the desk when requested (and chewed up a number of books as we found out the night we snuck into the space at the bottom). It was ancient, noisy, did not work well, had a certain wrought iron charm, and impressed upon me the privilege of being in its presence at all: something of a makeshift image for my education.

In graduate school at Northwestern suddenly things came easily. As soon as I passed my master's exam with a record score, I got scared. I can look at my fright one way as conventional female programming. I was married to a graduate student in physics. I dropped out to support him, although I was a better student. Failure brings emotional rewards to women; success brings penalties. Indeed all the men in my department used to insult me whenever they could get through.

But I wanted to write. I knew I was writing badly. I could not produce two lines without making five literary allusions, punning in Elizabethan English and dragging in some five-dollar word like *chiaroscuro*. I was assimilating. Graduate school represented the first financial security I had ever known (which may sound weird to you, but meant a meal ticket to me). I knew I could hack it and then I'd be safe, I thought. Actually now I see how shaky are the positions of women in universities, Ph.D. or not, fired just before tenure, shunted into cleanup courses. I didn't have the savvy then to guess that security might not apply to me. But it scared me anyhow and not entirely because I feared success. That wasn't success to me. It was just security.

Success was telling some truth, creating some vision on paper. I had to go back to my own roots somehow before I lost a sense of myself. I lived in Uptown in Chicago, on Wilson Avenue in a poor white neighborhood the JOIN project of SDS was later to work in. I was laboring for a sense of my self, origins, prospects, antecedents, intentions, a renewed sense of a living language natural to my mouth, even a mythology I could use. Some I tried to read from the city streets, some from my grim jobs, some from the library again. On a borrowed card I sought a mythology that centered on women. From 1958 through 1960 I read everything I could get into my hands on the mother goddess religions, mandalas, matriarchy, Crete, Amazons, Isis, Ishtar, Diana, Artemis, Cybele, Demeter. I read Margaret Murray on witches and poured over Jung's illustrations. It was all useless. I could not assimilate it usefully. I could not write out of what soaked dark and wet and fecundating into my brain. I could not make connections. Now of course the emerging women's culture draws on this stuff. But to be interested in Demeter in 1958 wasn't to be a precursor but to be mad, objectively irrelevant. Just as there was no community to mediate for me between individual and mass, there was nobody to write for, nobody to communicate with about matters of being female, alive, thinking, trying to make sense of one's life and times. I wrote novel after novel, poem after poem for no one: to lack a context and to create is to be objectively mad.

Within a year after leaving school I broke out of the box of my marriage. I remember my husband demanding to know what I wanted in leaving him, and yelling that I was pursuing a phoenix. He told me that both he and his shrink agreed I needed help badly, was frigid (I no longer wanted to sleep with him) and pursuing neurotic fancies. I stood there flat-footed and suddenly I could see the cramped, starved, supportive housewife relationship with my husband side-by-side with earlier, freer bondings with other men, and I started to laugh. He tried to tie the divorce to my being willing to go to his shrink or a shrink his shrink would choose, but I just left. I am surprised considering how timid and malleable I was then where the strength emerged to laugh and walk out, to cling to my own flimsy reality against official reality, husband reality, shrink reality, newspaper reality, sociological reality, the reality of everybody I knew telling me I was a self-destructive fool to walk out of such a good marriage. Good for what, I asked? I think only a hunger for reality, a large omnivorous curiosity that had led me to a certain breadth of experience by twenty-two gave me a courage based on having at least some few things to compare other things to.

That comparison was generally lacking: a sense of possibilities, of alternate universes of social discourse, of other assumptions about what was good or primary, of other viable ways of making a living, making love, having and raising children, being together, living, and dying. There was little satisfaction for me in the forms offered, yet there seemed no space but death or madness outside the forms.

II. Femininity as a Persistent Discomfort, Like a Headcold

Surely seldom has the role of women been more painful, the contradictions more intense, than they were in the fifties, when the full force of the counterrevolution struck us. Sick was a cant word of the fifties: if you were unhappy, if you wanted something you couldn't have easily or that other people did not want or wouldn't admit to wanting, if you were angry, if you were different, strange, psychic, emotional, intellectual, political, double-jointed: you were sick, sick, sick.

Women's clothing of the fifties, the purchased or stolen trappings of my adolescence: a litany of rubber, metal bands, garters, boning, a rosary of spandex and lycra and nylon, a votive candle of elastic, I consecrate to you. I think you were sick.

The skirts were long and clumsy. How we waded through summer as they hung from us in fat folds muffling our thin hips and flat behinds as if we were matrons vast as car barns. But sweaters were tight. Through the sweater you could see ridges of brassiere like targets for gunnery practice, through the fluorescent pilled nylon (like goosepimples), the more affluent pastel cashmeres (kept under the bed in trunks by girls in my dormitory, fingered like gold: a nice suburban girl counted her wealth, her worth in cashmeres), the ubiquitous flat lambswool cardigans and pullovers, playing their demure mother and daughter acts under the false teeth of pearls.

Sacky tweed skirts, little grey suits in which no one looked real. What you were supposed to wear to job interviews, along with some hat, white shoes, white gloves. In my drawer were two pairs of white gloves never worn except at job interviews: some mad connection between being paid $1.35 an hour to type and carrying a pair of white gloves. Purity. Virginity. We used to rub chalk on them to make them white.

The other choice besides the acres of swishing skirt was called a sheath. Those were alluring gowns into which we crept, first having squashed flat the belly, the hips, the waist, slowly, slowly, toothpaste cramming back into the tube. If a zipper broke, we spilled out. Bottles filled with our fizzing blood or stale water, it did not matter; they stood alone, their sex so much more definite than our own, hard and horny as the carapace of beetles. Our flesh served them in bondage: the bondage of which all these clothes speak.

What is a woman walking on high heels? What is a giraffe on roller skates? The platform shoes clumping along now depress me. Spike heels used to turn ankles and break legs regularly, catching in gratings, escalators, cracks at elevator doors, stairway treads. Who grows tumid at clumsy mincing, at the warped back of a woman bobbing stiffly—who cannot run if she has to, who is hobbled, distorted, learning to endure pain?

Longline brassieres underneath staved in the ribs, shoved the stomach up into the esophagus, raised the rigid breasts till their padded peaks brushed the chin. Breasts were hard and shiny as the apple stuck in the mouth of the roast suckling pig. Strapless brassieres dug into the skin to leave a red welt encircling. If you reached upward, if you moved suddenly, the bra would remain anchored like a granite ledge. The freed breasts would pop out. Suddenly you stood, Diana of Ephesus with four boobs. I remember my dormitory friend murmuring scorn of the boyfriend who thought he had caressed her breast in the twilit lounge. All he had contacted was Playtex padded perfect circle size 34A.

Girdles: my mother bought me one when I turned twelve, saying to me that now I was a woman. I weighed ninety-two pounds and cast no shadow standing sideways. Rubber coffins. They were diving machines that made of air a sticky sea to founder in. Who could eat with pleasure in a girdle? I remember pain at restaurant tables, the squirming, the itching, the overt tweaking and plucking. Who could dance? Run or bend over or climb a ladder? Fuck? Scratch? No, in a girdle you stand and stand. You sit rigidly and nothing jiggles, nothing bounces. You are looked at like an avocado tree in a lobby. The pallid flesh sweats coldly under the rubber mask with it smell of doctors' offices and baby cribs.

What do these costumes say with their high, conical breasts, deep waistlines, flat rib cages, and no bellies at all— no wombs in there, nothing to digest with? Girdles that chafed the thighs raw. It is not trivia, this catalogue of out-of-fashion clothes that arouse lust in middle-aged men. These costumes say that flesh must be confined, must suffer in rigidity. Women must accustom themselves to a constant state of minor pain, binding themselves in a parody of the real body to be constantly "attractive." A woman must never be able to use her body freely.

Before this armory of underwear, flesh was quelled, cowed. It had the shape divine. We didn't have bodies then, we had shapes. We were the poor stuff from which this equipment carved the feminine. Under all this clothing our meat, imprinted with seams and chafed with elastic, shuddered and waited in ignorance. Our bodies were blind worms, helpless under rocks. Secretly they turned to muscle or to flab as they would, but the clothes jailed us, trained us to await babies and cancer and rape, dumb as a centerpiece of wax fruit. I feel less vulnerable naked than in those trappings.

III. Daddy, Mommy, and The Bomb

The Bomb: like God, a central presence, hefty as in the Herblock cartoons. It blocked political thinking. It made us afraid of Them who presumably would drop their bomb on us rather than afraid of Us, who were our business to control and who policed us into complicity.

I used to dream eschatologically, New York Harbor choked with charred corpses, the blackened pit that had been Detroit. During my freshman year we spent time, the three of us roommates, fantasizing about what we would do when the bomb fell on Detroit. We had a feeble scheme of stealing horses from a nearby riding stable and heading north to the woods to live off the land—something we had as much idea how to do as construct an atomic pile. That was a big time for lists of necessary supplies to keep in the basement.

I suspect one of the grand sexual fantasies of the fifties was survival with a few choice members of the opposite sex—or same if you were gay. Miraculously saved in Mammoth Cave where you happened to be visiting at the time with a party composed only of you and whomever you wanted. It would be the end of anxiety. The worst would have come true and all the rules gone out the window. Back to the simple life to try it all again. Or wait for the end with fun and games. In any event it too was an outlet, a source of change in a static world. A persistent and obsessive fantasy I found in at least half the men I was involved with in those years.

I think people generally expect less of sex now and that works out better. If a woman obeyed Freud and togetherness and gave up everything for her femininity, she expected the earth to move and the sky to fall in bed. Men who conformed to the corporate image on the job expected to go home to warmth, intimacy, and a personal geisha.

Living was personalized, privatized. You had problems. Everything seemed to go on in small boxes. It was a time dominated by a Freudian theology of biology and childhood as fate. I don't believe there are greater incidences of rape and impotence now than in the fifties. I was a bit outside, and people came to me in crises. It was assumed I would know the abortionist or what to do. I functioned in that way for years, repository of sexual lore, like a crazy bank where people left stuff they didn't really want, to molder and gather slow interest. Then, as now, a great many women were forcibly raped, and then (as now enforced by the society and the law but just beginning to be fought by women), women were ashamed of that violence done to them and believed, as programmed, that to be violently entered was somehow their fault. The incidence of male impotence has always been high among any class of men I've ever known, age, background, race, level of education regardless. I suspect from conversations with much older women that it's held constant since 1910 at least. But nobody talked about it then. Men did not talk honestly to men, women did not talk honestly enough to women. Men talked to women individually but with a mixture of confession, propaganda, blame laying, and demand.

The myth of the vaginal orgasm (big bang theory of femininity) did enormous damage. It not only produced a generation of women alienated from their bodies, trained to deny actual pleasure and to act out fancied orgasms, but alienated from their minds, since generally in order to function and "be happy" in relations with men, women had to believe they were experiencing "fulfillment" in bed.

Mutually exclusive sex roles divided humanity into winners and losers, makers and made, doers and done, fuckers and fuckees, yin and yang, and who the hell wants to be passive, moist, cold, receptive, unmoving, inert: sort of a superbasement of humanity. Women still police each other, to keep each other in line, as men too police women, the range of permissible behavior for women remaining much narrower than for men. But women policed each other in the fifties with a special frenzy, being totally convinced nothing but death and madness lay outside the nuclear family and the baby-doll-mommy roles. How could we have believed that when we saw the toll of death and madness inside the roles?

Even the notion of acceptable beauty was exceedingly limited and marred a whole generation of women who grew up knowing they did not embody it (training in self-hatred) and a whole generation of men who felt they were entitled to it, and any actual woman not resembling the few idols was very second-best: or Everyman has the right to the exclusive possession of Marilyn Monroe. Just as the sex roles have widened, slightly, and loosened, a minute amount, so the range of people who grow up thinking themselves physically acceptable has increased perceptibly. Kinky hair is fine, afros are fine, straight hair is fine, you don't have to wear falsies any more. The common physical conditions still persecuted include being fat and ordinary signs of aging, i.e., flesh being less than brand-new as if from a machine shop.

What we were trained to respond to sexually in men can be roughly divided into two types. One was the Sensitive Hood, mean, destructive, self-destructive, sadistic but suffering. The other was Iceman: now Iceman might be the

Cold War cowboy, the suntanned tycoon; or might be the more ectomorphic intellectual with cheekbones and an ascetic air. But he was cold through and through, he was ungiving Daddy, the block of stone, destructive but not usually self-destructive. The perfect tool of empire, whether in his study or his factory or his trenchcoat. The essence of each was the inability to love, to feel in a useful way, while retaining the ability (usually) to act. The Sensitive Hood, the existential darling, feels but only pain or the pleasure of giving pain. A generation of women was raised to impale themselves on knives or pound themselves mushy on rocks, while fantasizing to order about womanly fulfillment, surrender, and the big bang orgasm. It would make me weep if I hadn't had to live through it, wondering what was hitting me. One is the Sinful Son and the other the Terrible Father, basically Puritan ghouls, competitive, alienated, death-dealing and empty, empty in the soul, useless to the preservation of life. Egoistic in quite different styles: insensitivity trained by the grueling rituals of American manhood, or narcissism ogling itself in the shine of a switchblade (usually imaginary).

The only road back from pouring affection down a rat hole lay in your children: creative motherhood. Of course we are approaching the great double bind by which a mother must give all of her attention all of the time to her children while they are growing up lest they become drug-dealing preverts, but a possessive mother kills . . .

We had not the active paranoia we have learned through the sixties and seventies, the Pychonesque government plot involving the CIA, the Mafia, the White House, and ITT: the knowledge that behind the bland or incoherent violent facade of newspaper "events" lie unimaginable writhings of interlocked directorates of multinational corporations. No, the facade was entire in the fifties: every Corinthian column in its place and nobody on the white marble steps but the D.A. taking his oath. Our paranoia was, first, petty: that "they," i.e., the FBI, would immediately know if I talked to a Communist or took Engels's *On the Family* out of the library. While I was at Michigan there was a minor furor when a student confessed to her boyfriend that the FBI had scared her into giving them a list of everyone who came to his many parties, for he was . . . an avowed Marxist! When I arranged for Pete Seeger to give his first concert there in many years, I felt incredibly cheeky. It was playing poker with monopoly money. The political dimension had been crushed from our lives, making it impossible to think about community, the state, the economy, history in any vital way.

The paranoia was massive on another level: enemyless. Life would get you. Life was obviously in the employ of J. Edgar Hoover and the *Ladies' Home Journal*. The conception of human nature was narrow: we are only now engaged in trying to knock it more open again. People were cardboard good, or inherently darkly evil. People may kill themselves more now, but they don't jaw endlessly about it.

The fifties, I cannot sentimentalize them. I hardly survived them. The idea that they might come back in some forms appears ahistorical to me but terrifying, like seeing a parade bearing my coffin down the street. They were a mutilating time to grow up female, and an ugly if more complacent time to grow up male. To grow up a gay male was to fit yourself for the closet or a minute bar world. To grow up a lesbian: you didn't exist. Without the dimension of the possibility of loving each other, our friendships among women were doomed to be shelved at the first approach of a male. To say something nice about the fifties. Well, people read less poetry then, but they did read more fiction, and take fiction more seriously. It's hard sometimes to communicate about ideas in the limited vocabulary currently acceptable in conversation. People's unwillingness to look up words they don't know has reached mammoth proportions. Large amounts of time spent with people who don't know how to do much besides roll a joint does inspire me with nostalgic respect for the work ethic (real knowledge about how to do things, like fix machines that break, build walls that stay up, speak Spanish, put in a well, look up something in a library, design a computer language), but I think that knowledge of at least manual skills is beginning to spread. Further, people coming of age now *tend* to be less hierarchical in their ranking of blue-collar, white-collar, black-coat work.

But I can't summon up any honest nostalgia for the fifties. In the fifties when I got pregnant I couldn't get an abortion, had to do it myself at eighteen and almost bled to death. In the fifties I was at the mercy of a male culture terrified of sex and telling me I was either frigid, a nymphomaniac, an earth mother, or stunted with penis envy, and there were no women's experiences available to compare with mine. In the fifties nowhere could I find images of a life I considered good or useful or dignified. Nowhere could I find a way to apply myself to change the world to one I could live in with more joy and utility. Nowhere could I find a community to heal myself to in struggle. Nowhere could I find space in which affluent white men were not the arbiters of all that was good and bad. I could not grow anywhere but through the cracks. I was not *for* anyone, my work burped in a void. I learned survival but also alienation, hostility, craziness, schizophrenia. Not until the slow opening of the sixties was I able to think I might begin to cease to be a victim, an internal exile, a madwoman. I might become an adult. I might be useful, I might speak and be heard, listen and receive. I might be delivered finally to a sense of a past that led to me/ us (Harriet Tubman, Sojourner Truth, Mother Jones, Susan B. Anthony, Rosa Luxembourg, Lucy Stone, Louise Michel). I might live in a community, however tacky and bleak at times, however scattered and faddish. I might conceive of my living and my working as a project forward in a struggle, however long and difficult and unlikely, tending toward a more humane society. Of course our recent past and present has also brought me beatings, gassings, danger, repression, fear, separation, demands, condemnation, physical collapse, overwork, exhaustion, petty bickerings, faction fights, fanaticism, hate mail, objectification, a more complicated life than I am at ease with, and a gallery of more judges than I need, presumably on my side but sometimes I despairingly wonder. I would not trade the worst of it for the isolation and dead-endedness of the fifties. To live in the fifties and think that the way this society distributes money, power, resources, prestige, and dirty work was wrong was to stand up in a stadium during a football game and attempt to read aloud a poem.

A Fish Needs a Bicycle

What I find absolutely essential as a poet and novelist to continue to draw from Marxism is a sense of class. With a few multinational corporations owning the media and the major publishing houses, the large chain bookstores screening out what isn't commodity literature, I find it important to remember to ask myself, on whose behalf am I working? Whose interests do I represent? Who benefits? Who are the people I want to reach with any piece of work?

The three equally old radical collections of theory and practice (Marxism, anarchism, and feminism) have shaped and actively shape my political activities, my political thinking and all my writing. You will never hear me talking about control of the means of production, but rather control of the means of production and reproduction; you will never hear me praise the dictatorship of the proletariat or any other authoritarian structure. But the imperative to ask who works and who owns, who gets the profits, on whose backs is this structure erected, sculpts the way I look at any institution I encounter.

Similarly, a sense of dialectical process is part of the way my mind works; I have a welcoming view of struggle and I expect conflict between opposing interests. I like it in the

---

From "A Fish Needs a Bicycle: Responses to a Questionnaire on Marxism and the Arts," *The Minnesota Review*, n.s. 9 (Fall 1977).

open. My appreciation of Marxism is also tempered by seeing its shortcomings as a body of thought rooted in the nineteenth-century attitude toward the rest of the living creatures we share the planet with and the resources available to all of us, and the racism that marred a lot of Marxist thought in the past and its practice since. To me patriarchy is the original contradiction, but we live in the center of a sophisticated empire. I cannot understand our relationship to our colonies or the wars that warp our lives every decade without a Marxist analysis of imperialism. I win from it the conviction that there are no private lives; we are all bound in an economic web, and we benefit and suffer from its tightening and its loosening together.

An Interview with Peggy Friedmann and Ruthann Robson of *Kalliope*

You've published a number of novels and many, many poems. What is the difference between writing poetry and writing prose?

In one the lines stop sooner. (Laughter.)

Poetry is more intense, more concentrated. It is more of a continuum of itself, except for *Breaking Camp*, [first volume of poetry] where some of the poems are to me very clearly apprentice work; overly literary, overly experimental, overly artsy. But even with a fair number of poems from that book, to me it is one continuity. I've improved, I've learned to do things, I've been able to grasp more, but it is all of a piece; the voice is somehow that same voice.

Whereas every novel is microcosm. It is a little world I create, live in, and depart. Each novel is a new world that presents new stylistic requirements, new things I have to learn—it is a self-enclosed thing. It is like, I guess, some small time construction people who build the house that they live in and then they sell the house out from under themselves and then they move on—there are people on Cape Cod like that—and they keep moving their families into other houses. In a way a novel is like that, you live in it and then sell it out from under yourself, and move on.

The novel, because of the size of it, you cannot encompass the way you can a poem. You can't turn it round and round

---

First published in *Kalliope*, Winter 1981–82.

and round and look at it from all sides. You don't have the absolute sense of understanding to the depths of what you are doing. With a novel, it goes on for so long, that it is less intense but more extended.

The difference between novels and poetry? It is the difference between a diamond and an elephant. And it is also a matter of what you are aiming to do. Poetry to me is the creation of this artifact made of human utterance. It arises somehow more directly out of human experience and it aims to clarify, preserve and communicate that experience.

But doesn't the novel do that in just a different form?

No. I think that the basic impulse of the novel is not that kind of utterance. It is not the lyric impulse. The basic impulse of the novel is narrative, stories. And stories are *about* time; their subject matter is time. They want to tell you what happens if you make certain choices, what happens then, what happens then. And then what happens. Novels are about human choices and the pattern of human lives through time.

And the poem is outside of time?

No, nothing is outside of time. Poems *use* time. They use time as music uses time, as part of the measure of the poem. But poems are not about time, in the sense of the novel. The novel's subject matter is time.

Judy Grahn has said that a characteristic of working-class writing is that it piles up events within a small amount of space rather than spinning out the many implications of one or two events. Your writing seems to me very working-class in that regard. Do you consider it so?

Yes. And I think that Grahn is probably hitting on something there. A lot of the most admired writing of our time has to do with a tremendous paucity of experience—an immense amount of style expended on a paucity of experience. I think that probably both she and I respond to that, viewing it in part as a class phenomenon.

You have just compared your novels to houses that you build and then move out of. Isn't it awfully difficult to move out of the house of the novel?

Capitalism is a great assistance in that. Since you sell your labor, in this case you sell the novel, it is literally bought by somebody else and belongs to them, so you had better cut your ties. Once the book goes into production, you must cut the ties. In fact I went through a very bad couple of days last week when the copyedited manuscript [of *Braided Lives*] left the house. I went into a three day depression, because that is the point at which you really have to cut the umbilical cord. It is gone. It is theirs, it is not yours, and you can't even change it anymore.

Do you feel the same way with a book of poetry?

No, because the poems go on being, somehow, because I'm always saying poems. The poems in their most real existence are spoken. They are either spoken by other people who hear them in their heads—whether they speak them out loud or not—or actually spoken. Poetry has to be heard in your head if not literally said. I am always standing up and saying poems that I wrote twenty years ago, or ten years ago, or last week. There is a continuity; the poem occurs when I recite it, when I perform it. So it is a different relationship.

Do you ever read aloud from your prose in performance?

Not if I can get out of it. Prose is not designed for that, and it is so hard to pick a little piece out of a novel. The scenes are only dramatic in context. It just seems pointless, although I do it when I am forced to. Poetry is designed to be read. It is an arrangement of sounds and silences. It has its most vital being when the sounds are actually being said.

So you think of your poetry as being in the oral tradition?

Yes. It works to the eye and there are a lot of people who enjoy it and do not hear it, but they will never realize, in a sense, how well it is crafted if they don't hear it in their heads. Poetry that isn't well crafted comes apart when you try to say it, and you see how it isn't put together.

When you first get a bound copy of one of your novels, do you sit down and read it?

No. Maybe five years later I'll sit down and read it and then I'll enjoy it. I don't read it immediately because I have to let go. By the time it arrives, I've already started the next novel. I have to be free of it. I reread *Small Changes* recently and enjoyed it immensely—I even felt some suspense.

Speaking of Small Changes, *what happens to Miriam after the conclusion of the novel?*

A book is an artifact. What occurs in it is what occurs in it. There is no afterwards, except in *you.*

But how did you decide to end the novel at that point?

It is like the quotation I have in *Going Down Fast* by Jay Gould, a nineteenth-century millionaire, that "I can hire one half of the working class to kill the other half." He was responding to why he wasn't worried about a revolution. And part of what I was doing again in *Small Changes* was saying that as long as women can be divided from each other, can be set to do each other in, it is hard to improve our lot. It is that dynamic where the oppressed turn and oppress. It is partly that I was dealing with there and partly that at this point Neil is really irrelevant to Miriam. She is being freed of him whether she wills it or not. The problems of her life are not of Neil. They are going to be a whole set of other problems. She'll be freer, living on a different level, more energy, more decisions, and also more monetary problems—the kind of problems any woman alone with children faces.

The men in your novels seem extremely real.

I always thought so!

Male writers have often been criticized, I think justifiably, for having unrealistic female characters. This criticism has also been leveled by men against women writers.

In my first two novels, *Going Down Fast* and *Dance the Eagle to Sleep*, (they are both coming back into print this year) there were multiple protagonists, a number of them male. Now, when I wrote those books no male reviewer ever said the men were less than tremendously real because the books had male protagonists and neither of them are feminist novels.

The men in *Small Changes* are always, except for Phil, seen from a woman's point of view. And they are seen, in a sense as men write about women, only insofar as they impinge upon women. That was very intentional. You don't, except for Phil, see them from their own point of view.

But I think Phil is an important exception. Also in Vida, *Joel seems particularly real to me.*

Well, other people have said to me that Leigh seemed tremendously real. There is a chemistry involved in a novel which doesn't exist in other forms of art. You respond to the characters in some ways as you would in life—you like some, you dislike others. No novelist can quite control that.

Yet even in your poems, some of the "characters" are capable of evoking a strong response, like for example "The Greater Grand Rapids Lover." How do you accomplish that?

I wasn't aware that the character did come through in the poems. I think it is nice if it does.

You have written a great deal about the relationships between men and women. On the back cover of your volume of poetry Living in the Open, *you explain that a number of the poems concern "why I still have and am fed by relationships with men." Do you feel that feminists have been put in the position of having to justify their relationships with men?*

Yes, and by now I'm extremely tired of that. There are always in movements pragmatists and purists. Purists want everything to be coherent and often care more for coherency than for impact. I care more for changing the real situation of most women. Frequently there comes to be an equation of lesbianism or lesbian-separatism with feminism. Now feminism has as an essential part of it a defense of the lesbian choice—the lesbian choice as being an equal choice, a wholly defensible and necessary choice for many women—but to me it does not mean it is a better choice, or by no means the only choice.

In a recent issue of Sinister Wisdom *(no. 17), you wrote a letter elaborating on the feminist critique.*

Yes—I was really upset at Joanna Russ getting attacked for writing what I thought was a very fine review, an honest review. If we cannot tell the truth when reviewing in feminist publications, I don't know where we are going to do it, ever.

I was very intrigued by your remarks in that letter that we feel we must be "nice in public" and ladylike. Do you think that most women critics have a tendency toward that attitude?

With most women intellectuals and critics, no. The niceness operates on one level. On another level operates the necessity to attack any woman twice as hard, because you really have internalized male values. That's often the public pose. If a woman writes or does something and it's not perfect, you have to stomp all over her. In establishment publications, you very frequently get women attacking women much harder than they would attack menor the same quality work, because if a woman does it, it has to be perfect. That is, it must meet criteria based on other critics and the work of dead male white writers.

About the "niceness"—there is a piece I wrote six years ago about the difficulty of disagreeing politically in the women's movement. We have trouble not taking it as personal betrayal when someone disagrees politically with us. We have to learn to be able to fight politically and disagree politically without experiencing it as personal betrayal or personal rejection.

You've also spoken about the writers obligation to give back to the community. To what extent do you feel writers recognize that obligation?

There is that whole mystique of the alienated writer who is a lone soul. Very obviously, you eat food that other people grew, you wear clothes that other people made, in the watch on your wrist are minerals somebody went down into the earth and mined. You live in a social web where other people's work sustains you—and you give back. I think that literary production is real production.

Is writing criticism and reviews like that?

Well, that is a simple kind of tithing, more akin to taking out the garbage. I don't think of reviewing as real production, I think of it as a service activity. You owe it to literature, you owe it to other younger writers, you owe it to your readers to call to their attention other writers who they ought to know about, and you owe it back to your constituency and the movement you're a part of, and so forth.

Do you see feminist criticism as a whole new genre and do you think of yourself as a feminist critic?

I don't think of myself as a critic. My problem is basically that I went to school in the 1950s at the University of Michigan and had a dose of the New Criticism so early as to fill me up with an immunity to criticism thereafter. Criticism as an activity in itself—well, I think it is nice that some people are doing that, but I'm not going to read an awful lot of it. In some ways, I'm more inclined to read criticism with a certain amount of sociological underpinnings or historical value, rather than a purely literary criticism. Although occasionally I'll read something very illuminating. I've been interested for example, in writing about feminist utopia. Joanna Russ had a piece in *Frontiers* which was marvelous. There was also a piece by Nadia Khouri called "The Dialectics of Power" which appeared in *Science Fiction Review* (7, no. 20 [March 1980]).

Your upcoming novel, Braided Lives, *is about the 1950s?*

Yes. About growing up before there was a women's movement.

Did you have to go back and do a lot of research to remind yourself of what it was like in the 1950s? How did you get in the right frame of mind to write the novel?

Partly music of the time. Pop music always has that effect. With the fifties, a lot of Black music, which is mostly what I listened to then.

Did you go back to newspapers and magazines?

Not on first draft, but when I was getting certain details for second draft I had to do research. Exactly when did the Soviet invasion of Hungary occur? What kind of clothes were high fashion in 1958? Most of the research was done between second and third drafts, but some was done before second in order to get straight the chronology of certain political events.

How many drafts did Braided Lives *go through?*

Three. That's normal, although there are parts of it that have been through a lot more than that. One particularly crucial scene, the self-abortion scene in the novel has gone through eight or nine drafts—that is always the case with crucial parts. In *Vida*, the part set in 1967 went through ten drafts. But generally, all the novel goes through three.

What else are you working on?

Two other books. One is selected poems, entitled *Circles on the Water*, which will be published by Knopf in 1982. The other is a book for the Poets on Poetry Series of the University of Michigan. That will be entitled *Parti-Colored Blocks for a Quilt*. I'm collecting reviews, fugitive pieces, interviews, etc., for the critical book, and I'm also writing some essays for it because I've never written that much about what *I* do. I tend to write about what other people do, I've an essay on Audre Lorde, one on Joanna Russ, one on Margaret Atwood.

I've also written an essay on my own lunar cycle. Since nobody ever writes intelligent criticism of my poetry, I feel as if I must make a bottom line by doing it myself.

You don't feel that anyone has written any intelligent criticism of your poetry?

There is a little bit. Eleanor Bender is probably the most serious critic I have and she has written an essay about my love poetry. I think if I scrabbled around I'd find a few others. There's been some nice pieces where people have called attention to poetry, but most criticism that has been written has been most unsatisfactory. So I thought I'd try to build a basement under it by doing some myself.

Obviously you agree with magazines that promote women artists and writers as Kalliope *does. What do you see as the function of little magazines devoted exclusively to women? Do you think there is a need for such magazines, still, even now?*

Yes. Because still, even now, most men don't read women or read very few women and leave us out of the literary landscape. I find the intellectual level higher—I hate to say it, sounding chauvinistic. Not always, of course. Some women's magazines have that very soft romanticism, that squishy quality where all real controversy, all real sexuality, everything really threatening gets edited out, and you are left with a girl scout camp and pajama party level of reality.

But we are just discovering what we can do. I read women's magazines with great interest and want to know what is being said and what is being done. There is so much that we have to say to each other, so many interesting controversies.

An Interview with Michael Luzzi

Do you keep a journal now or have you ever kept one?

I write for a living and don't have a lot of time free from writing poetry, novels, reviews, and giving readings. When I was an unpublished writer at times I kept a journal and often I wrote very long letters—as I mentioned in "Women of letters". That is no longer the case. When I'm done writing for the day, every day I'm here, I'd rather do something entirely different. The only time I make notes on my life is when I have an insight I want to hold on to or when I perceive something that might prove interesting farther on down the road. Or when I am troubled about a decision. Mostly the experiences of my life are transmuted into my work in an indirect way and every single hair and button will be used some time, some where, usually not much the way it really was.

Before you were published you did keep some notes or journals, etc. Why?

I wrote letters, especially. I was tremendously frustrated as a writer because I couldn't get published, so at least letters somebody read.

How important was it to you to be published before?

Desperately. I mean how important is it to feel your life is not a total failure? To feel writing was what I did and no one but me thought I did it.

Did you have many problems before you were published? Did you send out many things?

Oh, it took forever, ever and ever and ever, especially with the prose. The world had to change before I could get my prose published. There had to be a change in society. You could not publish what I wrote until there was an audience created for it. And you're not really allowed yet. You get punished: your books don't contain enough despair, they aren't proper politically. I happen to agree with Christians on one point and that is, despair is a sin. I don't admire despair.

I remember reading about Evan Hunter, author of Blackboard Jungle *in the early fifties and the writing done by critics about him at that point was that it was a fine first novel. Then we find out he had published a few hundred stories prior to that and had written three or four other novels and that it wasn't at all his first, but his first that achieved any critical aclaim. But they wanted to make it seem that the American dream had been fulfilled, by gaining all this notoriety and making all this money from his first novel. Was that the case with you? Have you published anything before something became famous?*

I'd been publishing poetry for ten years before I had a book, writing fiction seriously for twelve years before I had a novel published. *Going Down Fast* was my first published novel, but my sixth completed novel. I had only little pieces of fiction in print before. There was no place you could publish serious fiction about being a woman, no place. The few things that made it, like a story in the *Paris Review*, had male viewpoints.

Did the fact that you had been publishing poetry sustain you even though you were being frustrated by failure of the prose to get published?

It helped some, but it was so slow, five, ten poems a year. I think that I was sustained more by political activity at that point than by any recognition in writing until 1967. I didn't go crazy or give up or kill myself because of being politically involved so I had some impact in the world and some sense of feedback as a person and not a total failure. I had some sense of community; that saved me.

When did you become politically active?

I was active in college. As there were movements that arose, and occasion to do things, I duly arose. I think since I've been fifteen I've identified with the Left, and racism was a big festering sore out of my childhood I had to think about and deal with. I cared about women's issues before I could understand them. For so long I lacked a vocabulary. I'm a something but what that something was, I didn't know. Something's funny, something's wrong, but there were no words to think with: trying to figure things out with no words to name them. When I look at early notes I made I see myself trying to grapple clumsily without a vocabulary of useful concepts.

Do you have any special frustrations? Do critics comment on your womanness rather than your writing?

Mostly it's just bias. At a recent PEN meeting in Boston on a panel on reviewing, I said to the arts editor of the Boston *Globe*, why is it a book that is embued with politics similar to the reviewer's is reviewed as if it isn't political, but in terms of literary merit, readibility, excitement. Now, I may read that book and to me it is polemical, because it embodies ideas of right and wrong, male and female, who's smart and who's stupid, all the notions always apparent in a work of art. If I reviewed it, I might say that the sexual politics of the book offend me although I find it well written, but establishment reviewers will not do that. I commented for example that when a book of Thomist philosophy comes out, it's given to a

Thomist to review, but when a book of feminist philosophy comes out, it's given to someone who starts out by saying that feminist philosophy is disreputable. In other words, the book is reviewed in terms of why it shouldn't exist rather than in terms of whether it is a contribution to its field or a success in terms of what the book aims to do. He agreed and he said, yes, that's how it is. I was so stunned by his reply. I was naive enough to think he'd produce some justification, but he just said, sure.

At the beginning, you said you had trouble getting published. Now after being critically acclaimed, don't you think you're accepted as a writer?

I'm not respectable yet. I'm not part of the literary establishment.

Will you be?

Tell me some Left novelists who've made it there? I don't think we're that assimilatable. This isn't, after all, France. This isn't a country with an institutional left, or an institutional feminist left. We don't have our newspapers to review in, our radio stations, our television programs. The U.S. is a strange country: there's only a huge right and a center which is fairly far right of center. That makes discussion very lopsided. Nobody ever asks the hard brutal questions of the oil companies, the government, the corporations, the utilities, in public debate.

Do you see in the future a meaningful and successful relationship between men and women? I am reading Woman on the Edge of Time *now. There men mother also.*

I think that's a necessary step—that men be responsible for nurturing children—for things to change fundamentally. Being responsible for someone young, loving, and dependent changes your relationship to the world. You are one with that child for a long time and it makes you live differently, whether this is a child of your body or not. You open to seeing how responsible we are to each other and to all living.

I have heard men rearing their children in a household where the woman is the primary economic provider and they've expressed how very difficult it is, and how they've changed through their sensitivity to the woman's situation and how it's been portrayed.

There's a lot that begins to trouble you that didn't before, like what's in the water and what's in the milk and what's in the food? You start worrying about chemical additives that affect a young child more than adults. You start thinking about radioactivity and the land and the rain and you begin to understand how we are on this earth and how we are connected.

I remember at an Erica Jong poetry reading during a question and answer period, a man said, Well, who's interested in the things that women are writing about anyway? Your baby, food, etc. She said I didn't know men were not interested in children, in eating, in where they live, and such little mundane things.

When I was in college, that was a common response. Who would want to read women's work? People sneering because some woman wrote poems about her kids and domestic life, when real poems were about alienation, the meaninglessness of it all, or about religious experiences, or best of all, about other poems.

Do you have to be selfish with your time to the exclusion of many other things?

Whoa. If I went to a secretarial job every day, would you say I was being selfish about my time when I worked a nine-to-five job? I don't understand. I make a living off my writing, and if I don't write I don't eat: don't pay my taxes, oil bills, electricity.

Do you work on a set schedule. X amount of hours each day?

I can't write first draft for as many hours as I can do second or third draft. I work on my novels just about all the time.

Do you also write other things while you're working on fiction?

Yes. I don't like to stop first draft to write reviews, but sometimes I have to do that too. I write poems on and off all the time.

Is it difficult to get to that point, or is it just a routine?

I've gotten faster. I used to have this idea that I couldn't start another novel till the last one was out. But that's wasteful because they take so long to bring out. I take a couple of months and do other projects. When the novel has gone off to the publisher and is in production, then I take and collect all my poems and start going through them for a book. Then I develop the plan for what kind of theme that particular book of poetry will have, how it will be organized. The shape of a book is important, so it takes me a while to figure out which of the poems I consider good belong to a particular book. I usually write poems specifically for that book also.

Do you approach the two the same? I was surprised to hear you say you do both at once?

Well, I'm on the first draft of a novel now (*Braided Lives*) and I've written a number of poems this winter. I may not work on both in the same day. It takes more intense energy to write poems. The time it takes is shorter but the energy is more focused. Typically, prose takes a much longer pull. With poetry I can't imagine ever working a six-hour day, when in revising prose, sometimes I work more hours than that.

What do you do to relax?

Sometimes I take time off in the city, in Boston. For research, I need the Boston Public Library and the bookstores. I get more intellectual and political stimulation in the city, criticism of my writing, meeting other writers, political feedback. Home, Wellfleet, I garden for food and pleasure. I spend a lot of time especially in the spring in the vegetable gardens. But I love the flowers too. It's soothing and good exercise. I like to walk. I love to cook and to eat. I love to talk with friends. I love to read and never get enough time, ever. I find the company of my cats pleasing. I always want to be doing seventy-five more things in every day than there is time for. Woody, we live together now, he says that whenever I look at a man twice, which given that I am now together with him I don't do so much, it's because I say he looks as if he enjoys life. To be avid of life, I like that.

Do you have time to read for pleasure?

Sometimes I have no time and sometimes I have some time. When I travel, I read, often three or four books on a trip.

Do you believe in the Muse?

I believe I'm the conduit for energy from others. One of my duties is to articulate for other people what they need to have articulated, especially what has been buried and hidden and denied. Images of their pleasure and suffering and fears. Art lends dignity. It can help you to avoid feeling crazy because what you have been through and have not been able to name is saved and justified and perfected in form. Art validates experience. Only rich white men get much validation in this society. It's gotten worse. If you see thirties and forties films, note the difference between the way ordinary working people were depicted then and the way they are portrayed now. The intolerance for ordinary people in the media has grown and grown. The class lines harden, and contempt for ordinary people is rampant.

Do you have a responsibility to readers?

I have the same responsibility as someone who bakes bread, to the people who eat it. My writing is for others. Artistic production is real production. I'm not saying I want to be judged by some narrow political yardstick—that's tedious and depressing, and has little to do with what a novel is, which is not a roundabout way of saying something you could say straight out in a pamphlet. Novels are about the choices people make, out of their characters and their time and their class and their social circumstances. When you read fiction, you have an intimacy and understanding of the protagonist created for you you never possess of your neighbors.

Do you have control over your characters or do they get away from you?

I work a lot on characters before I start writing. Characters do have their own momentum and I can't force them to do things they won't do. Sometimes in first draft they disturb the neat outlines of the previously arranged plot, but mostly I try to understand them well enough before I start to have the plot issue directly out of the characters, so that doesn't happen.

Do the characters speak for you?

Directly, seldom. I rarely use a protagonist to speak my mind or my politics. I feel that the book as a whole is making a statement, and all the characters are saying things from where they stand. My protagonists may often say things they believe that I don't agree with, because that's their truth. I may try to indicate obliquely what I think the consequences are of such a belief, but to me the truth of the novel isn't in what any character says, but rather in the whole of the fiction. As a known feminist I find critics often naively imagine I am putting my politics directly into the mouth of my protagonist. That I could not possibly be amused, ironic, interested in the consonances and dissonances.

How do you mean, naive?

I remember Elizabeth Hardwick reviewing *Dance the Eagle to Sleep*, quoting a passage in which one of the four protagonists, Shawn, is engaged in a public sexual display and accusing me of "phallic narcissism"—a little weird for a woman anyhow. I had to be one with Shawn, in spite of what the novel makes clear happens as a result of him using sex with women as a means of impressing men. I get blamed for describing from inside Shawn what he is doing, as if I had invented sexism. Similarly, from the other direction, *The High Cost of Living* was attacked in *Heresies* because the three working-class characters, Leslie, Honore and Bernie, cannot love each other as they are, or love themselves. They have incorporated too much self-hatred or romantic and commodity dreams. Now I have created working-class characters with self-respect, such as Jill in *Braided Lives*, but I have the right and the necessity as a serious writer to explore those who are far commoner in our society, those who buy the values that degrade them.

I find again and again and again critics assuming that they see in my work not what I carefully put there but some insight available to them but lacking to me. They notice what I have created and assume I have done so blindly, instead of artfully, and I ask again and again, why? I think reviewers and academics have the fond and foolish notion they are smarter than writers. They also assume if you are political, you are simpler in your mental apparatus than they are; whereas you may well have the same background in English and American literature they have, but add to it a better grounding in other European and Asian and South American literatures, and a reasonable degree of study of philosophy and political theory.

Do you have a general outline of what you want to do when you begin a novel?

A novel is like a house; you don't just start improvising. There's an architectural shape to it and the parts must be properly proportioned. As a writer you're never intelligent and attentive enough, never. Always a little clearer intelligence and a little closer attention would flush out more connections and implications.

Do you feel a joy in actually giving a poetry reading?

I love readings. It's a direct recompense, immediate response.

What about things not yet published; do you read any poems just written?

Sure. But some people are familiar with your poetry and some aren't. If I read in Boston, for instance, I pull a big audience and all of them have some familiarity. I've read often enough in San Francisco, in Detroit, in New York, to have the feeling that I should be careful not to do many old poems. But when I read for the first time in an area, say a small college in Virginia, I wouldn't assume familiarity on the part of the audience, and I would be more inclined to try to cover some small portion of the central body of my poetry.

Before James Dickey and Erica Jong wrote their first novels, they were primarily poets and then they had enormous success. They found that economic success was better than poetry which wasn't a fruitful venture.

About a third of my income comes from poetry. So that's not the case with me. I give a lot of readings. Poetry pays its own way.

How do you feel about the place poetry has today in society? A lot of people are negative about it.

Many people read my poetry, though not as many as read the novels in mass paperback. I think poetry is an art you can reach people with. Often people who come to my poetry readings don't know the novels. Poetry and fiction do not always reach the same audience. Such people have stopped believing that fiction is going to say anything about them or their lives—it's just adultery, account executives, women married to wealthy men, actors, psychiatrists. Yet they believe that poetry has something to say or show them, so they respect it.

Don't you think a common problem is that people try to sit down and write poetry, but they don't read enough of it? They don't want to read other poets, they just want to be published.

That isn't as true of women poets, who do in fact read women poets, often desperately. We have—many of us—the conviction that everything is still to be done. We're not at the end of a long played-out tradition. We get very excited about what other writers are creating. Yes, now we can write about that, now you can say that. What a breakthrough! How illuminating! We lust for role models.

What type of advice can you give to someone early adolescent about where they go from here if they want to pursue writing?

To young writers all you can say is read and write and read and write and read and write. Try to know who you're imitating. Imitation is fine but understand it is only imitation. You can try on many different people's concerns and styles. It doesn't count against you for a long while.

What about finding your own voice?

It's difficult to find your own voice, whether you do it through trying on other people's or just keep plodding along as you develop. But it's meaningless to talk about finding a voice when a young person doesn't know who she is yet and she's still trying on selves. It's a slow process of coming to know what you have to say, how you really are, and who you want to be, and then you start figuring how to say it, to whom you're saying it, and why.

Some people are so vulnerable they turn away. Can they get over that point?

Probably extreme vulnerability doesn't go with being a writer. A lot of people write without being writers. It's like music, there's room for a whole groundswell of amateurs before you can reasonably have good professionals or appreciation of good professionals and what they're doing. Lots of people write and they might publish one or two poems in a lifetime or none. Just show a poem to friends, to lovers, or to their children. It's good to do that. Every poem doesn't aim to be a great poem, or good in a literary sense. That amateur stratum of people who dabble in an art is important. If you've never tried to write a poem, you don't have as good a sense of what a good one is. The private pleasure in an art is not to be condemned, the Sunday painter.

How do you feel about interviews, by the way? I heard you weren't crazy about interviews. Why?

Well, it's a weird conversation, when one person asks questions and another has to answer them. Don't you think it's peculiar?

If I had more time, I might have sent you a general outline of what I wanted to ask. I think the flow is better that way.

This is fine. The worst ones are those who haven't prepared by reading anything and they want to talk about my personal life. When they discover you won't do that, they become hostile, as if they are entitled to ask personal questions. I have always told them beforehand I won't do personal interviews but they think, she will when I get there, if I insist. The other difficult interviewers are the ones who sit and ask complicated long questions to which there is no response but yes or no, I agree or don't agree.

They have previous ideas about what you're like before they meet you?

Or they think how you theorize about your work is irrelevant, because they've already got you fitted into little boxes in their heads. Sometimes they come with a lot of quotations from other writers and ask you if you agree, and a lot of the time all you can say is no. You feel so prepackaged. They have a grand scheme you are being banged into.

Starting Support Groups for Writers

Every writer needs support and feedback to go on writing. Established writers can get some of that from their audiences, but until then, we can only get support and feedback from the people around us and from each other. In Chicago many years ago I had a support group, and then again for a while in New York. I still have a number of writers to whom I show manuscripts or my novels in second draft or with whom I exchange poems. This description of how to set up a support group was written initially for the Feminist Writers' Guild of New England, published in our newsletter, and then expanded some for the National Feminist Writers' Guild Handbook, *Words in Our Pockets*.

For publication here I have changed little. I have retained the female pronouns of its original publications; I am always reading "he's" that are presumed to include me, so why not vice versa? If these suggestions are to be applied to mixed groups, I think it even more important to stress the importance of not allowing one, two, or three individuals to dominate a group and especially to dominate reading or criticism. I once taught a workshop composed of eight women and two men. The two men always spoke first to every poem, and set

---

This essay is a chapter reprinted from the anthology *Words in Our Pockets: The Feminist Writers' Guild Handbook*, edited by Celeste West (San Francisco: Bootlegger Press, 1981).

the tone of reaction so that the women who were timid and had different aesthetic criteria tended to keep silent. I finally had to establish a rule that neither of the men could speak until two women had addressed any particular poem. After two weeks I could lift the rule because the women had begun to gain confidence and the men had become conscious of their overmastering behavior. The workshop was more useful to everybody in it once it reflected the opinions of more than two members.

Ground Rules for a Support Group

1. Respect

Everybody should be able to expect the group to listen to her work and accord it respect. We should try to give another writer criticism for succeeding or failing to do what she is trying to do, not for doing something we wouldn't do. We should not expect that other people want to write the way we do or with the style or content of writers we admire. We should respect women who write directly from their own experiences and women who write from their imagination or their research. A support group is no place to win converts to your ideas.

2. Equal Time

This is an ideal but not a rigid one. Everyone in the group should be able to claim equal time for her work. However, if somebody has low or slow output, the group should not put more pressure on her than she wishes. With a poetry group we might go around the room each time and read one poem by each of maybe half the group. In a drama, fiction, or article group, we might do two or three people each meeting until everyone has been heard and then repeat.

3. Everyone Participates

No one has the right to ask support, feedback or criticism if she is not willing to listen carefully and/or read carefully the work of others and give her responses freely. When we feel we don't know how to express what we sense about somebody's writing, we have to risk trying to say what we mean. We have to risk sounding silly or clumsy or wrong. Silence is not fair to the others in the group; being shy is a luxury. We must share our reactions to other's work so that we can give help as well as receive it. Learning to express my feelings and reactions, my evaluation of another woman's work is important to me because from that exercise I will learn observations I can bring back to my own work. Having to say what I feel is good discipline, and support groups are an environment, unlike a class or a formal workshop or writer's conference, where it should be easy for us to expose our reactions to each other, where we have a right to expect support and respect.

Not every writer can afford to be taking writing workshops all the time, nor are they necessarily the best source of feedback. Often what you learn when you "study" writing with somebody is their mannerisms and their prejudices. Some writing workshops tend to produce a product; a large number of the students who pass through them emerge with similar notions about poetry or prose revealed in their work. Sometimes you will do better with a group of peers.

Often what you learn in a workshop or in a support group is the questions to ask yourself when your poem or piece of fiction is not coming along right. What variables should you consider changing? That way you learn how to revise.

4. We Try to Help

The rule of thumb is always to think what to say to help the other become a better writer. Being witty at the expense of another group member or using their work to put out a pet theory about writing is not being helpful. Each group will set its own emotional tone: how blunt or how gentle people feel comfortable with. But everyone in the group must be able to live with that feeling tone. We should not lie to each other, as that does not help. But we should think how to give feedback that is truly useful.

We must try to be open to each other's criticism too. It's useless to be in a group at all if all we want is adulation. If every criticism is met with "But that's the way it was!," "That's just how I felt!," "That's how it came to me," you can't learn and there's no motivation for others to boil their brains trying to help you.

5. Copies

Each person should take the responsibility for making copies of her own work. Xeroxing is so popular, people often forget that carbon paper exists. Any typewriter will make six or seven legible copies if onion skin or carbon copy manifolds are used. If you give copies to your group, you can expect much better feedback. Many people simply can't get more from a poem or story the first time they hear it than a general emotional sense. That's fine for a reading, but defeats the purpose of a support group.

6. Who Talks

As said above, everybody should make a strong attempt to communicate about each piece of writing. It's also our duty to keep any one or two writers who are more articulate or experienced from dominating the group so that their taste has too much influence.

7. Support in Work Habits

Many of the problems writers face are not in our work, but in our lives. People around us give us little or no support for being writers, for writing. We can give each other that support. We may have trouble sitting down to write. We can encourage each other. We can work in the same building or at certain hours. We can share or circulate child care among our group. We can work out patterns of assistance that help individual women work. Some women want to be nagged. They want a phone call at 10:00 saying, "Have you got to work yet?" Some women need to be praised. They want a phone call at 5:00 saying, "How much did you get done? That's wonderful." Some women want to be let alone while working. They need encouragement in taking the phone off the hook and refusing to answer the door. Some of us need places outside our homes in which to write: we can share office space. Sometimes writers get stuck and need help getting unstuck. Sometimes being listened to about personal problems helps. Praise may be needed. Sometimes a writer needs a sounding board for ideas or needs some help or suggestions for solving a problem that has stymied her.

Mechanics of Starting

1. Somebody must take early responsibility. We need a leader for the first meeting or two. After that, we should rotate the chair.

2. Limit the size of your group. The group can be bigger for poetry than for prose. You do not want a group so big it takes two months before you get to read your work. People will drop out if that is so.

3. Make a real commitment to coming. Death, serious illness, and having to be out of town are valid excuses. Going to a movie, a party, not feeling like it, let other people down who want to read that night, who need help, who need encouragement.

4. Always inform the group if you won't be there.

5. Don't set a time for a meeting when people in your group usually are writing. If the group cuts into work time, it will be resented.

6. Things to do at the first meeting if you don't start right in with reading: You might want to discuss, going around the room:

What writing experiences you have had,
What you want to write and why,
What do you want/need from the group,
What obstacles do you experience in writing,
What has helped you to define yourself as a writer and
What has hurt you,
What do you hope and/or fear from the group?

7. In fiction or nonfiction groups, an agreement should be made about roughly how many pages somebody is going to read. It doesn't work well for somebody to read for two hours or even one hour. No matter how interesting it may be (especially to the author), everybody tunes out eventually and starts thinking about their dental appointment, kids, lovers, and how long it will be till they get to read.

8. Save some time in every other meeting at least to go around and get out anything that's needed. Groups can foul up on little bad interactions if there's no way to work out problems or hurt feelings that arise.

Things a Group Can Do Eventually

Our support group can also provide the beginnings of a group who gives readings. It's much easier for a group of lesser known writers to get a reading someplace together than for each woman individually to secure such a reading. You can each coerce enough close friends to come out to hear you to put together a decent-sized audience. Your writing often improves when you have to read it aloud. Once you have got over your initial fear and nervousness, you can hear what works and what doesn't in prose as well as in poetry.

Your support group can also put out a magazine, a journal, an anthology, or a chapbook. You can sell it at readings you do together as well as hustling it around in the usual bookstores.

Finally, your support group gives you an audience, something which an apprentice writer needs more than anything else except time and determination.

The City as Battleground: The Novelist as Combatant

Why do ordinary people read fiction? The most primitive answer is the most real: to get to the next page. To find out what happens next and then what happens after that; to find out how it all comes out.

That desire for finding a pattern in events—for not all happenings will satisfy us, not nearly, only the "right" ending, the proper disaster or the proper suspension or the proper reward—still functions as a major hunger we bring to the novel. We want stories that help us make sense out of our lives. We want to see all this mess mean something, even if what we discover is a shape perhaps beautiful but not necessarily comforting. After all the shape of a spiral nebula when I get into the country and can actually see it does not make me more comfortable—or more self-important.

We want to know when we read a story what happens when somebody makes one choice rather than another: speaks to a wolf in the woods, runs over an old man on the road to Thebes. Sometimes the pattern a novel traces on our mind is overt in the book and sometimes the most important pattern is covert, the kind of hidden myths that Sandra Gilbert and Susan Gubar have traced in *The Madwoman in the Attic* in nineteenth-century women's fiction. Of course, we

---

First printed in *Literature and the Urban Experience* (Newark: Rutgers University Press, 1981).

can experience resonance, counterpoint, conflict between the overt and covert patterns of a novel.

Fictions build us alternative cities superimposed on the city whose streets we walk or drive. Some of these paper cities seem close to our own, evoking the pleasure of reading a story set in a Boston you remember or an Upper West Side of Manhattan you live in. But some of these cities are exotic, threatening, enticing, cities of the dead and cities of the unborn.

Since our cities are grids of Them and Us experiences, fiction is a way of inducting you into the cities other people know: people who are poorer or richer than you are; people who speak another language; people who construct the world of different forces and different necessities and different desires; people who live down streets you fear or streets who fear you. Broadway is one street in songs and another to a bag lady.

As a woman I experience a city as a mine field. I am always potential quarry or target or victim. The first question that will be asked of me if something happens is, What were you doing there? Why were you alone? How were you dressed? In parts of some cities at night the police will stop any woman and question her as a prostitute, for she is presumed not to belong on the streets by virtue of biology.

The expectation of violence constricts our lives. We can't go where we should be able to go. The expectation of insult also harries us. We walk carefully and often more quickly than we desire to. We may not be able to look around freely or exercise curiosity.

The city of the old who are not wealthy, the ordinary aged whose lives have been passed in useful work, is a web of dangers the young pass through without imagining. In Boston there are neighborhoods where a Black person cannot walk down the street and sometimes cannot even drive through safely. These are truly forbidden cities. Similarly, and especially during times when violence against Blacks has been worse than usual, there are parts of Roxbury whites cannot pass through. Many children have grown up with the knowledge that being Jewish they could not go past a certain avenue or the gangs there would beat them, or being Italian or Puerto Rican, they could not violate certain arbitrary but very real boundaries.

In Europe just about everybody who is not a peasant speaks at least one other language and often several. Your average European has vacationed in other people's countries, and while chauvinism may be just as rampant, at least the knowledge that there are other ways of doing things is widespread. Americans often grow up never really speaking any other language and finding it intolerable that they ever should have to. But every language organizes the world in a slightly or very different way. I think fiction can provide that experience of a foreign kind of organization that makes experience appear quite different.

A novel can make us enter those other streets and corridors and hallways and alleys. A novel can reconstruct cities of 1840 and 1890. A novel can take us through cities that may be built in 2137. A novel can put up alternate cities of Atlantis to float like highly colored slick on the bubbles of the imagination. These cities of the past and the future and the never-was can also help us to grasp our own experiences in our cities. A past that leads to us validates us. A past that has created the problems we wallow in can help us to understand and to endure or attack our problems. A future we long for can draw us into activity that might help it happen. A future we fear can galvanize us to prevent it.

Actually few writers of science fiction or speculative fiction have created believable future cities. They tend toward creating simpler societies (after-the-holocaust novels) or they project capitalism usually in a more primitive stage than today or—somebody help us—feudalism as it existed in France around 1200 and add some lazer guns and rocket ships. Samuel Delaney is one of the few whose imagination can take us in directions that feel more sophisticated, more complex, more likely in sexual arrangements, families, socialization, pleasure, work, defense, intrigue, and art forms.

For an increasing number of us, the city as it is organized now doesn't work. That's why when I wrote *Woman on the Edge of Time* I decided to break with the urban tradition in utopian fiction and depict a society that used small units spread more uniformly through the landscape. I make no particular brief for the device; it was convenient in enabling me to deal with the changes in people and in the economic, social, and familial arrangements I wanted to depict. But I do stand by the statement that for most people life in cities is getting more difficult. Usually we feel we cannot influence or control the institutions we inhabit like goldfish in a small and poisoned tank: our schools, streets, courts, transportation system, parks.

The city formed and deformed me. Growing up in Detroit made me a novelist. I have a lot of early childhood memories about my mother and my father and my brother and my Uncle Danny but I also have in my earliest memories company violence against the unions at Ford, where a large percentage of the men in the neighborhood worked, and the Detroit race riots. I was in day care and we were painting plaster plaques of grapes when the mothers began coming. All the Black children gathered on one side of the room and whispered that the whites had knives and all the white children gathered on the other side of the room and whispered that the Blacks had knives. The mothers came one by one and took their children home.

I belonged among the white children but not quite. In my age group there were only two Jews, myself and Emily, who was Black, and even many years later we were put on hall guard together and got the same kinds of roles in the school plays (the storyteller, usually, unless there was an Oriental part, which I would play).

What impressed me most was that each side said the same thing with desperate fear and nobody had any knives—not us children. The next thing that impressed me was witnessing a Black man beaten by a group of whites on Tireman, which was just ceasing to be a dividing line between Black and white working-class blocks then. I recognized him although I did not know his name as he worked in the drugstore where I sometimes was taken by my brother to buy ice cream cones on summer nights. I did not know the whites and I would have nightmares about that beating.

Detroit was a violent place to grow up. Certainly as a child there seemed to me an excessive amount of cruelty from adults to adults, adults to children, children to children, and children to animals. As a child the latter most upset me. I preferred animals and would have liked to live surrounded by cats and dogs and rabbits and cows and almost anything short of tigers. Tigers I didn't need.

At the same time my area was a functioning working-class neighborhood, which meant that people helped each other through trouble and crisis. Women went in and out of each other's houses all day through the back doors and what you did not know about anyone on your block was simply too uninteresting to repeat. Every operation and drunken spree and lost son and marital squabble and letter from abroad was spoken in every other kitchen on the block before sunset the next day. There was no television, only your neighbor's soap operas to follow. My mother, as a gifted palm reader, knew everyone's secret troubles. She was gossiped to but she never passed on gossip. Except to me.

The buses were my instrument of class education. Whether you took the Joy Road or the Tireman buses, in one direction they ran downtown (where you still went to shop or for official things when you had to pay on a mortgage or delay paying it or when you had to deal with City Hall in some fearful negotiation or where you waited all day in a clinic or for some cheap Dr. Yankum). As you took the bus downtown, the neighborhoods changed from tough but stable working-class neighborhoods like my own with their Black blocks and white blocks like a checkerboard of turfs, their Irish gangs, their Polish gangs, the parochial school kids versus the public school kids, to ever Blacker streets and shakier housing. As the bus passed the ring of decaying grandeur—Victorian mansions now roominghouses, dog and cat hospitals, chiropractors—you entered the oldest and rankest part of Detroit, low to the ground huddled together ramshackle buildings of falling down slums.

If you took the bus in the other direction, the houses became single family homes. At first they'd be pastel cupcakes turned out in rows. Then they became what were called colonials, meaning they had two stories and maybe a perfunctory pillaster either side of the front door. Finally the houses were brick. Nobody from the old brick rowhouse East can understand how substantial brick houses appear in the Midwest. Brick houses were where rich people lived. Now I know they weren't rich, just upper middle class. We all make fine class distinctions near us and cruder ones farther away.

If you left the city altogether—not possible on public transportation—you found the palaces of those who lived off what burned up the air we tried to breathe.

The difference between what we were taught in school and what I saw bothered me and got under my skin. My mother taught me to respect what it said in books. She had not got to finish the tenth grade before being sent to work, but the house was always full of books she brought home from the library. But nothing—the relationship between the sexes, the races, adults and kids—was the way it was supposed to be.

What I saw was a place where people who had little enough devoted their best energy to fighting each other in small groups. My friends were outcastes. I was beaten up a great deal by the other whites for being a Jew and I went home to a father who told me I wasn't Jewish and a mother who would wait till he went to work and tell me of course I was.

I also had a lot of good friends who died in prison, on the streets, on drugs, from botched abortions, from getting pregnant at fifteen and drunk when it was time to deliver, in car accidents, of hypertension and bleeding ulcers in their twenties and thirties. The love I got kept me alive and I have tried to carry those friends and relatives in me and birth them again in my work. All the love I ever took in I feel I owe back in work that speaks for all the buried lives that want to be said through me. Detroit is a great place to come from, but it wasn't so easy on those friends who didn't leave their class to make it. I have the guilt of the one who got away.

I went to college on a scholarship—the first person in my family to do so—where I learned that politics was over and we lived in a classless society. I learned that poetry must be ironic and ambiguous and full of Christian imagery and that the proper novel was one of manners—meaning interior to the world of the affluent and excluding the rest of us. I learned I ought to write like a British gentleman. I learned that a few misguided pinko writers had fiddled with something called the proletarian novel in the thirties but that had been a mistake and you didn't have to read them. You had to read a great deal of Henry James.

You also read essays and wrote them on whether it was possible to have real tragedy any more in the age they called in the textbooks of the common man or whether only kings and dukes could be truly tragic. Obviously a king was more real than a bus driver or factory worker and suffered more and certainly louder. Kings suffered in blank verse while the peasants suffered in prose or silently in piles. Women had clearly been a nineteenth-century invention since we never read of any women before then. We hardly read any after that, but it's not easy to teach the nineteenth-century novel without reading a couple of women and women do tend to write about women—one of the factors that trivializes our output, we were taught.

I got a fellowship to Northwestern and went on in graduate school for about nine months, but instead of living in Evanston, I lived on Wilson Avenue in Chicago. It was a gamy neighborhood full of single room occupancy hotels, old people, recent migrants from Appalachia, Spanish-speaking people both Puerto Rican and Chicano, nightclubs and dim bars and the El that I travelled every day to suburban dry Evanston where in the imitation Gothic towers of the university we studied textual variants in Keats's *Endymion*. Keats was another word-drunk working-class kid with lung problems and one afternoon when I was getting ready to flee the University permanently I hallucinated a whole conversation with him up in the stacks of the library about loyality and stress.

I found that while the university offered the only security I could imagine and certainly would ever know, that class mobility was killing something in me I valued more highly than my busy and certainly necessary intelligence. I wanted to be a writer and had been turning out both poetry and prose since I was fifteen and got a room of my own with a door that shut. I thought that if I did not leave the university I would never write the novels I felt I was supposed to write.

The next four years I lived on the south side of Chicago doing part-time jobs and learning to write from the bottom up, for I found I had to unlearn much in order to get at where I came from. I am driven, and one force that impels me is the demand that I speak for those largely unspoken for. Art validates experience.

In college I had observed that whenever people like those I had grown up with, like me, appeared in fiction we read, they represented death or the flesh or simple folk wisdom or simple folk stupidity. When women appeared in fiction— and almost all the twentieth-century literature we read was written by men—we were objects granting or refusing sex or nurturance to men. That's all we were unless we too represented mortality or the flesh or the earth or temptation or redemption or anything else other than ourselves.

I was taught in school and I still hear all of the time statements that suggest people with less money are simpler than those with more money. This is an idea some writers of the Left have shared with right-wing writers. The notion prevails that people who cannot express reactions in the vocabulary educated people learn to use have less reactions worth bothering with.

The conviction that those who talk differently or look different feel less is exceedingly popular. "They don't know the value of human life in the Orient," you say, dropping bombs on them. Or the Middle East. Or Latin America. Or Africa. Or wherever you are doing business. One of the effects of the novel can be to induce the reader to empathize with different people. We may identify with a character who resembles us or whom we wish we resembled. As a novelist you can use that transference to get the reader to change her or his mind at least momentarily, as the character does. But you can also seduce the reader into identifying with characters whom the reader would refuse to know in ordinary life. Very few people who read *Woman on the Edge of Time* would talk willingly with its heroine, a middle-aged, overweight Chicana woman defined as crazy, shabbily dressed and lucky to get off welfare into any mopwoman job. Nor will many readers of *Vida* ever have met a political fugitive, at least knowingly.

I called cities grids of Them and Us experiences and I consider fiction one way of persuading people to cross those borders of alienation and mistrust into the existence of someone in whose mind and body they may find it enlightening to spend some time. Fiction works no miracles of conversion, but I guess I believe any white reader who spends a reasonable proportion of time consuming Black novels and poetry is less likely to be as comfortably racist in large and small ways; and any man who reads enough of current women's literature is less likely to be ignorant of what women want and need and don't want and don't need, and what patriarchy costs us in blood and energy day and night.

Basically all novels have a political dimension. That is, novels embody in their characters and what happens to them as well as in the language with which those characters major and minor are embodied and described, ideas about what's feminine and what's masculine, who's good and who's bad, who has and who deserves to have it, what behavior's on the side of the angels and who are those angels and what do they want. What's good sexually and economically? Who's allowed to get who and how? And will they die for it? Are uppity women heroes or bitches or upstarts? Whose pain is more real than other people's? What's pretty and what's ugly and who are we made to care about?

Now if the notions embodied in the novel are congruent with those the reviewer or the editor or the grantsgiver is used to hearing over dinner or at cocktail parties he (and I do mean he) attends, then he does not treat the novel as political. It's just a novel about how things are and it is reviewed or judged in terms of its literary merit or its entertainment potential. Reviewers generally demand the work coincide with the categories and obsessions they were taught characteristic of "serious literature" when they went to college, based generally on the work of a few men whose childhood was passed in the nineteenth century; or else they demand the work excite their fantasies.

But when a reviewer or a professor or an editor or a grantsgiver reads a novel that embodies a different standard of right and wrong, of masculine or feminine, of the good guys and the bad guys and the haves and have-nots in the brains and virtue and lovabilty departments, then the re-. viewer says "polemical." He will then explain to you that political fiction is bad fiction; which means that art is never supposed to embody different political ideas than the contemporary powerful hold. The notion that literature has nothing to do in the world but be consumed in a vacuum is a recent heresy. Go on, sit down with Aristophanes, with Euripides, with Catullus, with Horace, with Alexander Pope and Dryden, with Dickens and George Eliot and Georges Sand and Tolstoi and explain to them that art has nothing to do with our morals, our politics, and our behavior.

In truth every work of art changes our world a tiny bit simply because it uses up resources—trees died that this book might live—and it will take time from those who read it. Every work of art possesses some infinitesimal capacity to move us and affect our emotional and mental state. It occupies our mind and our attention and alters them as it goes into our memory. In that respect novels are like dreams. If you remember them and sometimes even if you don't, they never happened and yet they will influence the way you expect things to be, even what you will long for or dread or fear.

In a stratified society, almost all urban literature is engaged politically and morally whether it is perceived so by the author or not: it will be so perceived by the readers it validates and the readers it affronts. That I speak of the effects novels have upon us and their uses does not mean I believe a novel should be judged by some utilitarian criteria. Art is only partially rational. It operates on all the levels of our brain and influences us through sounds and silences, through identification and imagery, through rhythms and chemistry. But as writers and readers, the novels we read make us more or less sensitive to each other. They tell us how we may expect to experience love and hatred, violence and peace, birth and death. They deeply influence what we expect to find as our love object and what we expect to enjoy in bed, and what we think it's okay others should enjoy. They help us decide what war is like—hell or a necessary masculine maturation experience in a jolly peer group—and therefore whether we are willing to be drafted to fight one. They cause us to expect that rape is a shattering experience of violence like being struck by a hit-and-run truck or titillating escapade all women generally desire. Novels tell us how piggy we have a right to expect to be with each other. They influence our daydreams and our fantasies and therefore what we believe other people offer us or are withholding from us.

When the dismembered bodies of women are used decoratively as part of an aesthetic cool violence that has characterized a lot of American fiction something is deeply wrong in the heart of that fiction. It stinks.

What I am tired of is the pretense that when we write and when we publish, we don't understand what we're doing and what we're saying for and against others, like ourselves and different from ourselves, clothed in similar or dissimilar bodies and with more or less of the goodies we have or hope to have. I believe we are accountable for what we write just as we are for what we say to people we meet on the street. We are engaged in the wars of our violent times whether we wish we lived—as I surely do—in less interesting times or not; we are responsible for our choices the same as plumbers and politicians and bureaucrats, and our novels embody our values and our choices.

A Symposium Response

From the Sixties to the Eighties

Introductory Note

During 1979 we sent out more than 150 flyers to old friends and comrades, acquaintances of more or less note, polling them on the change of decades. Here were the formal questions:

> *1. When did the sixties end for you? How do you evaluate the culture work you were doing in the sixties?*
> *2. How did the changing situation of the seventies affect your work? Your idea of the seventies cultural accomplishments generally?*
> *3. If you "came of age" before the sixties, how do you evaluate the era compared to earlier times (1930-40) of radical cultural attainments? If since, has the 1960s heritage meant for you liberatory possibilities or mainly illusion?*
> *4. What do you see ahead culturally for the eighties? Is the sixties experience a positive or negative "useable past"? An inspiration for the Future?*

The response was, actually, slight. And many of the replies are marked by bitterness at the collapse of the Left, its cultural sterility, and the climate of relative isolation for artists and writers. These obviously are not our perspectives. But the answers speak for themselves.— Editors, Cultural Correspondence.

From *Cultural Correspondence*, nos. 12–14 (Summer 1981).

In the sixties the cultural work I did was treated by everyone around me as inconsequential and therefore tended to be pushed to the side of the organizing I did, the standard movement office work, the meetings, the writing of pamphlets, the power structure research. Political people in the United States do not express much respect for fiction in general and only slightly more for poetry. If they have any interest in literature, often their taste was formed by what they were taught to admire in Departments of English and has not broadened since. Therefore their taste tends either to the naive (Howard Fast fiction) or to the traditional canon of British-oriented modernists.

Most of the time my political comrades viewed my writing in the sixties as self-indulgence. I can hardly remember any encouragement to such pursuits, although people did like to hear readings and were willing to use readings to raise money. The big change for me came in the strong importance the women's movement placed and places now on cultural work. For the first time in years of being active politically I found myself respectable for the work I did, even though what I write always remains controversial within the movement as well as outside.

The women's movement has encouraged cultural work and also provided a home for thinking and working on the relationship between form and content, between tradition and oppression, between invention and communication. Mostly I have found people on the Left relating to the poetry more readily and the novels generally two or three behind where I am now. That is, *Dance the Eagle to Sleep* became visible to the Left after *Small Changes* and *Small Changes* mostly got respectable as a political document in the last couple of years. Feminists and even futurists picked up *Woman on the Edge of Time* about two years ahead of the rest of the Left; and the only serious attention *The High Cost of Living* has had in terms of a novel about class is in England.

Whenever a novel comes out, it always has the wrong line, fails to contain the moment's slogans, disturbs because it either has sex in it or too much sex or the wrong brand of sex or the characters aren't heroic and simple-minded enough. Fiction seems especially disturbing to political people. Maybe it's a puritan response: lies, all lies. What do you want to go around inventing stories for? Is that a good way for a responsible adult to behave? When I think about how the next novel will be received—*Vida*, about a political fugitive—I can hear it in advance. Ripping off the underground. She isn't perfect. None of them are perfect. You have written once again about humans, ugh.

Since I have a very strong sense of what I'm doing, I persist in my dumb way. Fiction that strokes our wish-fulfillment evaporates like popsicles with a little sticky wet stain and leaves nothing useful behind. We have to be willing to support art which hurts us, shakes us, moves us into more awareness, not less. I do not believe that reading about the amazing exploits of protagonists without flaws or hesitations or errors helps us to live our lives more usefully.

A lot of what I lived through in the sixties is inspiring to me, that molten and organic sensing of community for instance, the willingness to try to move past the nuclear family and possessiveness and rigidity. The beauty in daily things. I learned a lot about how people learn and grow in crisis and stress, how we act in danger, what keeps us from being about to work together and trust each other. I know that a lot of what I express as hopeful vision is based in experiences then that were powerful and moving.

An Interview with Allison Platt of *Sojourner*

The word for Marge Piercy is intense. Although physically small, she commands attention with her lively way of talking. When she reads poetry she chants, when she speaks she does so in bursts, with sudden exclamations and changes in pitch and volume. When we talked in early February, I found myself wishing there was a way to convey this personal energy to Sojourner's readers, but her own writing is probably the best witness to Piercy's energy.

Where did the idea for Vida *come from? What were your sources?*

I don't know why people talk about sources with novels. It's not knowable—what goes into a novel is so various and so mixed . . . I think I could say that I talked to some people who had been underground and are now "legal," but the funny thing is that I learned nothing that I hadn't already written at that point.

I think that everyone who has ever been politically involved in the U.S. has tried to imagine what it would be like to be a political fugitive. There have been a number of periods of our history when political people have been forced underground. One was during the abolitionist move-

This material first appeared in *Sojourner*, The New England Women's Journal of News, Opinions and the Arts (143 Albany St., Cambridge, MA 02139), March 1980. Reprinted with permission of Sojourner, Inc.

ment when a number of Black people had to go underground to survive. Similarly, around the time of the Palmer raids right after W.W.I, political people were forced underground. And again in the fifties a lot of people in the Communist party were forced underground.

Speaking of going underground, what do you think is going to happen with current political movements (feminism, gay rights, etc.) in the next few years?

Either the forces for social change are going to learn how to talk to more people or we will be crushed. We have to learn to reach more people, not talk to each other and stay in our little ghetto communities. If we don't, the Right will make us illegal, because they *are* talking to other people and they have more money.

The draft may make a difference, however.

What do you think should be done about the current factionalism in the women's movement?

I think that that's a terrible phenomenon. I mistrust purism—I mistrust it immensely. I have tried in my various novels to write about the problem of confusing morality and politics. Trying to force other people to be like yourself destroys the possibility of changing things. People spend so much energy on fighting people with whom they agree on nine points out of ten.

So what do you think the solution is? New Ideas? New Leaders?

You don't need new leaders, you need organizers. Organizers are just people who have credibility when they talk to other people and can *listen* and not get offended when other people don't understand their position or don't agree with them. The ability to listen is more important than the ability to be charismatic. Charismatic organizers often cause a lot of trouble. Women in the movement often guilt-trip each other on emotionally loaded issues. This is very destructive, whether the issue is motherhood, whether you're gay or straight, whether you're poor enough, or whatever . . . But we've been through periods like this before.

Are you suggesting that when things get bad enough that people will do something about it?

Well! (Laughs.) Things *are* pretty bad now. How much worse do they have to get?

It isn't that things have to get bad, it's that we have to get good. . . .

Could you talk a little about how you write your novels? Do you start with an idea for a story and build from that?

I write very character-centered fiction—the characters determine what issues are involved in the book and what aren't. I start with a theme that I want to deal with.

What would you say the theme was in Vida?

I actually found the original card that the whole book started from. It went something like: "Suppose you wrote about two sisters, one of whom is a woman whose politics is based on a sense of her own oppression, her own situation, and who becomes a feminist, and the other sister is a woman whose politics is based primarily on the oppression of other people, and who is involved in the more traditional causes? What causes one sister to feel one way and the other sister to feel the other way? They should remain close, argue with each other, disagree but be able to communicate." Natalie and Vida were the seed of the book.

But Vida seemed much more the focus.

Well, that seemed obvious to me—it's more interesting to explore the path not taken than the path taken. I've written about how women become feminists before. It was more interesting in a way for me to explore why a woman doesn't become a feminist, though Vida ends up very influenced by feminism. The experience of being a political fugitive, after all, is the experience of being an invisible woman, instead of a token woman. She was much less open to feminism when she was a token woman, a charismatic woman sharing the stage with men. As a fugitive, invisible and necessarily anonymous, she has none of that—her experiences are much closer to the experiences of ordinary women, and she becomes much more open to the ideas of feminism, though I would never call her a feminist.

How much time do you spend writing each day?

Except in spring planting when I stop for a while, probably 9:00 to 3:00 or 4:00 every day except when I'm travelling . . . I do perhaps thirty readings a year.

Have you always been able to work that steadily?

When I had to work at other jobs or when I was doing organizing that ate into the time, I wrote *Dance the Eagle to Sleep* by getting up at six in the morning when the rest of the movement was sleeping.

Many writers I know say the hardest part of writing is to start. . . .

Well, there's always a sense of nausea when you put paper in the typewriter and start chapter one, page one—the nausea of realizing you're about to start on a two or three year project. But once you've written a chapter or two, then you're *into* it.

But I don't sit down to write chapter one, page one before I've done a lot of work. Thinking, notes, dossiers on characters, the whole architectural shape of the book. I don't use a detailed outline, but I know the shape of the action and I know a lot about my major characters. I don't start and improvise the characters as I go, I improvise the details of the action instead. In chapter 12 of *Vida*, Vida and Joel get into a struggle about his jealousy, and when I *got* there I figured out what he got jealous about.

So you set up a situation and let the characters "speak for themselves"?

Yes, the momentum of the plot and a strong sense of the characters create the details. I also do three drafts, so there's a lot of opportunity to change things and shade things. Parts I rewrite more than that. The 1967 chapters of *Vida*, for instance, were rewritten again and again and again. It was very hard for me to get back to 1967 and get at what I really wanted to show.

The first draft establishes the major characters, in the second the book gets much more fully fleshed, and much more work on language, and the third time it's shading—the cross-hatchings, the subtleties.

Is the first draft much shorter than the last?

In some books it's longer, but there's not usually a lot of difference in the length, because you take things out as well as put them in.

Do you talk with anyone about your writing while you're doing it?

Ira Wood and I show each other our manuscripts as we go. I've never done that with anyone else, but we've gotten into doing that and it's lovely. It isn't that we don't scream a lot, but I find that it makes me more productive. That kind of feedback early on makes me work faster and better. To be forced to identify what it is you're trying to do . . . The way we talk isn't competitive—it's very supportive and has given me strength.

When I finish the second draft I circulate the manuscript. Some of the people I show it to are people whose literary judgment I trust, some are people whose political judgment I trust, some are people I consider good general readers. Sometimes I also want to check out some kind of technical expertise. . . .

Do you work on more than one book at a time?

No. I know what the next book will be, though, and I'm always working on poems and a novel at the same time. The poems are more spontaneous. There are days I set aside for it, but other times I will be working on a novel and get a strong poem idea. Also, poetry fits into the interstices of my life a lot more. I'll wash my hair and think of a poem and go and write it while my hair's drying, or something like that . . .

It takes fierce concentration to write poetry, but it's much more delimited than fiction in the amount of time and energy it takes.

What is your new book of poetry about?

It's called *The Moon Is Always Female*, and half of it is poems from the past two years, and half of it is poems from the lunar cycle. There are thirteen poems for the thirteen lunar months, plus an introduction and an epilogue.

The poems in the lunar cycle were incredibly involving and draining to write. I didn't write them like I usually write poems—they had to be written again and again. They were *so* intense and so complicated—not that I mean that they're obscure, they're not, but to manage to get at what I wanted to, I had to push and push and push . . . My secretary finally took them away from me and said "they're *finished!*" A lot of them are about nonrational aspects of being a woman. I'm going to perform the cycle at a benefit for *The Second Wave* on April 15. Karen Lindsey will read also.

Ohhh, they are strange poems. They deal with things like all the different lunar aspects of passionate love, despair, the relationship with other mammals, mother/daughter relationships, abortion, respect, sisterhood, the relationship between creativity and the earth . . . You'll see what they are. I'm very proud of them. I feel they are a major work of poetry I've produced.

Reading Recipes, or What I Have Learned on the Yellow Brick Road

I answered a questionnaire about poetry readings for a symposium published in *Some* magazine, in a special issue called *Poets on Stage*. The first section of this essay is from my contribution to that issue; my response has a defensive edge because the questionnaire seemed to imply a number of attitudes I disagreed with. I wrote my response ages before the magazine finally came out in 1978, no later than 1976 from the list of publications they credit to me.

Some Symposium, 1976

I consider myself a performer when I am performing the poems. For me the poem on the page is secondary; the poem uttered is primary. The ear or the mind's ear is the organ of the poem. The eye is basically the interpreter of the notation so that the poem can come to life. The poem is not necessarily knowable on first hearing. But it is experienced.

If a poem is emotionally clear and coherent, the imagery, the language, the thought can be quite complicated and it will carry. It is the strength that carries it. But I am concerned that the poem move well as utterance. I find a lot of poems written in a language for the eye and brain almost impossible to speak. I do not like an excessively literary language, poems that smell too much of libraries and other poems.

I am not able to make the distinction between the personal and the political that seems to come easily to people who have not lived their lives involved in struggle and group process. My writing and my readings are political as my life is. I do not know where the barrier between political and personal is supposed to be located. I do know that much poetry classified as apolitical supports the status quo. I find a political dimension in poems which treat women as stupid cunts, as myths about physical being, as fecundity, comfort, the earth, the ding-an-sich, or elemental grubbiness. I find poems political that assume the white knight is good and the black knight evil. I find poems political that carry in their rotten heart that ultimate aesthetic image of our culture, from comic book porn to men's mags to *Evergreen Review* and literary journal clottings, the mutilated, raped, dismembered body of a woman, as decorative object. I do not differentiate between my political poems and nonpolitical poems; I am not sure which are which.

Inert audiences depress me. I don't get much out of readings to superliterate audiences who make me feel like hors d'oeuvres. I want audiences who are able to respond. What I would like in dreams: the audience as participants, as celebrants with me, the congregation in a Black church who says "Oh tell it, sister!" I like to see women swaying to the rhythms of the poems, moving as they listen. Changes on the faces, something happening, the temperature in the room rises: then I can feel the audience, we are moving on the same wind. My best readings are those when I can enter the poems, when I read most fully but worry least about how I am doing it.

I learned a lot during the middle and later sixties from a number of Black poets, including Sonia Sanchez, Don L. Lee, June Jordan: learned a relationship I wanted with an audience, having a constituency. I learned that "a ritual of unity makes something of what it pretends." For women, a woman celebrating our female experience in strength of pain or joy and affirming what we experience that is denied by the whole culture can make us at least briefly sisters, as we see together a vision of what we have been and what we would like to be. What works if the reading works is the production of energy quiet but real. That is vital feedback for me and for some people a momentary knowing of forces in themselves too often choked. We remember together what we are supposed to be doing.

Poems I don't read? Some of the activist-to-activist poems like "The Organizer's Bogeymen" from *Hard Loving* or "When will we sit down together?" from *To Be of Use*. I don't tend to read these unless it's a special audience, from worrying that the nature of the poems might exclude many present. Some poems that I still like from my first book, *Breaking Camp*, don't go aloud well because they are just too damned literary. They are too much in the head and the eye. Or they assume more of a discourse of common information than genuinely exists. "Visiting a dead man on a summer day" from *Breaking Camp* would be a good example; also "A married walk in a hot place."

Reading has affected my poetry by making it much stronger. I have cleared out a lot of deadness and affectation. Anything inert, wordy, vague, dishonest, prosy seems to stand out when I say the poem to an audience. The poems I read most frequently are some fairly direct and simple and some dense and complex. They all make an effort to be as open and clear as they can.

1981

I really do like to say my poetry to audiences, as much now as when I wrote that rather defensive response. I'm just not as embarrassed about my pleasure in giving readings. I hate lots of things that go with readings: airports, planes, airport and plane food, if you can call it that; being away from home and my roots; some of the weirdness that goes with being at universities. But I like getting up before an audience and reciting my poems to them.

I don't read from my novels often. I'll do it if some place insists on it, but I feel awkward acting out the parts, the characters, as I never do reciting the poems. The novels read well enough out loud but they aren't designed for that, and a piece feels mutilated by itself. I have enough trouble making excerpts that are the size of short stories. The poems are strong in oral qualities, are constructed of sounds and silences, and I feel pleasure performing them.

The first time I read a poem in public, I rarely perform it well. I am listening too critically. I am testing it too consciously as a poem to pay attention to performance. That first time or two is probably the only time I feel susceptible emotionally to the poem, almost as if I were hearing it from somebody else. Once or twice I have cried when reading a poem for the first time, but fortunately, that passes.

When I am giving a reading I try to enter the poems and say them correctly, to make them belly forth on the air. I am conscious mostly of technical questions: saying the poems into the microphone, whether the microphone is working correctly or not, whether I can use a wide range of dynamics or whether I have to project every poem and cannot afford to let myself murmur or whisper occasionally.

Academics are forever telling me I don't need a mike in a particular hall where they lecture and I have to explain I am not lecturing. Of course I could project and make myself heard. I am probably better at that than most people by now. But I don't want to do that if I don't have to. It cuts down on what I can do with my voice. A mike gives me a chance at shadings unavailable if I have to bellow.

I come in with a list of poems typed up beforehand, page numbers noted and books for each poem, so I rarely have to shuffle papers, but I may depart from this program. If the circumstances are poor, I will not perform poems that require intense concentration either to read or to follow. Then I may cut the program short. I may become aware of some local situation I ought to speak to—a faction fight in the local women's movement or a series of rapes in the town. I look at the house and judge the proportion of women to men, of younger to older people, and alter the program accordingly if I am surprised. You have to keep a sense of your pace in a reading and be prepared to read different poems than you had planned if you guessed wrong. Sometimes I find I am doing too many nature/garden/outdoorsy poems for an audience. Some audiences can follow quite complex poems. I have learned to stick with short poems for a high school audience except for poems like "Burying blues for Janis" or "The Rape Poem" in which the subject matter compels their attention for a medium length poem.

A reading is a performance. I am concerned with working well and that means getting the poems I, after all, took great trouble to write well, across to as much of the audience as I can reach. I don't get stage fright and haven't for years, although when I began doing readings I could not hold my poems because my hands shook too much. When I began, I read with my hand before my mouth as if to deny I was actually daring to speak in public, and I kept my eyes down—all the mannerisms that put me to sleep when I see them in other poets. I learned to give the effect of confidence years before I felt it, because I observed that audiences prefer you to seem as if you know what you are doing. Years after people began to tell me I was a natural performer, I would get violent diarrhea right up till I walked on the stage. Then one year it was gone.

Especially if you are a woman, you must give an impression of having something to say and being able to say it, if you want to seize the audience's attention. Learn to appear as if you want to give the reading, enjoy reading, feel good about being up there, and you will eventually fool even yourself. Nothing is as unpleasant for an audience at a poetry reading than somebody who acts as if they are dying up on the stage and would rather be in a library or ten feet under. Nobody ever held a gun to any contemporary American poet's head and made them read, so why do some act as if they were doing so in desperation?

I try to get up for a reading, which means if possible having a little time to myself in my motel room beforehand, to change into a reading dress, to find my energy and concentrate on my program. If I am allowed some time alone, I have my energy together—almost a kind of physical sensation through my gut and chest and up into my throat— and I start higher when I go out onto the stage. Otherwise I start slacker and have to get my energy concentrated during the first few poems. Sometimes people insist on chattering with you right till you walk out on the stage.

I have certain garments I use only for readings. Putting one of them on starts focusing me. I feel less the daily harrassed me and go to the audience as a performer, a celebrant. I usually read in a long dress; sometimes in a three-quarter length dress. Long dresses have advantages. As I have heard that Edna St. Vincent Millay did, I have frequently read in a beautiful silk chiffon dress with long underwear beneath. Once in Buffalo I read in a long black lace dress wearing muddy combat boots. I discovered when I went to dress that I had forgotten to pack shoes.

I eat before readings, as I gather many poets don't. I get too irritable and crazed on an empty stomach. I try to avoid eating supper in the clothes I am going to perform in. With lots of readings to do in the school year, I prefer not to have to pay for cleaning the clothes I use all season; I am a sloppy eater, but I defy anybody not to the manor born to manage a potluck buffet dinner while ten people ask you questions and somebody sticks a book in your face to autograph, and not drop spaghetti sauce in your lap.

Some things I have learned about building a program I can share. I almost always begin with a handful of poems; in fact, nine times of ten the first poem I read is "To be of use." Often in a given year I have one or two ways to open a program—that pattern of the first three or four poems— which gives me a part of the program entirely memorized.

During those early moments I can concentrate on judging the set-up. When I was younger I made an effort to memorize my poems; I find now that I do so anyhow after a few readings. It's important to start with familiar material until I know whether I have predicted the type of audience correctly and can follow, more or less, the program I typed out, and until I can gauge the hall, the acoustics, the P.A. system.

Whenever I have done a few especially heavy poems, I do a funny poem. Otherwise the audience fades out. I cannot always follow this rule, actually. If I have only a twenty-minute slot to read on a program with others, if I am doing a specific sequence such as the Tarot poems ("Laying Down the Tower") or "The Lunar Cycle," I void my own rules. Normally, however, a program is composed of poems from every one of my books, running most heavily to the most recent and including new work not yet collected and sometimes not yet published.

Given the number of them I have written, I am sure to include some love poems, unless they are totally inappropriate. However I have learned not to read lots of love poems and never many in a row. You lose the audience into private musings. They sit there with their eyes glazed over after number four thinking about their last lover or the one they have now and the one they'd like to have—and they're off and running up their own mental trails. You may never get them back.

Unless I am on the program with other people and have too short a time, I always do some new poems. I need that test for a poem. I almost always cut after the first reading. Not infrequently I rewrite. Loose words, extra words, the wrong word—how they stand out when you say them to an audience. My ear is more critical than my eye ever is. Oftentimes my eyes will pass on lines I reject when finally said at full volume, even though I thought I was hearing them exactly in my head.

I like large audiences, I confess. Oftentimes I give a better reading, the bigger the audience. It's the politico in me: gee, all those people, I got to get to them, etc. The more responsive an audience is, the better I read too. I pick up their heat. I can feel the heat up on the stage from an audience that is with me, and it galvanizes me. I don't think I ever give a reading any longer below a certain point of professionalism, but I sure do give some readings that are a hell of a lot better than my average, when the audience is moved and I feel it. It's true that audiences like to laugh, but they like also to be moved. I find that people also appreciate poems that make them cry or simply touch them. Inert audiences give you nothing back: you are left with the bare bones of your skill. I come closer to chanting then. With an audience that loves the poetry, reciting approaches singing and high intense conversing, a music between us.

There must be a couple hundred poems I read regularly to audiences. Now and then I drop a poem for good or for a while. Sometimes I just get tired of it and can't hear it. It's gone stale. Sometimes I never will feel it again, but then often an old poem I haven't said in five, ten years comes back feeling fresh again. I don't organize a reading chronologically but thematically, by blocks or by contrast, sometimes by imagery, emotionally, for climaxes and resolutions and laughter now and then.

Occasionally I do quite long poems. I think the longest poem I do relatively often is "The homely war" from *Living in the Open*, which takes somewhere between twelve and fifteen minutes to read. That's at least a quarter of my program, so I have to be sure I want to do it that night. Some of your audience you will always lose during a long poem—their attention span is simply not developed—but some listeners will especially appreciate the extended development. I always do several poems that take around five minutes a piece. You can as readily lose an audience doing too many short poems in a row, especially poems around the length of haiku. It must take an entirely different style to put out an entire reading of haiku.

A piece of worldly advice: most people read too long. It is better to stop with the audience wanting, than to stop with the audience yawning. Don't cheat them, however. People feel short-changed if you read alone and only give them half an hour. An audience generally will expect forty minutes to an hour. I never read longer than an hour, and generally I aim for something like fifty minutes. But for every poet who offers too truncated a program, there are two-hundred fifty-eight poets who read too long.

It is especially nasty to read on and on when you are on a program with others. Perhaps they will stab you in the back some dark night in a parking lot or perhaps they will trip you tonight when you finally relinquish the stage. If dirty looks could kill, many garrulous poets would fall clutching their throat and be borne off to make way for the rest of the program. There are poets whose work I would have enjoyed had they only stopped fifteen minutes sooner and whose work I will never read because mention of their names produces a reprise of an earlier headache. The sense when to stop is not widespread, evidently, so buy yourself a digital watch (they start around $25), a big man's watch with clear numbers, and keep an eye on the time. Get off when you ought to.

I will never forgive or forget my early days at readings organized by SDS chapters around New York. The poets were always on alphabetically. If I had understood in time my quandary, I would have changed my name to Anna Aardvark and flourished. There was a poet whose name came ahead of mine in the alphabet and once he had the mike in his grasp, he never ceased until the audience had all stolen away—in ones at first, in nervous couples, threes, in fours, in whole rows they would flee. When I rose at last to read, no one was left, time after time, except the organizers and the other poets. I remember his name to this day as I remember his didactic crapulent poems, but I wouldn't give him one free line of publicity after fifteen years. Poets never forgive other poets who lose their audiences for them.

You can learn to perform by borrowing a recorder and practicing. Sometimes it helps to practice against music. I dislike reading with music, but I did so early and learned a lot, especially how to project to make myself heard. I always read standing for the same reason that you sing standing: you can't command the expanse of your lungs and control your diaphragm seated. A few times students have asked me why I tend to raise the inflection on the ends of lines. I do this a lot more when I am cool than when I am warm, but I do it to avoid swallowing the ends of lines. One of the commonest errors poets make is to dissolve line endings and sometimes the ends of poems into a collapsed mumble.

I try to enunciate clearly, although I don't like to read with an accent too different than I speak with normally. However, the importance of careful enunciation was brought home to me and I was humbled and abashed, when I was sent the transcript of a speech I had given a number of years ago. As I often do when I have to make a speech, I began and ended with one of my poems. A student had been hired to transcribe the tape. The poem she was copying was from the Tarot poems, "Laying Down the Tower," the last poem of the cycle, "The Sun." Here is that poem, the first half of it:

The Total Influence or Outcome of the Matter: The Sun

Androgynous child whose hair curls into flowers,
naked you ride a horse without saddle or bridle
easy between your thighs from the walled garden outward.
Coarse sunflowers of desire whose seeds birds crack open
nod upon your journey, child of the morning whose sun
can only be born from us who strain bleeding to give birth.
Grow into your horse, let there be
no more riders or ridden.

Child, where are you heading with arms spread wide
as a shore, have I been there, have I seen that land shining
like sun spangles on clean water rippling?
I do not know your dances, I cannot translate your tongue
to words I use, your pleasures are strange to me
as the rites of bees: yet you are the yellow flower
of a melon vine growing out of my belly
though it climbs up where I cannot see in the strong light.

My eyes cannot decipher those shapes of children or burning
  clouds
who are not what we are: they go barefoot like savages,
they have computers as household pets; they are seven sexes
and only one sex; they do not own or lease or control.
They are of one body and of tribes. They are private as
  shamans
learning each her own magic at the teats of stones and trees.
They are all technicians and peasants.
They do not forget their birthright of self
or their mane of animal pride
dancing in and out through the gates of the body standing
  wide.

Here is what the hard-working student heard on the tape:

The Sun

A drungeness child whose hair curls into flowers
Naked you ride a hose without saddle or bridel
Easing between your thighs and the walls garden outward
Of course sunflower is of desire who sees birds crack open
Not upon your journey
Child of the morning whose sun can only be born from us
  whose strain bleeding
to give birth. Go envy your horse! Let there be no more riders
  or ridden.
A Child, where are you heading with arms spread wide as a
  shore has I been there
Have I seen that land shining like sun, bangles on clean water
  rippling. I do
not know your dances. I cannot translate your tongue to
  words. I use your
pleasures are strange to me as the right of bees. Yes, you are
  the yellow
flower of a melon vine growing out of my belly. Till it climbs
  up where I
cannot see in the strong light. My eyes cannot decipher those
  shapes of
children or those burning clods who are not what we are. Go
  barefoot

like savages. They have computers, household pets.
They are seven sexes and only one sex. They do not own or
    lease or control.
They are of one body and of tribes. They are private as
    shavings learning
each or own magic at the teats of stones and trees. They are all
technicians and peasants. They do not forget their birthright
    or self
or their main animal pride dancing in and out through the
    gates of the
bodies standing wide.

Ever since then I have tried very, very hard to pronounce clearly (which doesn't mean that like most people from my class background who learned a lot of our vocabulary from books, I don't mispronounce a lot. I suspect I still do). You figure with the best of luck somebody in the audience who is not already familiar with the poems will listen to about two-thirds of your reading and hear about half of that.

Another common error is to go blah blah forever between poems. If the poems are good, they will read well once you have figured out how to say them. It's nice to say a word or two or make a little joke if you can, but to explain a poem for ten minutes is almost always a dreadful mistake, for the poem often feels anticlimatic. If you think there's a reference in the poem the audience might not understand (my poem "Laocoon is the name of the figure" requires explaining who he is to most audiences), you want to mention it before you read rather than afterward.

I know when I go to hear a poet and they lecture me half the evening on whatever is on their mind at the moment or explain, apologize, footnote every poem to death, I am hungry afterward. I wanted the intensity of poetry, not the roominess of prose. You can stop in the middle and make a brief impassioned plea about something or tell a story or pass the hat or whatever. I mean extremes of loquacity that are common as poison ivy.

Most poets seem afraid of being too dramatic, of making fools of themselves in public. You will hardly ever hear someone hamming it up too much, overdoing the emotion, whipping up a false storm. Earlier generations may have had that problem, but it is rare now. Our faults are flatness, coldness, the preference for being boring rather than taking a risk to get something across. The voice is your instrument when you recite your poems and you have to learn to use it, to indicate line breaks, the stanzas, the rhythms of the poem, to suggest emotional quality. You control the timbre, volume, resonance, tone color of your voice. You can learn to control your breath so that if you write long lines, you can say them properly; you learn to breathe in through your nose during a long phrasing without breaking the flow of sound through your mouth perceptibly.

Before you arrive where you are going to perform, specify the kind of podium or table, mike or not, water, whatever you need. I always specify water without ice because I've never figured out what I'm supposed to do with a mouthful of ice in the middle of a reading; spit it out, chew it into the microphone or just throw it into the audience?

The more practice in reciting your poems you get, the better job you will do. When I was too shy to read to people, I used to read to my cats. When I was in Scandanavia promoting a book, my friend Penny stayed at my home to take care of my very old Siamese, Arofa, who was dying. Penny kept her hanging on till I got back by playing poetry tapes. Arofa survived till I came home to ease her death and when I got there, Penny had memorized a great many of my poems, involuntarily. Arofa was my earliest audience and while never critical, her enthusiasm sufficed.

When I was starting out, other poets advised me to read to specific people in the audience, and sometimes I do that. You can also avoid focusing on anybody but rather read to the aisles or the back wall. Be careful with eye contact when reading poems with strong sensual or sexual content, or you may have a nuisance to deal with afterward. The most important single thing in reading to an audience is to care to get your poems across, to try to do that, to take the risks involved in projecting the poems, to approach the audience with a kind of alert respect. I think if you concentrate on the poem rather than on yourself, you will read much better, whatever the type of poem you write.

Looking at Myself

A Study in Focused Myopia

Personally, I would not be enormously impressed by a writer telling you about her writing, because we have a tendency to overemphasize the rational elements and the more respectable intentions. What I can give you basically is some of the ways I think about my own work; in this case my poetry.

I can impose a few different grids upon my work, different systems of classification, of bins and slots and file drawers. The first way of looking at the poems might be in terms of source. One class of my poems contains those whose strength lies in their clarity: in which something gets said boldly and simply which we need to have said. Usually such poems are brooded over for a time and then written for some occasion that demands them. "The Rape Poem"(5) was, in an earlier version, called "The Missoula Rape Poem" because I wrote it one night in a motel when I could not sleep after women at a meeting had described to me a series of brutal rapes and rape murders occurring in that town. They had had no satisfaction from the police, and the sheriff and the men around them treated the rapes as an occasion for mirth. The first time I read it publicly, in Missoula, a woman came up to me afterward and asked for a copy. I explained there wasn't any. She told me her twelve-year-old daughter had

First presented as a lecture to the Northeastern Association of Teachers of English, Washington, D.C., October 20, 1978.

been one of the rape victims and she wanted to show the poem to her because she thought it would help. So we copied it out.

Other poems in that category would include "For shelter and beyond"(6), "The secretary chant"(4), "Women's laughter"(4), "For Inez Garcia"(5), "To the pay toilet"(4), and "The friend"(2).

Another category of poems are those in which I am exploring some aspect of my own experience which I feel to be private but am not sure about. I am speaking as myself rather than as a spokeswoman or a medium or a channel through which energy flows. Often I write these poems with a sense of shame or trepidation. Instead of reading them first on a platform, I show them to women I trust and say, Is it okay? Can I say this? Is it ever that way for you too? I don't have the sense of speaking a basic truth but a smaller one which is true for me and maybe for some other women. "You ask why sometimes I say stop"(6), is a good example of such a poem. It was only when I showed the poem to other women and found it produced in several cases a discussion of feelings about orgasm—fear of the intensity, fear of too much, fear of being too excited or becoming too involved through the depth of sexual response—that I decided I could publish the poem. "Burying blues for Janis"(4) is another such poem, about female masochism. "Insomnia"(6) is another.

When writing such poems I always have a sense of pushing through a barrier, an inner barrier of shame and fear. I have the feeling I am talking about something I am not supposed to recognize in myself, something I am not supposed to name, to expose, to make public. I have to have a commitment to my own private truth wrung from myself as well as the truths already made public from our common struggle, to be able to write what I have to write. Feminism gives me that strength, even while I fear that what I say may not be well received, as in the poem about orgasm I mentioned.

I have to believe that when I go into myself and say what I experience that it is going to speak to you. Some of our experiences are similar and some are different, and the naming of both liberates us. The saying of the ones that may be different with some of us feels more dangerous to me, as if I am more alone in the saying; yet I think they are important too for us. We cannot define ourselves when we do not even have a set of possibilities of actively shaped womanhood to choose from.

Then there are simple lyrical poems like "Unclench yourself"(5), "We become new"(4), "Easy"(2), and "The cats of Greece"(1), where I am sure that such experiences and the utterances that come from them are accessible and common enough for the poems to work for others.

Then there are poems which try to fuse the personal and the political in a more complex artifact, as they are inherently fused in my life. For me, the political is not any more external than any other passion or any other set of ethical impulses and checks, any other hunger or need. Poems in which I have attempted to deal with the political matter of my own and other lives in the full context of daily bodily turmoil include "The provocation of the dream"(5), "The homely war"(5), "A gift of light"(6), "Women of letters"(6), and "If they come in the night"(6).

Some of my poems are rooted in the landscape, in a relationship to the soil and the other living beings around me, such as the "Sand roads"(5) sequence, "Kneeling here I feel good"(5), "Crows"(6), "The first salad of March"(6). These sometimes fuse what I would define as political feelings with feelings of tenderness and union. As I write this, three crows look at me from a distance of ten feet. Our communication is not a matter of words on a page but it works. I am honored by their trust, which is shrewd and canny. They aim to survive. So do I. None of us like men with guns.

Some of my poems are about poetry itself—not a lot, because I don't think poetry should often turn inward. But I do write such poems because writing is what I do and I must be conscious and critical and concerned about it as an act at the center of my life. Some of these poems are overtly about more general work, with my own work implied as I am really talking about work in general. "To be of use"(4) is such a poem. Others such as "Athena in the front lines"(6) and "Looking at quilts"(5) are making statements about women's art, my own only in the context of our common situation. But there are poems like "Sacramento, Geneva, Middlebury, Colorado Springs"(6) and "The new novel"(6) where I am talking directly about my own role and trying to understand it as it feeds me or wears on me. In "Memo"(7) I speak directly to other women writers.

An entirely different way I can look at my poetry is by the type of line I am using in each poem. Some of my poems (the entire Tarot sequence "Laying down the tower"(4), for instance) are written in the long prophetic line that comes out of the King James translation of the Bible into English, through Whitman and Ginsberg. Some are written in the short, breathier, more conversational, more gnomic line that comes out of Emily Dickinson through Williams, and some of the Black Mountain poets. Examples of that sort of poem would include "Market economy"(6), "The inside chance"(7), and "A work of artifice"(4). Some of my poems are written with reference to the old blank verse iambic pentameter line. Examples are "Learning experience"(2) and "White on black"(7). I am not inclined to write a whole segment of a poem and rarely two subsequent lines in iambic pentameter, since I dislike too regular rhythms. I find them boring unless sung. But there are poems where the line circles about pentameter and where I feel that ground swell under the line, pressing against what I choose as the rhythms line by line and paragraph by paragraph. I am always conscious of the rhythms of course, and my verse is strongly rhythmic.

Grid three: some of my poems are almost violently imagistic. Strong images are juxtaposed and the dissonance is as important as the image in itself. "Curse of the earth magician on a metal land"(2) and "Doing it Differently"(4) are examples. Others apply one sustained metaphor, such as "High frequency"(4) and "Concerning the mathematician"(1). Others use imagery sparingly, only to make what is described more vivid, such as "Gracious goodness"(5). I also write poems which are almost clear of images, such as "A friend"(2).

I have found it is possible to use very complex streams of images and ideas and references as in "The provocation of the dream"(5) if the sustaining emotional argument of the poem is clear. If the poem is emotionally coherent, convincing in its movements, audiences can follow it, no matter how complicated it may be when studied on the page.

For me the saying of the poem is its primary life and the record on the page is the notation by which you bring it to life when you say it, either actually aloud or in your head.

Another way of categorizing the poems is according to speaker. In a poem like "Crescent moon like a canoe"(7) the I is rather simply and bluntly me, the historical M.P. speaking out of my own life. In "The longest night"(7) I am only a shade farther than that I: I am myself with my life but it is not out of a particular moment or historical or biographical event I am speaking. The particular night is fictional, the particular landscape. It is a somewhat more generalized "I" a little way toward fiction or mythology. In a poem like "The perpetual migration"(7) the "I", like the "we" is impersonal—a political I, a human eye, in no immediate way attached to my body or history. In "Another country"(7) the "I" is a purely fictional construct, a "hairy/angular body," not at all my own, clattering with gadgets who goes to visit the porpoises. In all of my poetry I can find many voices that fall into one or another of the rough categories above. In a very few poems I have actually taken on a mask or persona. The two voices in "Embryos"(2) are examples of wholly alien persona, as is the old woman who wrestles the angel in "At the well"(7).

In many poems of course there is no "I" at all except for a narrative voice, as in "The cyclist"(2) where the male protagonist is described as "you," or "Juan's twilight dance"(2) where the same protagonist is "he," or "What she waited for"(4) where the dead waitress is addressed as "you."

I have noticed that readers sometimes misunderstand poems because of assumptions that any "I" in a poem is the historical, lyrical "I" of the poet, and they think that you therefore stand behind every "I" regardless of interior evidence in the poem, or try to fit the poem into what they know or imagine about your life.

I am conscious in my poems of exploring the experiences of being a woman in this society. I am consciously a feminist working with, by, and for other women. I feel an identity too with other people in struggle. I am conscious of being engaged on the Left and wanting to move the society constantly toward equality and to contribute to liberation struggles everywhere. I always remember our own struggle first and foremost, never forgetting us, never putting us second. I respect the choices of women who may feel more oppressed as a Black or a Native American, but I make no compromise with somebody who tries to dictate my priorities.

I have been aware also especially in my fiction but sometimes in my poetry of writing from the experience of the working-class woman in this country: a continued identification with my roots and the situation in which the bulk of my life has been lived. I try to maintain that class consciousness I came to in pain and to make it part of the work even at the cost of alienating or boring people whose class identification makes them uninterested in and rejecting of working-class lives and insights and experience.

I often see my own poems as fitted into a body of work being written by other women. For instance the core experience of giving birth to myself that was part of an acid trip in 1969, which I did not understand at the time and which produced hostility in the group I was with that summer of mostly gay men—strong hostility—was an experience I could only name, understand, and begin to integrate in my life and thought after I began to understand it was an archetype of women's thought. Only after I had encountered the image of a woman giving birth to herself in poetry, calendars, women's theater, graphics, could I know what my own hallucination meant. Only then could I learn from my own experience and could write "The provocation of the dream"(5).

Without the ongoing web of struggle, of exchanged idea, and insight and experience and organizing that makes up the women's movement, I would never be able to write those clear poems I described above, such as "Right to life"(7). They are clarifying poems because so many women have contributed to the analysis and understanding they issue from. We have all had a hand in making them. I see myself often as a channel through which that energy collects, narrows, intensifies into an artifact. Not that I do not work to do that, but that that is one of my functions, in the way that a baker of good healthy bread takes the grain raised by others and makes a whole wheat loaf of it. That is why I do not hesitate to write poems for occasions, as "For shelter and beyond"(6) was written to be presented at a rally in Government Plaza in Boston on August 26, 1976, when Women Support Women was the theme of the day and half the speakers were battered women. If I am moved by a theme and I feel in touch with it, why shouldn't I write something to order? Similarly, "For Inez Garcia"(5) was written for a benefit Karen Lindsey and I did to raise money for Inez Garcia, and "For Shoshana-Pat Swinton"(6) was written for another benefit, at a time I was passionately involved in Shoshana's case. I resent the implication so often laid on me that a poem written for delivery at a benefit and to be used in that campaign (as Shoshana used my poem in hers) is somehow less a poem than one written on the occasion of the poet's getting drunk or losing a lover or seeing a daffodil. I lose lovers and see daffodils and write poems about that, but I also support political prisoners and write poems about that.

I work very hard to make the meaning of my poems clear. If the images are surrealistic or dream images, I try to make the poem emotionally clear, clear in its drift, its context. If what I mean does not communicate well or is confusing without any gain for that confusion—and I can think of very few cases where I have desired ambiguity—then I rework the poem and rework it until I think it says what it must, on all the levels it says.

Recently a truculent young man heckling me called me a preacher. I guess it was the worst thing he could think of—a female preacher, he said. I cannot imagine taking the trouble I do as a writer only for my own glory or satisfaction or only to express my own emotions or opinions or tell my tale. If I didn't think there was some point to it all, some use to others, some function to my work, I would not keep at it in the face of the hostility that feminists and those identified with the Left arouse. The feedback that I get from audiences and from individuals who speak to me is more than my bread and butter; it's the energy that flows through me back to you, and it's the support that sustains me.

---

1. *Breaking Camp* (Middletown, Conn.: Wesleyan University Press, 1968).
2. *Hard Loving* (Middletown, Conn.: Wesleyan University Press, 1969).
3. *4-Telling.* (Trumansburg, N.Y.: Crossing Press, 1971).
4. *To Be of Use* (New York: Doubleday, 1973).
5. *Living in the Open* (New York: Knopf, 1976).
6. *The Twelve-Spoked Wheel Flashing* (New York: Alfred Knopf, 1978).
7. *The Moon Is Always Female* (New York: Alfred Knopf, 1980).

An Interview with Denise Wagner of *Plexus*

In the past four years I have had the opportunity to interview a number of women who have made what I would consider to be a significant contribution to feminist culture. This interview with writer Marge Piercy has been one of the most enjoyable. She was very personable and answered my questions honestly. Besides, she even fixed me lunch.

At what age did you start to think of yourself as a writer?

I have been writing seriously since I was fifteen years old. I started writing both poetry and prose, a novel actually when my family moved into a house where I had a room of my own with a door that shut, providing me with a bit of privacy.

What was your subject matter like at that time?

In poetry it isn't terribly different from what it is now. It was partly political, partly personal; a lot about being a woman, in that case a girl growing up. I then went to college and learned that you don't write about things like that. It took years of unlearning before I started focusing on a personal/ political pulse in my writing again.

From an interview in *Plexus*, March 1981.

In prose I think I started out with much weirder notions of what fiction was. The first novel I wrote was dreadful. It was a strange combination of observations of real life, terrible girls' books and Faulkner, all mooshed up into one terribly unhealthy stew. I should have burned it years ago. To think I could drop dead and someone could actually read it! It's a horrifying thought.

How did you get to the point where you could produce what you would consider a good quality novel?

It has been a very long process of learning what I wanted to do with fiction and being able to learn very slowly how to do it. I wrote five or six novels before my first published novel was released.

When did feminism first start to come through in your writing?

I think there was a resurgence of the women's movement when I was working on what was going to be my second published novel, *Dance the Eagle to Sleep*. The first time I addressed women's issues head on was in *Small Changes*. *Going Down Fast* had little feminist consciousness in it. It was written before there was an active women's movement. I think my poetry began coming around about the same time.

Is there a specific audience you are trying to reach through your writing?

I'm interested in reaching women who are not already in the women's movement. The main focus, especially of my fiction, is on reaching other people, primarily women who are not already persuaded. So I am not writing my fiction internally to the women's movement.

I remember in the early seventies there was some conflict in the feminist community that some artists were feeling a pressure to be "more political" through their art. How did that affect your writing?

Well I am quite a bit older than many women who are currently involved in the women's movement and because of that I don't find most conflicts quite as devastating because I have experienced similar situations many times in my political involvement before.

I think the women's movement has treated its cultural workers a lot better on the whole than the New Left did. In the past the New Left would guilt trip you all the time for writing. I think that the women's movement has an unusual number of people who had some sense of art as part of the oppression and therefore part of the solution.

So do you see art as something that is inherently political?

Art works on many different levels. The political is one of its dimensions. Art is not a totally rational thing. A work of art whether it is a piece of music, a painting or poetry speaks to you on many pre-rational and irrational levels. It speaks to you on all levels of your knowing and being. Some of those are rational and political and some are not.

There has been a considerable amount of mystification around "the Arts," and since that is such an integral part of a culture which many of us are working hard to further develop, I was wondering if you could share some of your thoughts about it with us.

I think the ability to derive pleasure from art is widespread in the population. Many people can dance enjoyably, a lot of people can sing enjoyably, others can write poetry for each other.

It is well to remember, however, not to confuse artistry with the ability to get pleasure through the arts. I love it when I can get at a piano, but the noises that I make should not be confused with what someone who is well disciplined and very good at it does. Nobody else is going to take pleasure in listening to what I might play. But I take pleasure in it.

Because I have taken some lessons and have played for a while in my life, I can understand music much better than I would have otherwise and certainly appreciate a good pianist beyond what I could have if I had never touched the instrument. Similarly, someone who writes poetry for pleasure or spends their Sundays painting usually possesses a deeper understanding of what is involved in the creation of that particular art form.

It is when you give your life passionately to something, and it is what you do, and you do it with great integrity, that increases the quality and enables your work to become art. Other people can relate to the work of an artist, or in my case a writer, because of the amount of intensity, reality, and energy, and the experiences of many people that have been put into it.

When I write I write of many people's experiences. Many people's experiences flow through me. To write of them is what I am supposed to do.

Mirror Images

Since I do writing of several kinds, I have to say that each feels quite distinct to me. I write essays, reviews, articles (like this one) in a spirit that reminds me of writing papers for school: almost always at the last minute to a deadline. There is usually a clear purpose to it, for instance, giving a push to some book I think important such as Alice Walker's *Meridian*, Audre Lorde's poetry, or Bell Chevigny's *The Woman and the Myth: Margaret Fuller's Life and Writings*. My aim is to be as clear as possible. The purpose overrides aesthetics. I usually try to make a few important points.

I tend to be open about the fact that it is my opinion I am putting forth and about what my political stance is, informing that opinion. I regard it as a duty that I carry with other women who have some access to print media. Writing reviews feels more like sharing the life-support jobs in a household than like creativity to me, although I know there are people who find the essay an exciting form.

My lack of commitment to reviews or essays does not mean I do not get excited about ideas, but that not enough of the rest of my psyche is involved for the act to feel to me as I am accustomed to feeling during writing. I do not respond the

Reprinted by permission from *Women's Culture: The Women's Renaissance of the Seventies*, edited by Gayle Kimball (Metuchen, N.J.: Scarecrow Press, 1981). Copyright © 1981 by Gayle Kimball.

same way toward other prose nonfiction: for instance Adrienne Rich's *Of Woman Born* moved and excited me and served me as much as any of her absolutely first-rate poems. I think of my nonfiction as impersonal, duty-oriented, like tithing: something you must put back in the movement, something you must do for others.

My only play I wrote in collaboration with Ira Wood. I worked with other people frequently in the past writing articles or pamphlets, usually in the course of political work I was involved in. Both in the North American Congress on Latin America, in Students for a Democratic Society and in the women's movement, I wrote with six or seven different collaborators. I had never, however, collaborated in something I viewed as art rather than as direct and immediate agit-prop or how-to information until I worked on *The Last White Class.*

Collaborating is interesting—which is like saying that marriage is interesting, and you wonder how other people manage it without murdering each other. It was hard, but it was hard in different ways than it is to work alone. It required a discipline of openness to ideas not originating with me and a stubbornness in defending my better ideas. I think it is good to have a relationship where collaborators can scream at each other and share some way to make up. We certainly screamed a lot. We wrote the whole play together line by line. In the different drafts we took different scenes to rough out, but then week by week we got together and did the actual writing. I might say I think in collaboration the ultimate advantage goes to the one at the typewriter because that person determines what finally gets typed. (We figured this out early and took turns.)

As for writing for the theater, it is still exotic to me and problematical. I remain unconvinced after many productions that plays are an effective way of reaching anybody. It feels very complicated and roundabout. I am familiar with the orneriness of characters in novels who won't lie down and die when you tell them to, but the orneriness of actors was new to me. I can imagine that the chills and fevers of opening night could be addictive, but probably more so if I were only a novelist and not also a poet who gets to experience my own opening night every time I give a reading.

My poetry appears to me at once more personal and more universal than my fiction. My poetry is of a continuity with itself and with the work of other women. No one who reads a lot in women's anthologies can avoid being struck by how we are all opening new ground for each other, how we create new kinds of poems, call attention to old daily experiences never named, and thus never recognized, how we help each other along the way.

I am constantly reworking the poems I read until they are published in book form. I consider magazine publication a halfway point. When I am putting a book together I rewrite forty percent or so of the poems. I don't always perform a poem the same way. I may put in or leave out. It is a performance, after all, and the form on the page is notation. Even when I am reading a poem from one of my books I may alter it. I have had members of the audience who have been following in a book tell me I made a mistake, which makes me smile. There are mistakes, certainly, when I miss a line or inadvertently transpose lines. But I also alter the poems experimentally or in response to something in the evening or the audience. However, the vast majority of the time once the poems have appeared in book form they are as I want them and I leave them and perform them as written.

Since I am still standing up and saying the poems I wrote fifteen years ago as well as some I wrote last week, I sense a continuity with my poetry inside my own career as well as across the boundaries of lives. Some poems I cannot any longer feel close to, can't feel good about saying, but others remain utterances I still want to say. I associate the strength of poetry with a sense of telling the truth: the truth of a moment, perhaps; the truth of the way the winter light falls on the path or the truth of a painful encounter or the truth of mass murder. I think of poetry as utterance that heals on two levels.

The first level of healing is that of the psyche. Poetry is a saying that uses verbal signs and images, sound and rhythm, memory and dream images. Poetry blends all different kinds of knowing, the analytical and the synthetic, the rational and the prerational and the gestalt grasping of the new or ancient configuration, the separate and fused hungers and satisfaction and complaints and input of the senses, the knotted fibrous mass of pleasure and pain, the ability to learn and to forget, the mammalian knowing (the communication you share with your dog), the old reptilian wisdom about place and intent. Poetry has a healing power because it can fuse for the moment all the different kinds of knowing in its saying.

Poetry can also heal as a communal activity. It can make us share briefly the community of feeling and hoping that we want to be. It can create a rite where we experience each other with respect and draw energy.

Fiction is as old a habit of our species as poetry. It goes back to tale, the first perceptions of pattern, and fiction is still about pattern in human life. At core, it answers the question, what then? And then and then and then.

Poetry is an art of time, as music is. Rhythms are measured against time: they are measures of time. A poem goes forward a beat at a time as a dance does, step by step, phrase by phrase. Fiction is *about* time. First this, then that. Or this— then before it was that. Therefore this. From the perception of the seasons, of winter, spring, summer, fall, of the seasons of our lives, of the things that return and the things that do not return, of the drama of the search and finding of the fruit, the seed, the root that sustains life, the looking and the hunting and the kill, the arc of the sex act, the climax of giving birth: these are the sources of the fictional intelligence. If you make such a choice (being kind to an old woman on the road, running down an old man, marrying Bluebeard against all advice, apprenticing yourself to a witch) what follows?

I do not write much short fiction. I used to, but I could not get it published. In the sixties there was no place open to me to publish most of my fiction, no place to publish serious short stories about the lives of women from a viewpoint anything like mine. The only stories of mine published then were a few with a man as protagonist and a couple about childhood. With the founding of women's periodicals, many of the short stories I wrote then could finally find a home. It made me feel very good to see them in print at last, as if the dead had finally risen, but the habit of writing short fiction has failed in me. Of course I have not been paid for them. The only short fiction I ever made any money on at all was a piece about a male religious fanatic who became a rock singer, published in the *Paris Review*, and then anthologized several times.

I have written a couple of stories in recent years, but only a couple, less than one every five years. Basically the decision is economic, and then habitual. I am accustomed to thinking of ideas for poems or novels but no longer invent ideas for short stories.

My novels feel very different to me, each a small world. A novel is something I inhabit for two or three years, like a marriage or a house. It owns me. I live inside it. Then it is done and I pick up and set out to build a new home, often with a feeling of terrible desolation and loss and depression. What will become of me? What will I do now? How will I live? What will I think about? While I am writing a novel, it occupies me and stains my life.

When I am writing first draft, it drains my dreams wan. I have simple anxiety dreams, simple sexual dreams, blatant wish fulfillment or terror. In later drafts my dreams flesh out again, rich and various. The first draft is scary to me. I can't risk interrupting it for long as the flow may be broken. The momentum is important, pushing off into space. I think of it as building a bridge in midair, from one side of a river. I am always terrified the whole thing is unsound. Sometimes my identification becomes dangerous. I lose a sense of myself in my characters until I have trouble functioning in my own life. I can't sleep, I can't get out of the character or the novel. Those are the dangers of first draft.

I like revisions. It's work that has more play in it, less spinning from the gut. I know I can get through it and the problems are large, perhaps, but smaller than the horizon. I can get my mind around them. Between the second and third drafts, I have a habit of circulating my manuscript to friends. I show it to seven to ten people, some writers and some not. I ask for criticism. That is the time I care most what people say about my work. I can put criticism to work then. I can accept or reject bit by bit but I need that kind of feedback, what works and what doesn't, what others are seeing when they look at the work.

As a political writer, frequently I have a fair amount of research to do on a novel. For *Going Down Fast* I had to understand the uses of urban renewal to the conglomeration of real estate and corporate powers that control cities, and I had to understand Chicago history and politics. For *Woman on the Edge of Time* I had a lot of studying to do about the brain and psychosurgery, about how it feels to be in a mental institution, and a lot of research to do preliminary to thinking about a good future society.

I have a very nice memory annex I use for just about everything from what I do instead of a diary (notes from time to time) to ways of keeping and organizing and accessing research data to notes on plot and character and future novels. The system uses edge-punched cards or edge-notched cards, however you prefer to call them, and a series of randomly generated codes which use one, two, three, or four hole codes according to the predicted frequency of use—according to my project, my habits of mind, what I think I'll be doing and caring about. I once wrote a book about this system of information storing and retrieval called *The General Practitioner*, but nobody wanted to publish it.

Anyhow, that saves me a lot of time in getting at the large amounts of information I use up and the large amounts of notes I take. Otherwise, I think I would drown in notes. I clip periodicals heavily and keep files on things I think possibly useful. Novelists are always hungry for information. I am always way behind clipping things, let alone reading them. My house is full of glaciers of yellowing newsprint creeping through the rooms.

I wrote six novels before the first one that was published, *Going Down Fast*. That had the least women's consciousness of any of my novels, but then it was written from 1965 to 1967 when I had the least of any time in my life. One of the earlier novels that could not be printed was close to a feminist novel, *Maud Awake*, and that was one of the things about it besides its great length that made it impossible to publish in the mid sixties. *Going Down Fast* marked the first time I had written with a male protagonist, in part, other than in short fiction. The novel is told from two major viewpoints and a number of minor ones, and is a fairly classy example of what you can do with multiple viewpoints in showing political process and the exercise of power and powerlessness. I find it a little "literary" and overwritten now but only a little. It was my love-hate musing on Chicago, where I lived for four years, the hardest of my life. So far that is.

Dance the Eagle to Sleep I still like a lot. Nothing else like it came out of the sixties, and I think it stands up very well. I doubt it would find a publisher today: the politics are too harsh and direct. It had enough trouble finding a publisher in 1969. It was turned down by twenty houses before Doubleday took a tiny chance on it with a miniscule advance, and a two-book contract that tied me up till 1975. It has more in it to me of what the heart of the New Left felt like than anything else I've read, and I think a lot of people who were passionately involved felt or feel that way about the novel. I did not try to write a realistic novel about SDS but produced a dream-nightmare version of what was going on in our psyches at the same time that I recreated a lot of the kinds of jargon, interactions, relationships, and political concerns that characterized that world. I think that choice was a wise one, and it certainly was a shrewd one in terms of being able to write about the New Left without describing events that might have proved useful to the government and its unceasingly multimillion dollar surveillance of all of us active then and now. You pay for that surveillance of political activists in all moments even slightly left of extreme right, and so do I. I don't think you get your money's worth. Wouldn't you rather spend it on a vacation or meals out?

Small Changes was an attempt to produce in fiction the equivalent of a full experience in a consciousness-raising group for many women who would never go through that experience. It was conceived from the beginning as a very full novel that would be long, almost Victorian in its scope and detail. I wanted, I needed that level of detail in the lives of my two women protagonists. The novel is as much about who is doing the housework at any given point as it is about who is sleeping with whom.

Woman on the Edge of Time is one of my favorite of my novels. My first intent was to create an image of a good society, one that was *not* sexist, racist, or imperialist: one that *was* cooperative, respectful of all living beings, gentle, responsible, loving, and playful. The result of a full feminist revolution. To try to imagine people of such a society was my hardest task. I think Consuelo Ramos is the best character I ever created, the fullest and deepest.

The High Cost of Living is about the price of moving from the working class to the college-educated working class. It also explores the limitations of cultural feminism and separatism; why I do not believe feminism without an economic and class analysis works. But it's also about loneliness and the rigidity that prevents us from being able to love each other. It's about labeling and lying.

Vida has as protagonist a political fugitive, a woman who has been living underground since 1970. On one level it is about the sixties and the seventies. On another level it is about two sisters, both politically committed, and some of the inner and outer forces that make one woman a feminist and another more oriented toward the male Left. On another level it is a love story about two people trying to build love and truth on the margin of danger and desperation. On another level it is a study of the destructive effects of male jealousy.

Braided Lives is set in the fifties, for the most part, and is about two friends who go to college from working-class families and work out their destinies in the world of rigid sex roles and Freudian orthodoxy of the years before the women's movement had made abortion legal and provided alternatives to women besides "marry or die." It is also a portrait of the artist as a feisty young girl, candid, independent, street-wise, buffeted, and hard-tried by the prevailing mores and values of those conservative times.

I think of each of my novels as being a different world, almost. I think each is written differently, and I think for each novel just as there is an appropriate length given in the basic idea (that *Small Changes* would be 500+ pages long, and *The High Cost of Living* less than 300), so there is an appropriate language for the character and the action. When I do what is popularly called fine writing, I do my best to strike it out. That wasn't true in *Going Down Fast*, but I think I have been more disciplined since then. However, I can imagine a novel where such literary language might be appropriate. I think *Braided Lives* necessarily is richer in its structure and language because it concerns creativity as a central focus.

Another strong difference between fiction and poetry is that poetry is almost independent of reviews for getting out to people. Poetry readings are more important, as is inclusion in anthologies. There are many alternate sources of information about poetry, and many shades of opinion are represented in writing about it. There is no single source or single few sources of rating, as novels have. With novels the reviews in a few New York-based publications can make or break a novel in hardcover and determine whether you will ever hear of it: whether it will be advertised, reviewed elsewhere, ordered by bookstores, or even printed a year to a year and a half later in mass paperback.

This gives a few periodicals whose opinions represent the interests of a few people who tend to be doing right fine under the present system a great deal of power to determine what fiction the rest of us are apt to be reading next year. Naturally I object to this system of screening books, since my novels always have something to offend everybody, but especially tend to offend the reviewers of those powerful periodicals. I'm a feminist, I'm of the Left, and I like to write about working-class people. When I don't offend, I am simply writing about people they don't tend to care about. I find suburban novels about adultery boring myself.

I find much more poetry I can enjoy than fiction. Among the fiction writers whose work I read with pleasure are Alice Walker, Toni Morrison, Alice Munro, Margaret Atwood, Joan Haggerty, Toni Cade Bambera, Stanislaus Lem, Gabriel Marquez, Thomas Pynchon, Doris Lessing, E. M. Broner, Rhoda Lerman, Joanna Russ, Suzy McKee Charnas, Vonda McIntyre, Samuel Delany, Fanny Howe, Tillie Olsen, and Grace Paley. There are so many poets I like I couldn't even make a short list. Adrienne Rich, Denise Levertov, Audre Lorde, and Diane di Prima mean a lot to me, and Margaret Atwood again. I probably read more poetry than I do fiction. I also read a great deal of nonfiction on a variety of subjects from natural history to economics to biography. Among other poets I read with more than usual interest are Marilyn Hacker, Susan Griffin, June Jordan, Faye Kicknosway, Etheridge Knight, Maxine Kumin, Phil Levine, Kenneth Rexroth, John Oliver Simon, Kathleen Spivack, Susan Fromberg Schaeffer, and on and on. I read a fair amount of poetry in translation and a great deal of older poetry, constantly.

Still, at the moment, there is more poetry that speaks to me as a woman, a feminist, a political person, someone hungry for ideas, information, confirmation of my experiences, knowledge of other people's, than there is in any other form of writing. I think many women share that perception, which is one of the reasons we fill poetry readings where women we respect say their poems to us.

In this book, for the first time, I have had to confront consciously my own aesthetics and try to articulate my practice. Of course I have collected interviews, reviews, a speech or two, some essays, but about a third of this volume I wrote directly for this volume. It has been an interesting if not wholly pleasant discipline.

This year has been marked by a formal stock-taking, quite unexpectedly. *Braided Lives* is of all my novels the closest to being autobiographical, although I am a novelist through and through and once launched on a tale, the tale is paramount. I have little interest in the accidents of how things were. In the same year that I finished rewriting *Braided Lives*, I have put together my selected poems *Circles on the Water* and this present volume.

I can imagine writing actual autobiography, if I live into a ripe and relatively safe old age. Two of my novels might be classified as science fiction; I can imagine writing more in that genre. I cast a yearning eye also at the possibilities of working in and against other genres. I can think of at least two I have definite plans to work in. I always know at least the next novel I am going to write, and sometimes the one after. I have put little in this volume of my theory and practice of the novel, and none of my political essays. What a pleasure it is to be a writer, in spite of the occupational hazards of backache and headache and social weirdness and the fluctuations of a never secure and often nonexistent income. I write my books as well as I can to last. If the world perishes, it cannot matter what happens to my books. I am writing them for the inhabitants of this and not other, perhaps saner, planets.

Fame, Fortune, and Other Tawdry Illusions

My name is not a household word like Drano or Kleenex. Mostly people have no particular reaction when they meet me, although you can never be sure. My gynecologist "knows who I am" because his receptionist Audrey read one of my novels, as has my accountant. However, from time to time people recognize me on the street or in odd and disconcerting circumstances like in a shopping mall when I was trying on a skirt, or another time in a restaurant when Woody and I were having a bloody if moderately quiet argument. I am not so bad about accidental recognition as I used to be. I do not try to crawl into my own pocket or pretend if I don't move a muscle or breathe, I will wake in my own bed, but I can't say I ever behave more gracefully than a sneak thief caught.

Publishing books, especially about women, brings letters that can break your heart: women losing custody of their children, women shut up in mental institutions because they rebelled against being an unpaid domestic or took a female lover, women in all shapes and colors of trouble.

> Women dyeing the air with desperation,
> women weaving like spiders from the gut
> of emptiness, women

First published in *New Boston Review* 8, no. 1 (February, 1982).

swollen with emotion, women with words
piling up in the throat like fallen leaves. . . .

"Women of Letters"

You also get flattering letters from women as well as some
men who tell you what your books have meant to them. You
also receive hate mail, if you have any visible politics.

The admirers who do not give pleasure are those who call
up, generally when you are sleeping or writing, making
supper, entertaining friends and say, "Hello, I read your
book, I happen to be in Wellfleet, and can I come over?"
There is no way to satisfy such a caller. When I was younger, I
was so astonished and grateful anybody had read anything
of mine and liked it, I would invariably say yes. Dreadful,
dreadful scenes resulted. Worse than that, whole boring
evenings and days and someone who felt they had the right
to invade again at will and at some point would have to be
dealt with forcefully. People who want to invite themselves
into your house to meet you generally are pushy and some-
times more than a little nuts, and nothing less than letting
them move in or letting them have at least an arm or leg of
their own will satiate a baseless hunger. The people I lived
with after *Small Changes* was published put their collective
foot down, saying they got nothing whatsoever out of tourists
who came to gape at me. Now I make excuses, unless I know
the person in some way, unless a genuine connection exists
so that we can hope for two-way communication.

Every week several books and at least one manuscript
arrive with requests for blurbs, criticism, help of some sort. I
used to try to respond to all those requests, but I got further
and further and further behind. The books I now put on a
pile in terms of when they arrived (I am currently a year and
eight months behind) and the manuscripts I promptly re-
turn, if the authors provided postage. I do not attempt to
read manuscripts at all, unless it is for someone I know. That
alone happens at least twenty-five times a year. All the books I
do finally glance at or skim at least and a certain number I

read, but I feel haunted, snowed in by them. I remember how long I was utterly unknown. I feel guilty, but I know rationally that if I was to read even a quarter of them, I would do nothing else; and I do not have a lot of time to read in the first place. Unlike academics, I don't have long vacations. I may take a two week vacation every couple of years, and if Woody can come with me, I will take a three or four day vacation once a year on a business trip to an interesting place. But to make a living at writing, I have to hustle and I have to work six days a week.

I travel a lot giving readings, and there the weirdness flourishes in some pockets like mold. People go through ego dances before me that I find confusing and bemusing. I do not have the middle-class patina and I am not much good at making gracious casual conversation. I like best to talk to people one on one, not necessarily about me. Women who go about giving readings are expected to act like ladies, like mommies, or like tough dykes, and I don't fit into any of those standard roles.

Joanna Russ says it's my body type and my style that gets me in trouble. Nobody tries to make her play mommy, or at least not quite as often at first glance. She's tall as the Empire State Building, lean and elegant, and dresses tailored. I am five feet four (almost), *zoftig*, and dress more or less peasanty.

I remember about 1973 or 1974, I was wearing my standard Women's Liberation Army garb, slumped way over so my boobs wouldn't jiggle too much because I wasn't supposed to wear a bra, dressed in about thirty pounds of denim, when I thought to myself, Why do I have to wear male drag to talk to and about women? I went back to skirts. I dress the way I feel good. And I always read in a dress: let there be no mistake I am a woman, proud of it.

What do people want from somebody they have heard of? It is not even, frequently, a matter of having read your work and formed expectations, for I have gone through upsetting pas-de-deux with individuals who had no idea what kind of work I produce. I was pure celebrity to them, some kind of superperson because a published writer. Of the people who have some familiarity, many are attached to one particular novel and express resentment that I do not resemble physically or in character either Miriam or Beth in *Small Changes*, or Vida in *Vida*—that I am not a native speaker of Spanish, like Consuelo in *Woman on the Edge of Time*, or a karate enthusiast like Leslie in *The High Cost of Living*, or a systems analyst like Miriam. I have had fans become hostile when I tried to explain that a novel was not autobiographical. The hostility seems to divide into those who feel put upon (I thought it was true and now I find it's just a story!) and those who suspect you're trying to keep the truth from them: all novels are thinly disguised autobiography and you're just trying to cover up being a lesbian or being a mother who has lost custody of her children, or whatever.

Readers of the poems tend to have somewhat more accurate expectations, although one of the first things always said when I get off the plane is, "I/we expected you to be taller" or "I/we expected you to be bigger." I intend to write a poem soon about being four feet tall, and then everybody will say, "Oh, but we expected you to be smaller." All microphones are preset as if everybody were five feet ten, and the podiums are sized accordingly.

Once in a while you arrive into a situation where somebody has decided beforehand you are their sex object. You land and are visited with this great rush that has nothing whatsoever to do with you, and which seems to assume you have no commitments, no attachments, but are really a figment of their sexual imagination capable of fitting right into the fantasies they have worked up. I find that so off-putting I don't even feel flattered. Mostly men do this, but sometimes women do it. There may even be the implication that they got you this real nice gig, paying more than they think you or any woman is worth, so you should thank them by rolling over belly up in their bed.

My advice to the struggling young writer is, never thank anybody sexually, and never use your body as payment or prepayment for help. Fuck only people you want, and then no matter what goes wrong and how you get clobbered emotionally, at least you will have catered to your own sexual tastes and you will not feel victimized. You have been your own free agent and will be stronger for it. If you are honestly turned on by someone who can help you, clear sailing. But if you are a woman, you have to be especially careful you don't get known as X's girlfriend, because then you can write *The Four Quartets* and still people will say you got published because you were X's girlfriend.

Every writer has some groupies, and how you deal with them is your own decision, within the law. You can sense that a great many of them would not like you as you are, as opposed to the idealized or otherwise fictional image they are toting around; or what they offer is a come-on for expecting you are going to be for them what Joanna Russ calls a magic mommy: solve all their problems, make them happy, get them published or produced or whatever, make the world right—for them—and have no real needs of your own to be satisfied. Since writers are generally pretty needy beings, such encounters are programmed for disaster.

On the other hand, one of the possible relationships that may work out for a woman writer is a relationship with a younger person who does know who you are and what you do, and who genuinely admires that before getting to know you—but does get to know you. Such an intimacy can contain a lot less bloody gutfighting than somebody, particularly a man, your own age. Oftentimes women who have achieved some small success find that the man or woman they lived with beforehand can not adjust to what they view as an unnecessary fuss about somebody they knew back when. Fame loses you lovers and friends, as well as bringing people flocking closer. It does, however, make it easier to find new relationships. You can pick and choose a little. That doesn't mean you'll choose any more intelligently than you did when you were seventeen and still squeezing pimples or twenty-five and invisible as a grain of salt at the seashore, but you may have learned something.

Many men and many women cannot bear success even of the most limited and partial sort coming to someone they married or whose life they have been sharing. They may feel they cannot hold on to their lover with all the new competition, real or imagined. More often they resent what they feel is the shift of emphasis from themselves as center of the marriage or life, to the other person who was supposed to dance attendance on them, not to be rushing off to Paducah to give poetry readings, not be signing books, making speeches, or giving interviews.

You will, as a traveling woman, find all too often that that fuss, however minor, also infuriates local men who feel that you are after all just a cunt and they've seen better, and why isn't everyone fussing about them? Similarly you will find as a traveling woman that frequently academic women in universities who may write a poem or two a year or always meant to write someday will look at you with annoyance and just about say to you, why all the attention on you? You're just a woman like me. Why should they pay you to come in here and read, lecture, pontificate?

People also commonly confuse three things quite distinct. As an American poet you can achieve a certain measure of fame, but you don't get rich and you don't acquire power. David Rockefeller is rich and David Rockefeller is powerful. Allen Ginsberg may be famous, but he doesn't own half of Venezuela or even New Jersey and he isn't consulted on the national defense budget or our policies toward South Africa. Morris the Cat enjoyed far more fame than any writer I know, but you didn't imagine him as wielding power.

Few writers are rich. If they are, maybe they inherited money. When you hear about a $100,000 paperback deal, the hardcover publisher usually takes $50,000, the agent $5,000, and the writer's share on paper is $45,000, except that she got a $15,000 advance to finish the book, so that $15,000 is taken out of her share. That gives her $30,000 minus taxes. Let's say it takes her three years to write a novel, I would think a decent average of what people need. My shortest book took two years; the others, all longer. That gives her about $8,000 a year income for the next three years. Happy $100,000 deal!

For a writer, having some fame is surely better than having none, since if people have heard of you they are likelier to buy your books than if they have not; but it doesn't mean you're drinking champagne out of crystal goblets while you count your oil revenue shares, and it doesn't mean you have any choice about how the world is run and what happens in the society you're part of. Similarly the writer above with the $8,000 coming in for the next three years is immensely better off than she was when she wrote for an occasional $5 or $50 fee from the quarterlies, or when she did a reading a week for twenty weeks at one hundred bucks per reading, ending up sick in bed and worn out with no writing done and having earned a total of $2,000 after her expenses on the road are deducted.

Make no mistake: I like applause. I adore being admired. I even like signing books, which I understand some writers don't. I'm tickled somebody is buying them. I work hard when I give workshops and try to make intelligent political points when students question me. I like having my books discussed; I passionately care to have them read.

But I resent jealousy, especially when beamed at me by people who have made as clear choices in their lives as I have. I know how invisible I was to the kind of people I meet around universities and other institutions in my nonfamous life, when I was poor and subsisting on various underpaid part-time positions. I know how they treat their secretaries, waitresses, telephone operators, cleaning women, store clerks. I was living in a slum, eating macaroni and wearing second hand clothes (not then fashionable) and chewing aspirins because I couldn't pay a dentist while I wrote the first six novels before the one that got published.

If I could possibly forget how little respect or understanding I received from other people when I was a serious but largely unpublished writer, I'd get a refresher course every day. I live with a young writer, Ira Wood, and I see how little respect he gets because he has not yet been sanctified by the fame machine. It's hard getting started in the arts, and one of the things that is hardest, is that nobody regards you as doing real work until somebody certifies you by buying what you do. "For the young who want to" was written for him, to cheer him on a few years before we were actually living together.

Another kind of irritation I provoke in resident or visiting male writers is drawing larger audiences or selling more books than they do, whereupon they are careful to inform me it's because I "jumped on this women's lib bandwagon." I'm fashionable, but they're universal. Universal includes only white men with university degrees who identify with patriarchal values, but never mind even that. If they imagine it helps me to be known as a feminist, they have never read my reviews. The overwhelming majority judge my work solely in terms of its content by a reviewer who hates the politics and feels none of the obligations I do when I review works to identify my bias and try to deal with the writer's intentions. Jealous males also seem to have failed to notice that the women's movement while touching the lives of a great many women no longer has access to the media, and enjoys little money and no political clout. To try to bring about social change in this country is always to bring down punishment on your head. My grandfather, a union organizer, was murdered. At various times in my life I have had my phone tapped, been tailed, been beaten very, very thoroughly with a rich medley of results to this day, gassed, had my mail opened, lost jobs, been vetoed as a speaker by boards of trustees as in Utah, been heckled, insulted, dismissed, refused grants and positions that have consistently gone to lesser writers, and they imagine there is some bandwagon I am riding on. A tumbril, perhaps.

Then there are local politicos. A phenomenon I have noticed since my antiwar days is how rank and file in American movements for social change treat those who have assumed, perhaps fought for or perhaps had thrust upon them, some kind of leadership. Frequently the mistrust with which your own treat you is sufficient to send people into paranoia or early burn out, away from political activity damned fast; it certainly contributes to crossing over to the

Establishment where at least you can expect that people will be polite to you.

If you are effective at anything, you will be sharply criticized. The real heroes of many people on the Left and in the women's community are failures who remain very pure according to a scriptural line and speak only to each other. Also many harbor fantasies that you are rich. The creeping desire I suppose is to believe that if you sacrificed a principle or two and perhaps actually spoke in American rather than jargon, you would instantly be pelted by hard money. At every college where I go a feminist will demand to know how I dare publish with New York houses rather than the local Three Queer Sisters press—as if the point of feminism isn't to try to reach women who don't agree already, rather than cozily assuming we are a "community" of pure souls and need only address each other. Often women who have some other source of support (husband, family, trust fund, academic job) will accuse you of selling out if you get paid for your writing or for speaking.

Feminist presses have an important function, as do all small presses. With the New York publishers almost to a house owned by large conglomerates, they are the one hope for freedom of expression and opinion. The all-pervasive electronic media are not open to those of us who do not share the opinions of the board of directors of Mobil Oil Corporation and Exxon, of I.T.T. and Anaconda Copper. What was true in the days of Thomas Paine and what is true today is that you can print your own pamphlet or book. The printed word is far more democratic than television or radio. You do not need to be a millionaire to acquire and run a printing press.

Just as a small press does not take much capital to set up and run, owners whether collective or individual of small presses can and do take chances on books that will make little money, that appeal to a small group. Most of the important writers of our day were first published by small presses and some such as James Joyce were published by small presses for their whole professional lives.

Conglomerate publishers may not be interested in a book because it is too original. They may be offended by its politics. I found out with *The High Cost of Living* it is still impossible to write a novel with a lesbian as a protagonist and have it reviewed as anything but a novel with a lesbian as the protagonist—nothing else is visible behind that glaring and overbearing fact. A book in fact may appeal to only a small audience, quite honestly, but appeal strongly to that audience and thus remain a good backlist item for a small publisher who can keep that book in print.

You can print a book as fine and beautiful and much more attractive in fact than the big publishers. The nub is distribution. The women I most want to reach do not come into feminist bookstores and may not walk into bookstores at all. They buy books at the supermarket, the drugstore, the bus station, the airport. I cannot reach those women if I publish with small presses, because small presses do not get their books into such places.

At a certain point I may be forced out of the mass paperbacks. I am always aware of that political and economic squeeze. But as long as I can get into mass paperback, I will. And I will resent the attempt to make me feel guilty for (1) lacking inherited money, the security of any other profession, or a husband to support me; and thus needing to make my living by the work I do; (2) trying to reach as many women as I can through the system I am trying to change, until it is changed enough to bypass it.

Fame has a two-edged effect on the character. On the one hand, if you suffer from early schooled self-hatred, then fame can mellow you. If you like yourself, you may be able to like others better. Naturally I apply this to myself, believing myself easier-going since the world has done something besides kick me repeatedly in the bread basket. However, I would also say that fame—like money and probably like power—is habituating. You become so easily accustomed to being admired, that you begin to assume there is something inherently admirable in your character and person, a halo of special soul stuff that everybody ought to recognize at first glance.

Fame can easily oil the way to arrogance. It can as easily soften you to cozy mental flab, so you begin to believe every word you utter is equally sterling and every word you write is golden. There is a sort of balloon quality to some famous men—including famous writers—and you know they may never actually sit alone in a room agonizing and working as hard as it takes to do good work, ever again. You may even come to regard yourself as inherently lovable, which is peculiar given how writers actually spend a lot of time recording the bitter side of the human psyche and our utter foolishness. Having a fuss made over one leads to the desire to have more of a fuss made over one, and even to feel that nobody else quite so much deserves being fussed over.

We can easily confuse the luck of the dice and the peculiarities of remuneration in this society with inner worth. I recently overheard an engineer who writes occasional poetry berating the organizer of a reading because he felt he wasn't being given a prominent enough spot in the line-up. "My time is worth something," I heard him announce, and he meant it: he considered what he was paid by the hour and day as an engineering consultant somehow carried over to his poetry and meant that his poetry was more to be valued, since the time he spent writing it was worth more an hour than the time of other poets. A fascinating assumption, it launched this particular observation about the confusion between what the pinball machine of financial rewards and public attention spews out at any given moment, and the assumption that the subsequent money or attention reflects some inherent superiority over the less lucky.

Once in a women's workshop at a writer's conference, several of the mothers were talking about feeling guilty about the time they took to write, time taken from spending with their children. I asked one woman who had been published a goodly amount by now if being paid for her work didn't lessen her guilt, and she agreed. Finally the group decided that if enough people seemed to value your work, whether by paying for it or just by paying attention to it, showing that they read or listened to your work and got pleasure and/or enlightment, something real, out of what you wrote, then you felt less guilty for demanding from the others in your life the time and space to write. Certainly attention paid to your work and even to you seems to validate that work and make it easier to protect the time necessary to accomplish it.

I suppose the ultimate problem with the weirdness I encounter on the road is that it makes me wary. It's hard to respond to people I meet sometimes, when I am not at all sure what monsters are about to bulge up from under the floorboards of the suburban split level where the reception is being held. I also find demands that I provide instant intimacy, or the idea that I should walk in to rooms ready to answer probing questions about my life and my loves patently absurd. The books are public. They are written for others. They are written to be of use. But I am not my books.

I never doubt that:

> the best part of me (is)
> locked in those
> strange paper boxes.

But I don't believe that people who have bought or read the books have a right therefore to sink their teeth in my arm. I had an unpleasant experience at a fancy Catholic school recently where a group of women made demands on me I found silly. I gave a good reading, worked hard to make the workshop useful, went over their work. Then I was attacked because I was not "open emotionally." One of them quoted to me a phrase of mine from "Living in the open" which apparently meant to her that you must "love" everybody you meet and gush and slop on command.

For some people admiration of something you have done easily converts into resentment of you—disappointment you are not Superwoman with a Madonna smile, or resentment if you do not bear obvious scars. They can forgive accomplishment if the woman who arrives is an alcoholic, suicidal, miserable in some overt way. To be an ordinary person with an ordinary life of ups and downs and ins and outs is not acceptable.

That admiration that can sour into hatred, sometimes off by itself, is frightening. Bigger celebrities inspire it far more than small fry, for which I am merciful, but I would rather not inspire it at all. It is sometimes as if when people meet you if you do not work a miracle—light up their life, change things, take one look at them and say, Yes, you are the one, then they have been failed in some way.

If what people want in a place is a good energizing reading, a useful workshop, an honest lecture, answering questions as carefully and fully as I can, then they are satisfied. If what they want is a love affair with a visiting Mother Goddess, a laying on of hands to make them real, a feeding of soul hungers from a mystical breast milk fountain, then they are doomed to disappointment. For that act, I charge a lot more.

II
Reviews

An Appreciation of Audre Lorde

> Hear my heart's voice as it darkens
> pulling old rhythms out of the earth
> that will receive this piece of me
> and a piece of each of you
> when our part in history quickens again
> and is over
> > "Prologue," Audre Lorde,
> > *From a Land Where Other People Live*

For the quality of her work, Audre Lorde has received re-remarkably little critical attention. About the only time I can recall her getting the kind she deserves is when she was nominated along with Adrienne Rich and Alice Walker for the National Book Award, when the three chose not to compete for the award but accept it jointly on behalf of all the women whose voices have not been permitted to be heard.

Even after that brief recognition, Audre Lorde remains one of the least read and least celebrated poets of her stature. Of all the anthologies that have made readers more aware of women's poetry (*No More Masks, Rising Tides, This Is Women's Work, Mountain Moving Day, Psyche*) she is included in only one: *We Become New*, edited by Lucille Iverson and Kathryn Ruby. The standard run of white male anthologies she is of

First published as a column, "From Where I Work," in *American Poetry Review* 5, no. 1 (1976).

course excluded from. But some Black poets are gathered into the predominantly white women's anthologies, making their work more familiar to our increasing audience: June Jordan, Lucille Clifton, Alice Walker, Gwendolyn Brooks, Margaret Walker, Sonia Sanchez, and Nikki Giovanni, for a few examples.

One piece of explanation may be that most of the Black women known to white anthologists and white readers are published by big commercial houses, even if they do a bad job of publishing and hold up a book for a year the way June Jordan's brilliant volume *New Days* was sat on. Audre Lorde's earliest book, *The First Cities*, was brought out by the Poet's Press in New York in 1968; her second *Cables to Rage*, was published only in England by Paul Breman Ltd. in 1970. The 1973 book nominated for the NBA was *From A Land Where Other People Live*, published by the Broadside Press, Dudley Randall's invaluable Black press in Detroit, as was by far her finest book, *New York Head Shop and Museum*, in 1974. The first two books are out of print. Selected poems from both of them will be published early this spring by Norton under the title *Coal*. That may help to bring some attention to her work at last.

That more women are not yet acquainted with her work is even more amazing since she served as poetry editor of *Amazon Quarterly*, and was in large part responsible for how much weight that cranky and beautiful separatist journal swung. The poetry she was able to draw for it and what she chose to print was stunning.

Diane di Prima first called my attention to the work of Audre Lorde. Di Prima had just returned to publishing, having just brought out a handsome collection *Arches* by Jackson Allen, and then Audre Lorde's *Between Ourselves*. The first real encounter with a chunk of Lorde's work I had was at the National Women's Poetry Festival in Amherst, Massachusetts, in the spring of 1974, where we happened to read together, along with Shirley Kauffmann. Audre Lorde is a powerful rather than a dramatic reader (in an irrational subliminal way she reminds me of Alan Dugan or vice versa on the platform), a big Black woman with enormous presence. The poems she pronounced were complex and moving. I have observed many times that you can read a long work successfully to an audience, almost any audience of high school age or older, no matter how dense or complicated the imagery and thought may be, if the emotions are coherent. The moving force of her work is strong and clear.

Lorde is a serious poet: serious in her craftsmanship, serious in what she is saying, serious in why she is saying it. I don't think, indeed, that there are more than three poems in her whole published output that could be called light or funny. Her poems often glint with wit, but a somber bony wit.

> Have you ever risen in the night
> bursting with knowledge and the world
> dissolves toward any listening ear
> into which you can pour
> whatever it was you knew
> before waking
> Only to find all ears asleep
> or drugged perhaps by a dream of words
> because as you scream into them over and over
> nothing stirs
> and the mind you have reached is not a working mind
> please hang up and die again? . . .
>
> Talking to some people is like talking to a toilet
> "A Sewerplant Grows in Harlem"
> *The New York Head Shop and Museum*

She is moral and political. She is heavy. She is trying to embody in hard-wrought poems truths frequently unpopular in her various overlapping communities: Black, feminist, lesbian, those conflicting demands and conflicting loyalties and contradictory pulls and pushes. She does not have an urge to simplify, a trait that must get her into a lot of difficulty but surely does make for poems that wear well. I would like to quote two of her plain but nice ones entire:

There are so many roots to the tree of anger
that sometimes the branches shatter
before they bear.

Sitting in Nedicks
the women rally before they march
discussing the problematic girls
they hire to make them free.

An almost white counterman passes
a waiting brother to serve them first
and the ladies neither notice nor reject
the slighter pleasures of their slavery.
But I who am bound by my mirror
as well as my bed
see cause in colour
as well as sex

and sit here wondering
which me will survive
all these liberations.

From a Land Where Other People Live

Separation

The stars dwindle
and will not reward me
even in triumph.

It is possible
to shoot a man
in self defense
and still notice
how his red blood
decorates the snow.

The New York Head Shop and Museum

Hers is certainly not a poetry of alienation, but of embattled connection and opposition, often intermingled. She is one of the most completely urban of poets: the landscapes of the inner city dominate her poems. Her imagery is of streets, alleys, tenements, and the city psyche: images of coal, mirrors, windows, coffee, fire, ash, wind against the seventeenth floor, cockroaches, seagulls, supermarkets, beggars, subway cars. She writes no poems about trees, except to say to a friend who has gone off to Honduras to live a simpler rural life:

> My mothers nightmares are not yours but just as binding.
> If in your sleep you tasted a child's blood on your teeth
> while your chained black hand could not rise
> to wipe away his death upon your lips
> perhaps you would consider then
> why I choose this brick and shitty stone
> over the good earth's challenge of green.
>
> Your mothers nightmares are not mine but just as binding.
> we share more than a trap between our legs
> where long game howl back and forth across country. . . .
> You will see it finally as a choice too
> between loving women or loving trees. . . .
> "To The Girl Who Lives in a Tree,"
> *The New York Head Shop and Museum*

A strong sense of New York City wracks her poems, that impossible dying metropolis, a sense of being harried on the street, institutions rotting, the press of problems, the casual hatred flicking across her:

> A bus driver slowed down at the bus stop one morning—
> It was late it was raining and my jacket was soaked—
> and then speeded past without stopping when he saw my
> face.
>
> I have been given other doses of truth—
> that particular form of annihilation—
> shot through by the cold eye of the way things are baby
> and left for dead on a hundred streets of this city
> but on that captain marvel glance

brushing up against my skull like a steel bar
in passing
>
> "Cables to Rage,"
> *The New York Head Shop and Museum*

Her poems typically are of and about connection. She writes most commonly as a mother, often as a daughter or a sister, not infrequently as a lover.

> And I knew when I entered her I was
> high wind in her forests hollow
> fingers whispering sound
> honey flowed
> from the split cup
> impaled on a lance of tongues
>
> "Love Poem,"
> *The New York Head Shop and Museum*

But most characteristically she is speaking as a mother. That has not been a common role for poets in our literature, for reasons I trust by now the women's movement has made clear enough so I don't have to waste a paragraph saying roughly what for instance Tillie Olsen has said eloquently in her book *Silences*. What interests me is rather what Lorde's writing a mother's poems means, a mother alone with her children, a daughter and a son. A mother alone with children she must support, love, teach, let go of, entrust to the callous violent world, be judged by: a mother aware of her mother in herself, herself in her daughter.

Generation II

> A black girl
> going
> into the woman
> her mother
> desired

and prayed for
walks alone
and afraid
of both
their angers.
              From a Land Where Other People Live

The First Cities contained one of the best childbirth poems
to be written recently. From her poem with the punning title
"Now that I am Forever With Child":

> . . . you growing heavy
> Against the wind. I thought
> Now her hands
> Have formed, and her hair
> Has started to curl
> Now her teeth are done. . . .
>
> I bore you one morning just before spring—
> My head rang like a fiery piston
> My legs were towers between which
> A new world was passing.

Time haunts her poems, the history of generations giving
birth to each other and carrying the previous generations
within. She has a sense usually reserved for novelists of
consequences worked out through lifetimes, the weight of
oppression crammed into the smallest inherited and imi-
tated, refused and transmuted gesture:

> A little boy wears my mistakes
> like a favorite pair of shorts
> outgrown. . .
> he toys with anger like a young cat
> testing its edges.
>   "As I Grow Up Again"

To her mother:

> I cannot recall you gentle
> yet through your heavy love
> I have become
> an image of your once delicate flesh
> split with deceitful longings. . . .
>
> But I have peeled away your anger
> down to the core of love
> and look mother
> I am
> a dark temple where your true spirit rises
> beautiful
> and tough as chestnut
> "Black Mother Woman"

To her son:

> Rain falls like tar on my skin
> my son picks up a chicken heart at dinner
> asking
> does this thing love?
> "New Year's Day"

> History
> bless me with my children's growing rebellion. . . .
> I have loved them and watched over them
> as the bird forgets but the trap doesn't
> and I shall be buried with the bones of an eagle. . . .
>
> When agate replaces dead wood
> slowly the opal and bone become one
> "Relevant is Different Points on the Circle"

Often the grasp she takes on more public events involves a sense of, What does it mean to the children. That is the heft of what I mean when I say that mothering is one of the basic ways she relates to the world and one of the basic postures and strengths of her writing. Speaking to Black women in "The Winds of Orisha" she says:

This land will not always be foreign.
How many of its women ache to bear their stories
robust and screaming like the earth erupting grain
Or thrash in padded chains mute as bottles. . . .

Tiresias took 500 years they say to progress into woman
growing smaller and darker and more powerful
until nut-like, she went to sleep in a bottle
Tiresias took 500 years to grow into woman
so do not despair of your sons.

From a Land Where Other People Live

When she wants to talk about the waste of Black lives she
thinks of, concretely:

Six Black children
burned to death in a day care center . . .
firemen found their bodies
like huddled lumps of charcoal
with silent mouths and eyes wide open.
Small and without song

"The Day They Eulogized Mahalia,"
The New York Head Shop and Museum

A sense of the waste of human lives torments her. In the
powerful poem "A Birthday Memorial to Seventh Street" she
creates a train which takes her lovers processed "through the
corridors of Bellevue Mattewean Brooklyn State / The
Women's House of D. St. Vincent's and The Tombs" and
once a year returns them "dried up bones sucked clean of
marrow" to all the American towns that spawned them. A
teenaged addict on a subway train she sees as her own
daughter and thus seizes and registers the loss and waste:

A long-legged girl with a horse in her brain
slumps down beside me
begging to be ridden asleep
for the price of a midnight train

free from desire.
Little girl on the nod
if we are measured by the dreams we avoid
then you are the nightmare
of all speeding mothers
rocking back and forth
the dead weight of your arms
locked about our necks. . . .

> "To My Daughter the Junkie on a Train,"
> *The New York Head Shop and Museum*

Pollution is the Con Edison soot that blocks her son's nose. The crippling hand of a colony-based economy on the ghetto means:

We are raped of our children
in silence
giving birth to spots quickly
rubbed out at dawn
on the streets of Jamaica
or left
all the time in the world
for the nightmare of idleness
to turn their hands
against us.

> "Viet-Nam Addenda"

I don't mean to suggest that she hasn't written many poems of loving, losing, friendship, city circumstance, but that built into the basic stance of her body of poetry is that watchful wary timebound helpless hopeful mothering: what we are that embodies the dreams and fears and losses that came before and what we are and do that we intentionally and unintentionally pass on. A number of contemporary women poets have children, but few besides Alta have written so powerfully and pervasively as mothers.

Even when she writes about herself as poet, as Black teacher/prophet/priestess/dreamer, the consciousness I have been describing informs her argument and choice of images. Both *From a Land Where Other People Live* and *The New York Head Shop and Museum* collections end with a poem in which she examines her role as writer including her speaking her own personal piece as she sees it at the risk of being called "too much or too little woman" or "too Black or too white / or too much myself." She is concerned with herself in community, in struggle, in history, and in need. I would argue that her conception of her professional role is shaped and tempered by her experience of mothering.

The palms of my hands have black marks running across
   them.
So are signed makers of myth
Who are sworn through our blood to give
legend
children will come to understand. . . .

though I fall through cold wind condemned
to nursing old gods for a new heart
debtless and without colour
while my flesh is covered by mouths
whose noise keeps my real wants secret. . . .

I am afraid
that the mouths I feed will turn against me. . . .
they will kernel me out like a walnut
extracting the nourishing seed
as my husk stains their lips
with the mixed colours of my pain. . . .

The chill wind is beating down from the high places.
My students wait outside my door
searching condemning listening
for what I am sworn to tell them
for what they least want to hear
clogging the only exit from the 17th floor
begging in their garbled language
beyond judgement or understanding
"oh speak to us now mother for soon
we will not need you

only your memory
teaching us questions."
                    "Blackstudies,"
                    The New York Head Shop and Museum

Quoting bits and pieces of the longer poems does an injustice to Lorde, because interest builds in the argument, the development of her mind's strong web. It is certainly true that there are good poets who are not intelligent—poets we do not approach to enjoy the flow of ideas, the sinew and gristle of mental work and the crackle of mental play—but poets who think well offer additional pleasure, especially when their intellect is neither academic, self-admiring, or self-serving. Her brain I suspect has been for Audre Lorde only one more tool for survival, for combat, occasionally for victory, although she has a more profound sense of losing. Loss is an experience she has been studying a long time, but not in a masochistic desire to perpetuate it. When I find poems in which not only the language, the imagery, the rhythms work, but also the thought is lively, I am excited. Finally her strong regard for homely realities and her commitment to speaking frequently awkward truths are good reasons to respect her work.

Contemplating Past Youth, Present Age

The title of Robert Penn Warren's new collection, *Now and Then Poems 1976–1978*, implies both the occasional nature of some of the contents and its concern with past youth and present age. Over his long career as a man of letters, Warren has published ten novels, eleven books of poetry, a play, biography, criticism, historical and political thought, while winning a healthy share of the prizes available to a writer of his time. When a prolific writer brings out a new collection of recent work at seventy-three, it is not really the moment for a lengthy summary of his career. He is not ready for his Collected Poems; and *Now and Then* is comprised of work written after his last of several Selected Poems.

Warren divides the volume into the Nostalgic and the Speculative, a little arbitrarily since what interests him in the past is what he seeks in the present. Mostly the poems he labels nostalgic are Wordsworthian in recollecting scenes from his childhood and early adolescence lived in nature—specifically the hills of Kentucky. The first poem in the book, "American Portrait: Old Style," defines where we are being taken:

> Beyond the last house, where home was,
> Past the marsh we found the old skull in, all nameless
> And cracked in star-shape from a stone-smack

First published in *Book World, Chicago Tribune*, August 1978.

> Up the hill where the grass was tangled waist-high and wind-
> tousled,
> To the single great oak that, in leaf-season, hung like
> A thunderhead black against whatever blue the sky had. . .

Our destination then is the moral and physical landscape of the Southern rural past.

As a sophisticated gentleman he occasionally fumbles the countrified tone, but what he's after is a philosophical or religious truth. The stronger poems resist this tendency to yank some abstract point out of the matter, as in "Orphanage Boy." This fine stark poem recounts a hired boy being forced to shoot a dog he treats as family. Warren is delightful too in his sometimes amused and jaundiced view of himself as boy in "Amazing Grace in the Back Country," an account of a gospel meeting where he didn't get saved. What is desperately exasperating to me is the combination in some poem of vivid description and banal generalization. He is marvelous at the creation of the landscape and "the landscape of my heart" as in "Mountain Plateau," he says:

> At the center of acres of snow-whiteness
> The snag-oak reared, black and old, boughs
> Crank. Topmost twigs—pen-strokes, tangle, or stub-fretted
> The ice-blue of sky. A crow,
> On the highest black, frail and sky-thrust support,
> Uttered
> Its cry to the immense distance. . . . .

Or, in "Amazing Grace in the Back Country":

> In the season of late August star-fall
> When the first crickets crinkled the dark, . . .

Then immediately, as in "American Portrait: Old Style," he can knock out lines of the most appalling dullness and generality and prosiness:

> Yes, a day is merely forever
> in memory's shiningness. . . .
> and in that last summer

> I was almost ready to learn
> What imagination is—it is only
> The lie we must learn to live by, if ever
> We mean to live at all. Times change.
> Things change. . . .

Sometimes he will craft a solid vivid poem and then throw it away in the very last line, often set off from the rest so you can glare at it and grind your teeth. "Boy Wandering in Simms' Valley" will do as a perfect example, tough and fine till an end that suddenly peters off in abstraction.

He works in a long line, conversational in its rhythms. Surely he must be one of the only poets working now who can carry out a perfectly conversational poem ("Heat Wave Breaks") that rhymes regularly. He uses an irregular meter and long lines that lap over, the sentence flowing on down the page. This is rather philosophical discourse, high toned, Latinate, and not infrequently grim, but still colloquial and very successfully so.

Two love poems I particularly liked. The first, "Love Recognized," is a nice courtly conceit in which he compares the impact of unexpected love to a snowstorm that ties up a city. The imagery is fresh and the wit delightful. "Waking to Tap of Hammer" is a poem of paternal love for his son building a boat, and the images of sailing and the ocean are crisply sensual.

An extraordinary poem that never flags is "Heat Lightning," supple and startling. The heat lightning observed is visible, almost tangible. First it is "memory purged of emotion," a storm seen in the distance. Then it is the heat lightning of sexual passion, an affair captured in a few details (the awkward embrace on the stairway, the bruise from a bite). Then the heat lightning far away is the report of a death and the memory, too, of the small death of the sex act itself. The silent lightning is a powerful image and the poem immensely evocative.

If Warren wouldn't allow himself to strain for the Truth about Time and God and Death but stay in the gritty emotions and the beauty and orneriness of the landscape he does so well, I'd probably like every poem in the book.

An Appreciation of Joanna Russ

Literature is ghettoized, at least as much as it ever was. Women's books are read by women, Black poets are heard by Blacks. I had a recent instructive experience in which I was invited to take part in a program in Washington, D.C. to speak about how I saw my role as a Black poet in the United States. Er, ah, uh, I said at some length into the phone, uneasy on that ticklish edge of possible racism, well you know, mmm, I can't exactly speak on that subject with authority, giggle. It turned out that the program director assumed I was Black since I've written not infrequently about Black writers, June Jordan, Audre Lorde, Alice Walker, and when I'm asked to list influences, I talk about Black writers, too.

Now I think the basic reason women demand the right to review women and Blacks to review Blacks and so on is because reviews by standard white reviewers tend to be offensive or defensive or if sympathetic, say the equivalent of "Gee, X can write good, almost like a white man, just the way we learned to expect the world to be seen and with a politics that is so similar to ours we don't notice it's there and call it not at all polemical. That's art." I read writers like Toni Cade Bambera and Toni Morrison because they write fiction that is not boring or alienating to me but moving, and I review

First published in a column, "From Where I Work," in *American Poetry Review* 6, no. 3 (1977).

novels like Alice Walker's *Meridian* because I want others to read them, and because I know damned well these writers won't make a decent living unless a lot of white people buy their books, too.

But there are other ghettos. If you write what's labelled as a genre—science fiction, mysteries, gothics—then you are considered by definition a hack. You get paid less for what you write than mainstream writers, you get no serious critical attention, and people who ought to read you don't. The better writers who produce science fiction either turn it out on the run like John Brunner, who writes one extraordinary book to ten into-one-end-of-the-typewriter-and-out-the-other, adventure by the yard commodities; or they get by the same way other writers do who cannot make a living in the New York marketplace: they usually teach. Joanna Russ works at the pace of most serious novelists: a book every few years, occasional short stories that are sometimes sketches for coming novels. She has three novels published and a fourth in press.

One advantage of working in a genre is that things have to happen, you must create a moving plot, and that discipline keeps Russ's springy intelligence at least somewhat anchored. If she is like any other writer, she makes me think sometimes of Swift. She is as angry, as disgusted, as playful, as often didactic, as airy at times and as crude, as intellectual. The quality of outraged, clear-sighted, pained intelligence, at once incandescent and exacerbated, is one of the major experiences for me in reading her work. Her critical essays tend to be witty and savage. Boredom is a torture to which the world obviously condemns her a lot.

Her first novel and still her easiest to approach is *Picnic on Paradise*. Why write what is called science fiction? Because science fiction offers a situation in which it is possible to be conscious of the variables and to alter one or two of them. Therefore, it can be fiction quite efficiently about some of the predominant themes in Russ's work which might be run down as survival, alienation, loneliness, community, violence, sex roles, the nature of oppression, the necessity of further civilization, and what is gained and what is lost by its progress.

Her protagonist Alyx is a Greek thief who was in the process of being executed in Tyre some centuries B.C. when she was accidentally picked up by an archeological survey operating far underwater from a future society. She is being used to shepherd a party of tourists across a resort world that is involved in a commercial war: she is accustomed to walking, living off the land, defending herself with weapons no more complicated than a knife, and above all surviving on little, on nothing if necessary. The tourists are all affluent, drug-saturated technology junkies whose primary activity is psychologizing about each other's small interactions.

At one point Alyx discovers that the "baby" of the group, whom she thought of as adolescent, is thirty-three—older than Alyx herself, who is covered with scars, has born three children, has gray in her hair and lines on her face at twenty-six.

> "Twenty six and dead at fifty. Dead! There's a whole world of people who live like that. We don't eat the way you do, we don't have whatever it is the doctors give you, we work like hell, we get sick, we lose arms or legs or eyes and nobody gives us new ones, we die in the plague, one-third of our babies die before they're a year old and one time out of five the mother dies, too, in giving them birth."
>
> "But it's so long ago!" wailed little Iris. (who is of course a couple of heads taller than Alyx—my comment)
>
> "Oh, no it's not," said Alyx, "It's right now. It's going on right now. I lived in it and I came here. It's in the next room. I was in that room and now I'm in this one. There are people still in that other room. They are living now. They are suffering now."

Of course Alyx is right in any sense because *Picnic on Paradise* is about underdevelopment versus overdevelopment, or the colonized vs. the folks in the center of the empire. Alyx is a fully realized character, tough, emotional, irritable, likeable. The jargon Russ invents for her characters has of course its satirical point here and now. Here is Alyx listening from outside the circle of her charges after they have made camp in a cave.

> They all got together; they sat down; some of them threw back their hoods; and then they began to talk. They talked and talked and talked. They discussed whether Maudey had behaved impatiently toward Iris, or whether Iris had tried to attract Gunnar, or whether the nuns were participating enough in the group interaction, with due allowance made for their religious faith, of course, and whether the relationships between Raydos and Gunnar were competitive, and what Gavrily felt about the younger men, and whether he wanted to sleep with Iris and on and on and on about how they felt about each other and how they ought to feel about each other and how they had felt about each other with an insatiability that stunned Alyx. . . .

We are dealing with someone accustomed to a visible economic base and to questions of survival, viewing people who have been removed from any real economic or political involvement or choice: in one sense they are freed, in another limited. That grid of ideas is the basis of *Picnic on Paradise*. It also contains a love story hardly conventional except in the context of Russ's other books, between Alyx and a young rebel who calls himself Machine.

And Chaos Died is the most benign of her novels. Her protagonists are always lonely and alienated. Now what does the isolated intelligence dream of? What do women really want, as Freud asked, and never stayed for an answer. The prevailing fantasy of *And Chaos Died* is a society in which upon reaching puberty, you become a telepath. Communication and community! When the minds can move mountains, nobody labors and machines are obsolete. Making love really works. The drama is partially the absorption of Russ's only male protagonist, a gay man named Jai Vedh, into the good community of lively connected souls, and partially the threat from Earth to this society. But Russ gives so many powers to her good people that the threat is never real. Jai Vedh's

Vedh's conversion to heterosexuality and togetherness is painless. For me it is a fascinating failure. And Jai Vedh I have always suspected of being a woman in male drag. The book is somehow slanting on its head and the ending is so oblique and impressionistic it is hard to figure out what exactly is happening.

The future utopia in *The Female Man* is a more believable one. There is nothing superhuman about it. They have a few gadgets but basically they would be in much the same shape without them. They would have a longer work week.

There are four protagonists in *The Female Man*, the same woman in different social contexts: Jeannine lives in a New York City where World War II never happened and the society is still slowly coming out of the Great Depression. It has less technology and drabber fashions than ours. The sex roles are based on forties movies. Joanna lives here and now. Janet lives in Whileaway, an all-female society far in the future after a plague has carried off the men. They practice genetic engineering and live in large nonmonogamous families. Mothering a child for the first five years of life is a time of self-indulgence, time to study and play and take it easy and plunge into the arts: to be taken care of. The first five years of life are for pleasure and being spoiled. "On Whileaway they have a saying: When the mother and child are separated they both howl, the child because it is separated from the mother, the mother because she has to go back to work." We are told, from Janet's viewpoint, how hard Whileaways work. They consider themselves hard laborers. They look forward to old age when they will be freed from ordinary work and able to do pure intellectual labor. Their work week, we learn, which they consider so onerous, is sixteen hours.

It's a rural society. War is unknown but dueling is common if frowned on. It is not that there is no violence but that it is not institutionalized, and not common.

On Whileaway eleven-year-old children strip and live naked in the wilderness above the forty-seventh parallel, where they meditate, stark naked or covered with leaves, sans pubic hair, subsisting on the roots and berries so kindly planted by their elders. You can walk around the Whileawayan equator twenty times (if the feat takes your fancy and you live that long) with one hand on your sex and in the other an emerald the size of a grapefruit. All you'll get is a tired wrist.

The Female Man is studded with jokes, vaudeville routines, addresses to the reader, instructive vignettes. "Praise God, Whose image we put in the plaza to make the eleven-year-olds laugh. She has brought me home."

> This book is written in blood.
> Is it written entirely in blood?
> No, some of it is written in tears.
> Are the blood and tears all mine?
> Yes, they have been in the past. But
> the future is a different matter.

Chapter 15 is a list called "What Whileaways Celebrate," which begins:

> The full moon
> The winter solstice (You haven't lived if you haven't seen us running around in our skivvies, banging on pots and pans, shouting 'Come back sun'. . . .)

Basically the Whileaways have sent Janet into our present where she plays the noble savage. Each of the women finds herself in the other probabilities from time to time. Eventually they are collected together when late in the novel we meet the fourth woman, the fourth 'J': Jael. She is an agent and an assassin from the near future, part of the "plague" that gave birth to bucolic Whileaway, in essence, a woman at war. She is Russ's most serious consideration of the nature of political violence, an extraordinary and chilling character. In her world the war between men and women is a hot war. She is interfering in the times of the other characters because she wants help in her war. She wants to win. The women of the present and alternate present, Joanna and Jeannine, agree to help her, but Janet, the woman of the peaceful future, cannot see past the violence that offends her, although Jael is what has caused her world to exist.

Russ's new novel, *We Who Are About To*, is about a group of travelers spaceshipwrecked with a handful of tools and a small supply of food on a planet devoid of anything but vegetable life. None of the themes are strange to her work, except the interest in death and the preparation for death. This time there is no one used to life in the wild to shepherd the civilized people through. Their skills are all verbal, manipulative; they do not know how to do anything "useful" in the ultimate sense. They fear deviance so strongly they will not let one of their group choose to die rather than go primitive, and finally she kills them in order to be allowed to die. She is the least attractive of Russ's heroines, the most devious, the most desperate. She was a person committed to social change, terrified into inactivity and a purely aesthetic life by repression, who has internalized hatred and has been slowly dying for years as have most of the others. Against the complexity and multilayered quality of *The Female Man*, *We Who Are About To* is a return to a simple, tight, chronological narrative.

All of Joanna Russ's novels are interesting beyond the ordinary. They ask nasty and necessary questions. They are always asking who owns things and what does it cost to survive, how and what do you eat and who do you use, what do you dare to do to make your own choices. They offer a gallery of some of the most interesting female protagonists in current fiction, women who are rarely victims and sometimes even victors, but always engaged sharply and perceptively with their fate.

Shining Daughters

The Two of Them is an extraordinary novel. I expect extraordinary novels from Joanna Russ; she's a novelist whose work I await with impatience. I would like her enslaved to produce books more swiftly, but each is too carefully thought out and too carefully written to be turned out any faster.

The Two of Them combines the fast pace and charm of her earlier novels with the overtly feminist concerns and political maturity of her more recent novels. It has a solid gripping plot, good characters—including one of the most real children I've encountered in fiction lately—and a focus passionately interesting to women.

Because Joanna Russ writes science fiction, expectations soured by an unpleasant adolescent exposure to Heinlein or paperbacks with women in Fredericks of Hollywood attire mangled by monsters in dinosaur skins may keep some women from reading her. You can be a little haughtier by calling the genre speculative fiction. But whatever you label it, some of the most talented feminist novelists (including Russ, Suzy McKee Charnas, Vonda McIntyre) work by changing some of the variables in order to write about the situation and lives and adventures of women.

This material first appeared in *Sojourner*, The New England Women's Journal of News, Opinions and the Arts (143 Albany St., Cambridge, MA 02139), October 1978. Reprinted with permission of Sojourner, Inc.

Joanna Russ's heroine grew up on earth around the same time Russ did. She was a frustrated, daydreaming, physically adventurous but blocked adolescent doomed to some secretarial job who grabbed the chance to escape into an interplanetry CIA called The Gang. She has been working since with an older male agent who saved her from her class and caste fate by taking her along, as she insisted. He is her lover. He is finally also her limiting factor. Their interests, their politics are in the end not the same but inimical.

Irene Waskiewicz and Ernst Neumann have been sent on what should be a routine, a pussycat mission to a planet Ala-ed-Deen where a highly artificial world beneath the boiling surface has been set up composed of small people imitating a simplified Islamic culture. To Ernst they are merely silly, boring, uncivilized. To Irene they are committing crimes against women. In particular she cannot endure what is happening in their host's family where a young, bright daughter is knocking hard against what women can and cannot do. In this instance she wants to write poetry. Her mother the Wezeereh is maintained in purdah on heavy tranquillizers (this science fiction invention is wildly improbable, of course; we are lucky to live in a culture where middle-class, middle-aged women are never sedated into endurance of increasingly boring sex roles and powerlessness). Her aunt, prevented from writing and defined as mad for her ambitions, has been kept in a cell chained alone for twenty years, mad now indeed.

Irene wants to free the bright and lively child Zubeydeh, the mother, and the aunt. She is successful only in forcefully stealing the daughter and running off with her. Ernst does not prevent her; but once they are underway she realizes that he finds her behavior out of line and plans to report her. He begins stripping her of the extraordinary powers that have enabled her to intervene on Ala-ed-Deen, and in fact, to escape her own programmed fate on earth. He wants to retire; he wants to keep his nose clean. He wants to operate inside the rules that do not interfere with anything he truly wishes to accomplish.

Joanna Russ told me perhaps a year or two ago that she thought one of the important themes in contemporary feminist fiction is the loss, search, rescue of a female child. The adventure of the lost daughter. She found this theme in *Motherlines* (Charnas), in *Dreamsnake* (McIntyre), in *Woman on the Edge of Time*, and other works. It is certainly a strong element in *The Two of Them*, in which the couple changes from the male-female love and work dyad to the dyad of older woman-younger woman, basically the helpful mother and desperate daughter. Of course, mothers have no power and must seize what power they can if they are really to protect their daughters and free them: even surrogate or mothers-elect.

This being a novel of strong realism in the characters, the daughter is not exactly grateful but resentful, sulky, teasing, bargaining. All the relationships are well filled-in. It is a book both strong in its actions and subtle in its perceptions, violent and cozy at once, a very female work. The way that Ernst and Irene speak, are silent, make love, bump against each other, fight, manoeuvre in silence, cut, chide, force roles on each other is exquisitely done. Much in the novel proceeds by small flashes.

What is shocking in the novel is that Russ creates a woman who can act. She can protect herself; she can protect the girl child she has seized from one destiny to choose another. Irene is a woman who has given way many times, but ultimately will not. In *The Two of Them* the ultimate political act and the act at once of self-definition and growth is the ability to kill. The novel leads to that act inevitably. It is disturbing but quite canny and clear.

The concern with how a young girl child shall be saved turns into a concern with how a young girl child shall come to maturity through adventurous testing in *Kittatinny: A Tale of Magic*. This is a story of initiation for daughters about how Kittatinny goes out adventuring, returns home, and goes out into the world for good. It should serve as a welcome antidote to most fiction designed for younger readers. Kittatinny encounters some frightening creatures, rocks that have huge mouths, a sleeping beauty who has become a vampire, some enchanting creatures, and some enchanted ones. Her dragon is a wise goddess who gives her a sword. She does not end up as a prize for a prince but with a woman companion.

What *Kittatinny* is not is a mirror image of boy hero books. This heroine is not eager to fight, although she acquits herself well. She does her wandering with a baby on her back, although a magical one. The only princess she encounters has been warped by overprotectiveness into a monster. The dragon is beautiful and helpful. The end of the journey is more traveling, for there is no home she can be welcomed to as hero, even in a fairy tale.

A Plea for Honesty in Reviewing

A few years ago I was asked to give a reading and workshop at an elite western school. What the women had decided would happen during their writing workshop was that each woman (it seems to me in retrospect to have been some hundreds, but must have been forty or fifty) would read to me a poem as I sat there. I was not to give criticism, for that would be intellectual and male.

I have given workshops that people have commented were helpful; that I was very critical and some of what I said was painful; that they carried away some kind of energy; that they learned practical information, techniques, at least addresses. Nobody from that day got anything out of it. Certainly not me.

The basic problem for me was to keep an interested smile on my face and look entranced as one poem succeeded another in a blur, while all attention was focused on me as if to gauge by dilation of pupils or respiration and heartbeat the response they had forbidden me to utter. Not being able to engage the work critically meant I tended to like none of it. It felt visited on me. Certainly I did not believe any of them were serious about their work if all they wanted was that I be paid to sit and endure it. A window mannequin would have been more satisfactory conducting that workshop.

A letter written by Marge Piercy in *Sinister Wisdom*, no. 17 (1981).

Writing for yourself or your friends is fine. A healthy amateur substratum in any of the arts produces people who understand what's really involved in that art. Studying the piano or the violin may not lead you to perform, but it may give you pleasure and it may help you appreciate someone who has spent the necessary years and passion learning how to use that instrument to capacity.

Performing publicly or publishing your work means you are addressing it to your contemporaries and to posterity and that it belongs to everybody intellectually and emotionally.

Reviewing is a thankless task I view in the same way I do tithing, as something you pay back into the community. Mostly when I review, I do so to call attention to the work of women that has not, I feel, had enough attention or enough understanding. I also review when I think something being admired is less than admirable; perhaps meretricious, perhaps dangerous. Reviewers also use on occasion a text as a way of talking about a cultural phenomenon they feel ought to be addressed. That is partly what Joanna Russ was doing in her by now notorious review in *Sinister Wisdom.**

I am sure that Russ would have written differently if she had been reviewing for the *New York Times.* (This is speculative fiction indeed: Joanna being asked to review three lesbian novels for the *Times.*) If we cannot tell the truth as we see

---

* Joanna Russ reviewed three books in *Sinister Wisdom,* a feminist review now edited by Adrienne Rich and Michelle Cliff. One of the books she reviewed was written by a young writer and published by a feminist press. Because Russ used the review to discuss a certain kind of sentimentalism she thought was becoming an accepted mode in some feminist fiction, because she tackled the fudging of sexuality and the lack of clear thinking, she was denounced in subsequent issues as being too harsh—not sisterly, not sympathetic to younger writers. In response to the charges that Russ and other feminists should be less stringent in our criticisms of each other, I wrote the letter printed here.

it, if we cannot be honest in women's publications for our own audiences, when do we tell the truth? Never? Then let's cash it all in now. If reviewing means patting on the head and on the fanny in mindless approbation whether we think what is being done is worth the price of admission or not, then it's patronizing mush. Traditional feminine behavior. "Oh, darling, you look fantastic in that dress." Then afterward, "Where did she get it? That's the sort of thing your maid gives you when she wears it out." Class example intentional, because we're discussing, after all, ladylike behavior. Be nice in public. Say something nice no matter what you think. After all, you can say in private what you like later on.

We have tons and tons of leftover middle-class niceness. What we need is more intelligence, more originality, more winged women who take off and head on out, and more heroines of culture who do the thing the first time, when it is not even beautiful yet, let alone pretty. And never comfortable. Instead of trying to cut Russ down to size and make her fit into a teacup, let us enjoy her as one of our great resources. She is never easy but she is always worth the climb.

Published writers are not children bringing home drawings from school to put up on the refrigerator and not siblings to be treated exactly the same; and feminist presses are not, as Marion Zimmer Bradley would have it, places where amateurs publish their little attempts before they grow up to mainstream presses. Feminist presses publish what is too political, too experimental, too specialized, too frightening, too hostile for the large factory presses to touch. A writer may publish her whole career with small presses, as many poets have throughout the twentieth century, as James Joyce did, and be a giant of letters.

If we are not honest in our evaluation of each other's work, where shall a feminist aesthetic arise? If we abandon the effort to set our own criteria, we have left standing the old values and failed to create our own to replace them.

Two Books by Susan Fromberg Schaeffer

Susan Fromberg Schaeffer, best known as the author of long, serious historical novels concentrating on the domestic lives of our parents or great grandparents ("Anya," "Time in its Flight"), has published her first collection of short fiction and her fifth collection of poetry.

The middle section of *The Queen of Egypt*, called "In the Houses," contains strong stories focused on love and its failures. They are not concerned with romantic love. In "His Daughter's House," Schaeffer writes beautifully about a stubborn old man, who has gone back into the clothing business after retirement, paying an unwilling visit to the home of his daughter, a successful singer in her forties. "Advice" centers on the failure of an immigrant Jew to send back the money he had promised to his father and his inability to love his own family thereafter. "Antiques" is about the strength of the bonds of another immigrant family, a sensuous, compelling story that takes place entirely within a New York antique store.

In "The Fairy Priest," a pregnant housewife, who loves a tomcat with a passionate will to survive, enters a silent struggle with a priest and her husband. When Schaeffer writes about the affluent, the upper middle classes of obsessed businessmen and mothers, of families and professionals, her evocation of a scene is good enough to cut like a pie:

First published in *Book World*, *Chicago Tribune*, January 27, 1980.

In neighborhoods like this, it is inevitable that everyone knows the rough lines and perspective of everyone else's lives, for the children belong to the same troops of Girl Scouts, and always have cookies to sell so that the desperate mothers band together in threes and fours, each mother buying one box of cookies from the other two or three children so that their own child will not have to sell cookies to strangers and cross too many streets. . . .

Unfortunately when she writes about gay men, feminists, working-class Irish, Guatemalan Indians, they issue from cartoons or other people's books and are weakly imagined. In "Destinies," one of the two novellas, Marcel is unlifelike in his Marblehead childhood, quite believable as a student at the University of Chicago—the wit of those passages will be relished by anyone acquainted with that peculiar institution—and slowly fades into caricature when he moves into gay life in New York. Here Schaeffer provides us with a glamorous alter ego, Diane, proving she is quite willing to exercise her bracing wit at her own expense: ". . . The manuscript from the nameless female in the shoe store arrives, and seen cynically, could be described as a work extolling the joys of sex, family life, and standard commitment to all values extolled monthly by Redbook, McCall's, and Ladies' Home Journal. Moreover, the book advocates psychoanalysis and clearly assumes the values of doctors, even witch doctors. . . . "

Of course what carries Schaeffer beyond this are her imagination, and her uncompromising awareness of our mortality, the fragility and power of our arrangements with each other, the pleasures and erosions of daily life. "Destinies" explores the attachment between Diane and her first editor, Marcel—an affection and mutual dependency that has no name at all but survives all their other attachments.

"The Queen of Egypt," the novella for which the collection is named, is a witty parable about beauty. The protagonist, Abigail, is herself only when she weighs 400 pounds and stomps about, a spinster elephant, pursuing her own ends. Fat, she is a person, isolated. Thin, she is a thing, enmeshed, defined as beautiful, desirable, and caught up in the machinery of male power.

The last section "Parables" is the least exciting, except for the first story, "The Exact Nature of Plot," in which a writer goes mad disappearing into her own book. The characters based on her parents take flesh and chide her, arouse her guilt, finally take over her work. ". . . It bothers me . . . when, in the middle of a chapter the baby began to cry; it wasn't that I had any doubts about whether or not she had been fed; I simply couldn't remember her name. . . ." Although I think any reader will find the story brilliant, the real connoisseurs have to be other novelists who will recognize their obsessions and quibblings.

The problem with the stories "The Yglesias of Ignatius Livingstone Island" and "Why the Castle" is the same weakness that often guts the less successful poems. We don't believe in these people or landscapes. They are not rendered *necessary*. They don't feel real, as good fantasy does. They're hollow inside, props of cleverness.

"The Bible of the Beasts of the Little Field" is a powerful collection of poetry, a sturdy book in which about two-thirds of the poems work. When Schaeffer fails, she falls into the portentous, the dead hand of symbol. When she succeeds, the music, the imagery, the intelligence charm and stun. "The Book of Hours" deals with a kind of female experience I have never before seen celebrated. The poem is about being overextended, a million things to do in the house and garden and family that batter one, and yet each is precious and good.

"This is the book of the hours of busyness," it begins. Sometimes I can almost taste Emily Dickinson, but delightfully, an influence well-assimilated in this description of a city graveyard:

> And the inhabitants,
> With their stone pillows over their faces,
>
> Can make themselves heard.
> They go together so nicely
> In that plain, shadowed green parlor . . .

In "The Windows," she deals superbly with women's daily life.

> . . . the serviceable dishes,
> Which return in their tiny orbits again and
> again
> Like used moons. . . .

Two of the most moving poems—like her short story "The Fairy Priest"—center on cats. In the title poem, it is the breaking of the back of a stray cat that is the pivot for Schaeffer's rage against the cruelty toward animals other than ourselves, in this case those of the "little field," the urban backyard. In "Jubilate Agno: Thomas Cat," she writes a love poem to a gray tom. Her best poems start from the ordinary, as in the fine erotic poem, "The Frog Pond":

> We went down to the frog pond,
> Stood in the center, learning
> The hoarse voice of love.
>
> Green bodies sped about us
> On important missions. . . .

When she's done with the ordinary, it is extraordinary to us.

A Rich Gift for Us

Another book on motherhood. Another? We have how-to books for painless and painful childbirth, we have histories of midwifery, gynecology, nursing. We have novels in which women have babies, an increasing number of poems by women about their children, their mothers, their experience mothering. We have endless books by men blaming the bomb and impotence, falling hair and falling stockmarkets, too much or too little or too hot or too cold sex on Mom, who made the world nasty and rude. There's Alta's remarkable novel *Momma*. But why in fact have we had to wait so long for a book considering that which all women are assumed to be sooner or later: mothers?

> All human life on the planet is born of woman. The one unifying, incontrovertible experience shared by all women and men is that months-long period we spend unfolding inside a woman's body. . . . most of us first know both love and disappointment, power and tenderness, in the person of a woman.

That is how Rich begins her study of mothering under patriarchy, *Of Woman Born*, one of the important books to

---

This material first appeared in *Sojourner*, The New England Women's Journal of News, Opinions and the Arts (143 Albany St., Cambridge, MA 02139), December 1976. Reprinted with permission of Sojourner, Inc.

appear in the current wave of feminism. She is careful to make clear that motherhood has two meanings. The first is only potential, the relationship of a woman to her powers of reproduction and the products of that, her children. The other meaning is the institution of motherhood "which aims at ensuring that that potential—and all women—shall remain under male control."

A great deal of research and much analytical thinking went into *Of Woman Born*. The notes are extremely useful. But *Of Woman Born* is not primarily a scholarly work. It proceeds in dolphin leaps and dives. It arches into the air of facts, history, anthropology, political annals, arguing as it goes. It dives far down into the painful dark regions of Adrienne Rich's own buried experience as the mother of three sons, as wife, as daughter, her guilt and rage and confusion and sense of betrayal. It is alternately dry and wet, reasoned and impassioned, analytical and intuitive. Rich remarks that under patriarchy sanity has become confused with rationality. I am sure that the book has been attacked because it is a profoundly feminist book in idea and argument and impact. But I am equally sure it has been attacked because the form of the book itself is the product of feminist discipline.

Of Woman Born is grounded in Rich's own most painful experiences, necessarily re-experienced, understood honestly and without, as she would put it, "false-naming." She believes that our best thought is rooted in our body, not alienated, and this book is a powerful example of what she means.

> I believe increasingly that only the willingness to share private and sometimes painful experience can enable women to create a collective description of the world which will be truly ours.

She has done so, using her old journals, her memories, her childhood, and that of her own children: ". . . only in shedding the illusion of my uniqueness could I hope, as a woman, to have any authentic life at all."

She discusses the importance of the control of female sexuality and fecundity and of childrearing by the State, by the Church, by the other institutions of patriarchy, for fun and profit and convenience, and to preserve the power of patriarchy intact. "Institutional motherhood revives and renews all other institutions." Many years ago a Frenchwoman said to Rich, when she heard that the poet had three sons, "Oh, you work for the Army, madame." The cynicism in that comment and its shrewdness got to Rich and remained under her skin for years until a chapter of the book is in fact an explication of exactly how women do work for the Army, the State, the corporations, the powers that be.

There is a fascinating chapter about male obstetricians taking over assistance at childbirth from female midwives at high cost to women, and a discussion of recent developments in the technology of birth. "Alienated labor" is one of her wittiest chapter titles. The most exciting parts of *Of Woman Born* to me, however, were about the guilt at the core of mothering, how we are estranged from our bodies at the same time that we are defined by them, how we are prevented from experiencing tenderness at the same time that we are denied our anger, the insightful chapters on "Mother and Son, Woman and Man," and "Motherhood and Daughterhood." Another of the fascinating strands in the book is Rich's attempt to understand men's fear and hatred of women and how pervasive it is in our culture. She discusses how "numbing this mysogyny is to women in all our dealings with men. Power prevents men from perceiving women"— or needing to. Our experience with men's power over us, and their perception of our autonomy as power over them, cripples us both. She sees this male mixture of anxiety, tension, loathing, and resentment as rooted in the institution of motherhood under patriarchy; but she is hopeful about new ways of mothering that can break the cycle. In all, the book is moving and involving, full of information and provocation, and studded on the way with marvelous insights about sexuality, sensuality, ambition, and creativity. Rich is perhaps a little unrealistically sanguine about the acceptability of lesbian daughters to their heterosexual mothers.

Of Woman Born has been violently attacked. Some of the vehemence is the standard anger which greets any feminist book now: why don't we all go back where we came from? Some of the hostility the book has engendered has to do with its subject. I have noticed in years of starting consciousness-raising groups and dealing with occasional ailing groups, that mothering is perhaps the hardest subject. Women who have had children feel threatened by women who choose not to have children; women who decide to get pregnant threaten women who decide to get sterilized; women who talk about the pain of raising sons or daughters from the viewpoint of having children about to leave home reach only shut ears of women who have infants. Maybe motherhood is the heaviest subject women talk about, scarier than death to us. Any discussion about motherhood touches my mother, my abortions, my guilt, my blood, my daughter, my son, my failures, my bad scenes in the middle of the night, my secret inadequacies, the children I did or didn't have.

The final reason Rich's book has disturbed reviewers is because the form is unconventional. We are used to books that are personal and confessional or else books that are objective, about things out there. The first are emotional (feminine?); the second crave to be scientific. We are not used to books that are rooted in the deeply, painfully personal and move from what is learned in the examined emotional life out to scholarly overviews of prehistory and a critical discussion of medical practice. In this instance, the form itself is a product of feminist discipline. Rich believes thought is most useful, most authentic when rooted in our body, our experiences, not alienated, and this book is a powerful instance of that blend of objective and subjective, personal and political thought that is felt and feelings intelligently analyzed.

On Lies, Secrets, and Silence

On Lies, Secrets, and Silence collects essays, lectures and speeches written by Adrienne Rich over twelve years centering on questions of our culture and its effect on all of us who read and write, especially on women. The best are written in a mood of intense and lofty passion, and all issue from an original and penetrating mind.

The tradition of American poets writing about language and what society does with it leads back to the Transcendentalists, and on through Pound and Eliot, whose ideas I may dislike but whose essays I had to read. Poets who carry on the practice of not merely rating the work of others but examining the philosophical and moralistic assumptions that weight and often rot our thinking have frequently been women of late: Denise Levertov, Susan Griffin, Margaret Atwood, and eminently Adrienne Rich.

However, the tradition she is working in is double, and its other component is a conscious and critical feminism that holds itself in a partially antagonistic posture to the language and culture that has and does regard us as other. Lies: Women have been forced or bribed to misname our experiences. We have been told much nonsense about ourselves. Silence: We have only begun to be able to tell our stories.

Secrets: Sometimes we have been able to tell a little in fables or slantwise. Our own past is a secret from us.

Some of these essays are appreciations of a specific literary work (such as the delightful essay on *Jane Eyre*) or particular writers ranging from colonial poet Anne Bradstreet to Soviet dissident Natalya Goranevskaya. The discussions of the poetry of Judy Grahn and Emily Dickinson impel us to turn back to these writers. The clarity and tenderness in Rich's criticism form a remarkable combination, an intelligent affection for good writing that invites our approach to diverse talents.

"When We Dead Awake: Writing as Re-Vision" is Rich on her own poetry. Perhaps it is in the nature of such pieces by any major writer to provoke excitement and disappointment. I found her most interesting on her early work and on the difficulties overwhelming and overcome. What she means by re-vision is: ". . . The act of looking back, of seeing with fresh eyes, of entering an old text from a new critical direction . . . (is) for women more than a chapter in cultural history: it is an act of survival. Until we can understand the assumptions in which we are drenched we cannot know ourselves . . . the very act of naming has been till now a male prerogative. . . . "

She is as much concerned with the difficulties she had in writing as she is with her achievements. Like Tillie Olsen she digs to discover why mothering can mean a loss of other ability. "For a poem to coalesce, for a character or an action to take shape, there has to be an imaginative transformation of reality which is in no way passive. And a certain freedom of the mind is needed . . . knowing . . . that the buoyancy of your attention will not be suddenly snatched away. . . . You have to be free to play around with the notion that day might be night, love might be hate; nothing can be too sacred for the imagination to turn into its opposite or to call experimentally by another name. For writing is re-naming. Now, to be maternally with small children all day in the old way, to be with a man in the old way of marriage, requires a holding-back, a putting-aside of that imaginative activity. . . . "

Some essays concern Rich's experience as a faculty member. "Teaching Language in Open Admissions" is an honest and moving essay on that short-lived experiment. Rich must be a fine teacher, for her perception of and commitment to students comes through in her writing. "The student who leaves the campus at 3 or 4 o'clock after a day of classes, goes to work as a waitress, or clerk, or hashslinger, or guard, comes home at 10 or 11 o'clock to a crowded apartment with TV audible in every corner—what does it feel like to this student to be reading, say, Byron's "Don Juan" or Jane Austen for a class the next day?

"Towards a Woman-Centered University" and "Taking Women Students Seriously" discuss restructuring of the university and suggest exciting prospectuses for large volumes still to be written. Sometimes her passing insights touch exactly the point that has needed to be made, as in her comments on Philip Slater and Robert Bly, who want to "feminize" men while ignoring a women's movement and leaving women out. The "female" in man is one more entreprenarial area to be exploited—by men.

Finally there are fine essays about motherhood as institution, about paternal kidnappings, on the love of women for women, on the relationship of white and Black women in the United States. As a woman born in the South, racism is not an issue Rich can comfortably forget and she is better read in contemporary Black literature than most white writers bother to be, to their immeasurable loss.

One of the most moving pieces is "Women and Honor: Some Notes and Lying." It is different in form from the other essays, being more of a meditation than an argument, close to a prose poem sometimes, sometimes a series of maxims suggesting La Rochfoucauld or Stein. It is one of the most passionate with a control of rage and pain that make them sing almost quietly in a pure silvery tone. Most essays are prefaced by a small note on the circumstances of the authorships or presentation and what Rich now thinks of her earlier opinions.

Monster by Robin Morgan

Monster is an extraordinary and uneven book. The raggedness is not a defect but the litter, the rubble of breaking through from something smaller, habitual, measured, familiar, to something far more interesting. What Morgan is doing is striving hard to move through and beyond the poetry of victimization.

The book is divided into five parts. The work in the first sections can be loosely described as more controlled in form, more literary in expression. These are the familiar tones of the poetry of resentment, the small ironies, the careful turns, the suppressed, slightly sour, essentially passive poetry that women frequently write to, about, around a man: Sometimes suppliant, sometimes tart, sometimes menacing, but with the knife carried handle out, blade in. Many women have written this poetry as well; a number have written it better.

The language is not vital. The imagery is too much imagery, the stuff of mental and verbal associations.

> Familiar demons frolic
> in the orchard of your face, my dear,
> more perfect than a prince's death-mask. . . .
> "Love Poem"

First published in *New* 21 (Spring-Summer 1973).

All seem begotten by books.

I don't mean that all the poems controlled by a conscious form are weak. "Freaks" builds well. Interestingly, the germ of the poem is an intellectual anger. It consists of a series of contrasts between the easy mystical unconcern admired in subculture and the common agonies of those too poor and exploited to afford that pose. The power of the images carries what is essentially a conceit past the idea into passion.

> the perfect lotus of unconcern
> whiter than a phosphorus wound
> in some child's eye.

The poems based on Vietnamese texts are also strong.

In the third section, "Matrilineal Descent" is the sort of poem in which I find the gathering power of emotional truth and increasingly complex and powerful statement shaping the poem, not gutting it, as the literary reader might expect. The language early in the poem is still a bit inert.

> Yet I wear mourning whole nights through
> for that embrace that warmed my ignorant lust
> even past intimacies you had dreamed.

But it improves. The language grows harder, springier. The strength of this poem, as of many in this book, is incremental and hard to capture by quotation— whereas the weaknesses are easy to pick out in lines out of context.

> Meanwhile my theories rearrange themselves
> like sand before this woman whose flaccid breasts
> sway with her stumblings. . .

> . . you stood. . .

> burning poems I no longer sent you
> like Yahrzeit candles in my name, unsure of me at last
> who sought a birthright elsewhere
> beyond the oasis of your curse,

even beyond that last mirage, your blessing.
Mother, in ways neither of us can ever understand,
I have come home.

In the later sections of the book many poems have the kind of strength I'm trying to describe. The imagination is stronger, the images are sparer and surer, there is a weight, a thrust of meaning holding them taut. More is comprehended, included.

The slow gathering power of that language—still a very literary English, often basically iambic—moves with a surer sense of hearing itself and being heard. She strains less for cleverness and has more confidence in what is felt and said. Sometimes the power is lean enough:

> After all, the dog was only stunned:
> a handsome bitch gulping for air
> in the road where a car had left her lying
> unmangled, nipples hard with fear. . .
>
> She rose on slim forelegs and fell
> back with the rest of her polished body,
> nails digging at the pavement to rise
> again, trot normally away.
> Then the blood blossomed from her mouth
>
> "Elegy"

Some of the strong poems, like "The Invisible Woman" are spare and exact. Many of the better lines have an idiomatic simplicity. "Dying faster than usual lately," "Static" opens. In striving to break out of the old masks and old poses, she collapses at times into lax, flabby writing that is a misnomer to call prosy; it is bad prose.

> It's funny, now, to write like this:
> a letter I don't even dare shape like one

> (not that you'll probably ever read it. which may be
> the reason it can now be written)
>   "Letter to a Sister Underground"

Her language fails her oftener than her nerve or her vision, although a few of the poems fail just at the end, trailing into clumsy vagueness ("Elegy") or subsiding into coyness, like the otherwise fine "Lesbian Poem." There she seems till the weakness of the very end to be fusing the power of polemical thought and energy with her sense of form using Thesis, Antithesis, and Synthesis as if they were parts of an ode. Wit is more frequent in the latter poems.

> nor will we lie on a plank
> in someone's correct political platform.

The poems I find most exciting are very much poems of the women's movement, although not by any means ag-itprop. They are as much and more often poems of the pain of struggle, of loving the enemy, of defeat carried within, of the fear of person madness that comes from battling on too many fronts at once, of lack of sanctuary and space-time for recovery. Poems of anger and pain, yes, but not the passive acceptance or the controlled resentment, not the playing out of master and victim, hunter and prey, the giver and taker, the sensible and the insensate. They struggle to go past, through, beyond not in simple affirmation but in struggling up through the center of the poem to what fighting tran-scendence she can honestly muster. You don't get the sense with these poems that they were written for the sake of producing a poem, or being a poet, or because it was time to write a weekly poem.

"War Games" is a brilliant long poem. Subtitled a mes-caline quartet, it combines a hallucinogenic sort of jewelled mythological imagery with paranoid suspicions of what's happening between the others, surfacing in an articulate sense of betrayal. What should have been, the communica-tion, the open relating, the attempt at honesty, is superimposed on the small manouverings for position and satisfaction among the four.

I find the already infamous "Arraignment" successful. Random House refused to publish the original version (finally printed in the *Feminist Art Journal*) in which Morgan accused Ted Hughes of the indirect murder of Sylvia Plath. In this version Morgan conducts her arraignment in a series of questions and disclaimers of intent, crackling with a controlled rage. I find this version superior, but would hardly care to compliment Random House for forcing it from Morgan. The question so used is a piercing weapon.

"Excuses for not moving" is another poem that contains its own negation—fear, defeatism, apathy—and breaks through in a last image blending Jewish, Cretan and women's movement mythology that I find powerful:

> the axblade, rampant, carved in the profile
> of a woman's face.
> It is my own unutterable name
> which I cannot
> yet
> pronounce.

"Monster," last in the volume, has harnessed in it enough pain and rage to light a city block. I saw an excellent novelist pick it up, read it for the first time, and burst into tears. Should poems make us cry? Yes, why not, when like this one they contain so much which they transmute, barely but finally. A defense of these poems has to base itself in part on what they are doing—on the depth and breadth of the attempt, the profundity, moral weight, serious passion—a lot of criteria that went out with Matthew Arnold and were presumably buried forever by Eliot and Pound. I don't think so. Any attempt to define a women's culture, any attempt to define criteria that will do justice to poems that do not measure up by criticism based on a canon of poetry which excludes them—Black poetry, American Indian poetry women's poetry—will talk about execution, technique, will talk about language, but will also, inevitably, talk about subject, intent, vision.

Margaret Atwood

Beyond Victimhood

Margaret Atwood is an extraordinarily good writer who has produced widely different books: so far, two novels, five books of poetry, and a critical guide to Canadian literature. She possesses an unusual combination of wit and satiric edge, a fine critical intelligence, and an ability to go deep into the irrational earth of the psyche. Her books are varied in genre yet through everyone of them run victor/victim and quest for self-themes, a set of symbols, and a developing underlay of theory. Some themes she shares with other Canadians, and others are characteristic of our developing women's culture. All are vital and juicy. Technique she has in plenty; what I want to look at is her matter.

In *Survival: a Thematic Guide to Canadian Literature*, Atwood finds throughout a preoccupation with survival; survival in a bare and hostile place; survival in crisis—shipwreck, snowstorm; cultural survival for the French; survival as obsolescence (those who consider Canada a relic); survival in the face of economic take-over by the United States. Considering Canada as a colony, she finds this obsession with the obstacles to physical and/or spiritual survival unsurprising. She outlines what she calls the Basic Victim Positions.

First appeared in a column, "From Where I Work," *American Poetry Review* 2, no. 6 (1973).

1. Deny that you're a victim. Direct anger against your fellow victims.

2. Acknowledge victimhood but explain it as God's will, history, fate: you may play it out as resigned or rebellious, but of course you will lose. The explanation displaces the cause of oppression to something too vast to change.

3. Acknowledge victimization but don't accept it as inevitable. This dynamic position can slide back to no. 2 or attempt to move on to no. 4. Here you can make real decisions about what can be changed and what can't; anger can be directed against what is oppressing you.

4. Be a creative nonvictim. She describes this as almost impossible in an oppressive society. I would conclude from her work that basically position 4 is achievable in moments from which insight can be brought back to the normal life of struggle and confusion in no. 3.

Survival is an extremely canny and witty book, but I am using it, or misusing it, not for its insight into Canadian literature, but for what it tells us about Atwood's ideas. I find in *Survival* a license to apply it to her own work, as she argues that discovery of a writer's tradition may be of use, in that it makes available a conscious choice of how to deal with that body of themes. She suggests that exploring a given tradition consciously can lead to writing in new and more interesting ways. I think her work demonstrates that a consciousness of Canadian themes has enriched her ability to manipulate them.

In both *The Edible Woman* and *Surfacing*, the protagonist is a woman who becomes aware she has lost her identity—her self—who comes to experience herself as victim, and finally to reject that state. Although a lacing of terror runs through *The Edible Woman* especially in the chase scenes in which Marian tries quite literally to escape her lawyer fiancé, it is a comic novel, clever in details and language—the endless playing on the metaphor of eating and food—and successful as slapstick. Although *Surfacing* has a satirical side (the description of the fashionably mindless and exploitative film making of Random Samples), it is in effect and intent a grim, desperate novel. In yet another narrative, *The Journals of Susanna Moodie*, Atwood uses a series of poems to embody a historic nineteenth-century Englishwoman who moved to Canada and did keep journals of her experiences as an immigrant. Atwood follows her through a sense of loss and alienation into an even more bizarre transformation than we'll find in the novels, into a kind of local ghost or chthonic presence.

In *The Edible Woman* Marian, who works for a market research firm at a job she finds unreal among women she cannot relate to (the office virgins decorating themselves to snare, passively, the man who will become their lives), agrees against all her stronger impulses to marry her boyfriend. Although a Canadian lawyer, Peter is a type Atwood identifies elsewhere as an American, whether or not he is born and bred in Ontario: slick, ambitious, empty, laden with expensive gadgets that give him a sense of power (fancy camera, fancy guns, the accoutrements of the businessman playing sportsman), conscious of his image and locked into his head, alienated from his body, his sexuality, his emotions, whatever they may be, most happy when he is destroying something or consuming something.

Marian tries to tell herself she is happy and lucky, moving inexorably toward marriage and only thinking beyond in advertising images. Her head does not save her; but her body rebels. She stops being able to eat first meat (animal victim), then fish, then vegetables, and finally anything at all. She slowly identifies more and more with things consumed. Marian's breakout comes at a party at Peter's. Under pressure from him she has had herself "done" until she feels even further alienated from what remains of her sense of self; uncomfortable exotic dress, hair processed, face altered, scent manufactured. The moment when Peter prepares to consume her image with his camera, for the second time she runs from him, this time successfully.

In "Camera" from Atwood's first book, *The Circle Game*, we find what bothers her in the use of photographs as an attempt to control reality and fix it in stasis.

You want this instant:
nearly spring, both of us walking,
wind blowing . . .

you want to have it and so
you arrange us:

in front of a church, for perspective,
you make me stop walking
and compose me on the lawn;

you insist
that the clouds stop moving
the wind stop swaying the church
on its boggy foundations
the sun hold still in the sky

for your organized instant.

Camera man
how can I love your glass eye?

The speaker escapes into the distance "at almost the speed of light."

Marian bakes a cake in the form of a woman and ices it carefully and cosmetically. "You look delicious. . . . Very appetizing. And that's what will happen to you; that's what you get for being food." When Peter comes she serves him the cake. "You've been trying to destroy me, haven't you," she said. "You've been trying to assimilate me. But I've made you a substitute, something you'll like much better."

What bothers me in *The Edible Woman* is, first the lack of awareness written into the character of Marian *or* the novel itself, about the programming inside her that makes her cooperate so neatly with Peter in her consumption. Second, the relationship with Duncan, sloppy self-centered graduate student, who is presented as the opposite of the perfectly packaged playboy prince, strikes me as no great leap forward. The relationship into which Marian seems headed is surely not conventionally bourgeois but conventional in the subculture and basically about as masochistic. He may not consume her, but use her he certainly will.

In both the novels, the women quit or are about to quit unreal jobs (the protagonist in *Surfacing* illustrates books and has learned to compromise before she starts drawing) but there is not much indication what on earth (what in Toronto) they are going to do next: where the real work that presumably will replace the alienated labor is going to come from.

The awareness of programming I miss in *The Edible Woman* is present in the title poem of *The Circle Game*, where children move in circles on a lawn:

> We can see
> the concentration on
> their faces, their eyes
> fixed on the empty
> moving spaces just in
> front of them.
>
> We might mistake this
> tranced moving for joy . . .
>
> . . . the whole point
> for them
> of going round and round
> is (faster
>   slower)
> going round and round

The poem shuttles between a man and woman in a room who are not communicating, who play mirror games, control games; and children learning fear from the adults, learning defenses and weapons, learning to keep others at a distance, learning to need to control, define, keep out, destroy. The poem ends: "I want the circle / broken." The circle of protection, lying, custom, fear, gamesplaying, roles that keep people "neither / joined nor separate." Atwood's latest book of poetry, *Power Politics*, explores the area of victor, victim games, pain and loss games, the confined war in intimacy between a woman and a man. The conception of the book and individual poems are brilliant:

> you fit into me
> like a hook into an eye
>
> a fish hook
> an open eye

Between the first and the fifth book of poetry, she has gained enormously in compression, daring, shape of the poem, precision of language. Here is a poem about the game of mutual losers admiring each other's style:

> My beautiful wooden leader
> with your heartful of medals . . .
> you long to be bandaged
> before you have been cut.
>
> . . . General, you enlist
> my body in your heroic
> struggle to become real:
> though you promise bronze rescues
>
> you hold me by the left ankle
> so that my head brushes the ground,
> my eyes are blinded,
> my hair fills with white ribbons . . .
>
> Magnificent on your wooden horse
> you point with your fringed hand;
> the sun sets, and the people all
> ride off in the other direction.

Love, in Atwood, is often an imitation of the real: an aquarium instead of the sea, in one poem. Rather than communicating her people evade each other, are absent in

their presence, try to consume, manipulate, control. By say-
ing, "in Atwood" or "her people" I'm not implying I find
such behavior unusual. What she describes is dismally famil-
iar; only the precision and the very shaped often witty an-
guish of the descriptions make them unusual.

> . . . pretending to love
> the wrong woman some of the
> time, listening to your brain
> shrink . . .

Still I find both *The Journals of Susanna Moodie* and
Procedures for Underground finally more successful as total
books. Few of the poems have individual titles, and we are
clearly to find *Power Politics* not a collection but a book. Why
does the shape of the book, especially toward the end, bother
me? When she says:

> In the room we will find nothing
> In the room we will find each other

why do I not believe? Perhaps the language does not change
enough, the terms of the struggle deepen mythologically
but do not change in any convincing way from the conven-
tional power struggle. Some fear seems to prevent her break-
ing through in this book as she breaks through with her
protagonist in *Surfacing*. To put it another way, she doesn't
seem able to imagine the next stage, and a book that remains
caught in its first terms while seeming to suggest that it will
transcend them, is frustrating, but brilliantly so. It is still a
strong and good sequence and a far more satisfying book as a
book then 90 percent of the poetry collections I read. Only
in reading her work I have come to want more than that. A
talent like hers needs to transcend its own categories, to
integrate the preconscious and conscious materials, the im-
agery and ideas. Her wit can lead her into trivia; just as her
passion for the omen can lead her to see the portentous in
grains of sand and jam jars, as in "Two Visions of Sweaters"
(*Procedures for Underground*).

At one point in *Survival*, she applies her chart of victim positions to attitudes toward nature. Meaningful connection with the environment is important in her values. In position no. 1, the writer goes on about Beneficent Nature the sublime while sinking in a mosquito-ridden bog (in *Surfacing* Atwood describes the sound of love in the North as a kiss and a slap). Canada was too hard for Wordsworthian sentiments to last. Next the harshness of the land is admitted and nature is seen from dead and indifferent to downright nasty. Nature becomes the enemy. Often the will to lose merges with a willing of the role of victim in a hostile universe. From there, one can decide to "win the war against nature." Since success in that war has brought us to ecological disaster, one can then identify with weak nature, attacked by man.

Atwood posits that in position no. 4 nature exists as itself "not as a collection of separate and inert objects; rather it exists as a living process which includes opposites, life and death, 'gentleness' and 'hostility'. . . man himself is seen as part of the process. . . . He can accept his own body, including its sexuality. . . ."

Her immigrant heroine Susanna Moodie, experiences the new land at first as a loss of self. She:

> entered a large darkness.
>
> It was our own
> ignorance we entered.
> > "Further Arrivals"

She knows "fears hairy as bears." She needs to become different in order to communicate with the land, in order to live with this new place. At first she holds on to her identity with all her strength and loss is all disaster and attack. But when she leaves the wilderness she realizes she is losing something she did not yet have, that she needs:

> There was something they almost taught
> > me
> I came away not having learned.
> > "Departure from the Bush"

They: the alien animals, plants, beings of the real woods.

> I need wolf's eyes to see
> the truth.

In "The Immigrants" Atwood encompasses a depth of the personal and social, the historical realized as living pain, that is breathtaking and leaves me wondering why I can't think of an equally powerful American poem on what should surely be a common topic. Here is a little of it:

> I see them coming
> up from the hold smelling of vomit,
> infested, emaciated, their skins grey
> with travel; as they step on shore
>
> the old countries recede, become
> perfect, thumbnail castles preserved
> like gallstones in a glass bottle, the
> towns dwindle upon the hillsides
> in a light paperweight-clear.
>
> They carry their carpetbags and trunks
> with clothes, dishes, the family pictures;
> they think they will make an order
> like the old one, sow miniature orchards,
> carve children and flocks out of wood
>
> but always they are too poor, the sky
> is flat, the green fruit shrivels
> in the prairie sun, wood is for burning; . . .

Susanna visits an insane asylum and there she experiences again that glimpse of the other place, the reality she craves:

> The landscape was saying something. . . .
>   . . . the air
> was about to tell me
> all kinds of answers.
>   "Visit to Toronto, with Companions"

Susanna is trying to love the land, but something is wrong. Not what seemed wrong at first, that it wasn't a great good friendly place. Something else is going rotten. She curses

> the invader of those for whom
> shelter was wood,
> fire was terror and sacred
>
> the inheritors, the raisers
> of glib superstructures . . .
>
> god is not
> the voice in the whirlwind
>
> god is the whirlwind
>
> at the last
> judgement we will all be trees.
> > "Resurrection"

Susanna scorns those who think "we will build / silver paradise with a bulldozer" and returns after her death as a demon of the place: a crazy old lady on a bus. She has finally "changed" and she is at home, prophesying.

In Atwood there is the old dichotomy between the city as a place of artifice (associated with being armored, becoming a machine or a thing), a hollow place as Edmonton is seen:

> a tight surface covering
> panic or only more
> nothing than I've ever seen
> > "84th Street, Edmonton,"
> > *Procedures for Underground*

And the cabin in the woods as a place where reality is approachable, where the self can be reintegrated. Yet she has none of the romanticism about nature that usually goes with such a dichotomy. Her rabbits are very much rabbits, they have real fur and bones and fleas and use their hind legs to give warning. Her blue jays and herons are more alive than those often overly symbolic props in writers—names, exotica, stuffed feathers inhabited by bits of human psyche and projection. She contrasts the two herself in the title poem of *The Animals in That Country*, and in another way in *Surfacing*, where the protagonist and her brother as children pretend there are "good leeches and bad leeches."

Yet finally her animals too are something else in their alien and irrational aliveness, as is the landscape itself. Both are at once themselves and transmitters of energy, the doorways to another level of reality at once alien and inner. The source of integration of the self, the reservoir of insight in Atwood lie deep in a wild and holy layer of experience usually inaccessible in modern life—in how her characters make a living, how they act with each other, how they respond or fail to respond to birth, death, loss, passion, how they permit themselves to live out of touch with what they want and what they feel. The landscape of the psyche in Atwood tends to be a cabin in the Canadian woods, on a lake, on a river—the outpost of contact between straight lines (roads, houses, gardens) and natural curves (trees, deer, running water): the imposed order and the wild organic community.

Every place the fundamental fact of being alive is being eater or being eaten. "The food rolls over on my plate" ("Creatures of the Zodiac"). The authentic way of approaching this revelation involves experiencing the reality of the victim you are consuming. Both her heroines go through a sense of the awfulness of taking life to eat. Some of this is, especially in *Surfacing*, a function of animals as totems. But the vegetable world is also sacred with life:

> . . . potatoes curled
> like pale grubs in the soil
> the radishes thrusting down
> their fleshy snouts, the beets
> pulsing like slow amphibian hearts . . .
> When I bent
> to pick my hands

came away red and wet . . .
> "Dream 1, The Bush Garden,"
> *Journals of Susanna Moodie*

In *Surfacing* the protagonist thinks of the green blood of weeds.

This strand in Atwood is an emerging theme of women's culture, I believe, for women have been forced to be closer to food, to know more of where it comes from and what it looks like raw (I think of a poem I saw in *Off Our Backs* in which a woman sees herself in the plucked chicken ready for the oven, sprawled on its back with a large hole between its legs from which its guts have been torn out), and where the garbage goes afterward. Perhaps societies in which meat comes sanitized in the supermarket wrapped in.transparent plastic and advertised by Disney pigs in aprons offering with big grins to be eaten, produces more vegetarians finally than societies in which everybody has seen a pig carried squealing to be slaughtered and the disemboweling of its warm carcass.

In killing too there is a proper natural and an improper and inauthentic attitude in her work. For instance the invaders, in their costumes as hunters, are seen with that terrible naive deadpan stare she can muster (somehow I think of Breughel, then of Bosch): the hunters are dressed up in their red suits for a ritual occasion, though obviously an unsuccessful one.

> They must be waiting
> for the god to appear,
> crossed in the sights of their rifles . . .
> > "The Festival,"
> > *The Animals in That Country*

In *Journals*, Brian the Still-Hunter embodies the other way. When he hunts, he says "I feel / my skin grow fur / my head heavy with antlers." Like an Indian he feels kinship with what he eats. Unlike the tourist sportsmen in *Surfacing*, he enters the animal imaginatively and risks death: he has "a white scar made by the hunting knife / around his neck."

Those "holy and obsolete symbols," gods, are best perceived (as the Egyptians, or more to the point, the Indians grasped them) as creatures emerging through and of the animal, like ourselves. In "Dream: Bluejay or Archeopteryx," a woman kneeling on rock by lakeside sees herself in the water, a bluejay reflected, then:

> in the water
> under my shadow
> there was an outline, man
> surfacing, his body sheathed
> in feathers, his teeth
> glinting like nails, fierce god
> head crested with blue flame

If the god does not surface, you may dive. Drowning occurs again and again in Atwood, appearing to represent going down and not coming up like insanity with which it is sometimes linked. In "The Death of a Young Son by Drowning" (*Journals*) drowning is entry to "a landscape stranger than Uranus / we have all been to and some remember." In the title poem of *Procedures for Underground* are the instructions for such a "trip": the other reality there is the country beneath the earth, inherent in nature and in your head at once. It's impossible to read this after Casteneda without making connections, but never in Atwood are there guides, old men, or sorcerers, no wise old women even, only the enigmatic dead, as we will see in *Surfacing*, and the individual vis-à-vis the ground of being as never unsavage nature:

> The country beneath
> the earth has a green sun
> and the rivers flow backwards;
>
> the trees and rocks are the same
> as they are here, but shifted.
> Those who live there are always hungry;

> from them you can learn
> wisdom and great power,
> if you can descend and return safely. . . .
>
> For this gift, as for all gifts, you must
> suffer. . . .

As she makes clear in *Survival*, Atwood is aware of Indians in literature as victims, avatars, symbols useful to whites. She uses Indian materials very sparsely in an overt way, but I feel under the surface of her work a lot of material learned from Indian sources, Indian thinking, Indian religion and mythologies and practice. The procedures for getting in touch with the power in a place that can connect you with the power in yourself in Atwood include openness to knowledge received from other living creatures, fasting, and usually physical exposure, a respect for the earth, a concern with taking only what you need, respect for dream and vision as holy and instructive. In Atwood the trip to be taken is something like this: you go into the forest, the natural and wild ground that is the past inside, the deep collective mostly unconscious past not knowable with the logical controlling brain, the ground of being, food and terror, birth and death: you experience the other which is yourself, your deeper nature, your animal and god half. The experience of transcendence is the gift of the totem animal and the god who is both human and animal and something else, energy perhaps. The procedures by which the protagonist in *Surfacing* finally comes to her vision would be familiar to just about any forest or plains Indians who inhabited the area Canada and the U.S. were carved out of. I wonder if the protagonist in *Surfacing* has no name because she has not, till the end of the novel, earned one. In *Surfacing* ancient pictographs provide the link between the generations, the dead father and the "dead" daughter.

In *Surfacing* of course the primary metaphors are of a descent through space, time, and water, and then a hazardous return to the surface.* The protagonist returns to a cabin where she spent the heart of her childhood, to look for her father who has disappeared there. Lacking a car, with a typically female inability to drive, she has got home by persuading two friends to bring her and the man she's living with. Though her mother has died recently in a hospital, she has not been back to the lake since she left abruptly under circumstances she does not remember herself till she can force herself to remember—pregnant by a married man who was her teacher and who manipulated her into an abortion. She drifted into a plastic marriage, then "running off and leaving my husband and child, my attractive full-color magazine illustrations, suitable for framing." The couple, David and Anna, praise marriage but are busy throughout torturing each other, role playing (he says constantly he married her for her ass, humiliates her by forcing her to strip for the camera, then complains she is not smart enough). Joe, the protagonist's boyfriend, is a loser. "That's how he thinks of himself, too: deposed, unjustly. Secretly he would like them to set up a kind of park for him, like a bird sanctuary." Their relationship is a cipher best summed up by the fact that the first time she went to bed with him, he was impressed by her cool, that she showed no emotion. But she felt none. "Perhaps it's not only his body I like, perhaps it's his failure; that also has a kind of purity."

Thus the relationships are empty; the aesthetics of the two men making a faddish movie are empty; the politics of David are empty. Anti-American, he posits guerrilla warfare against imperialism but as soon as the protagonist becomes interested and asks him how, he says "Organize the beavers." "Now we're on my home ground, foreign territory," the protagonist thinks as they cross into Montreal. The setting is a colony inside a colony, marginal economically. The lake will or will not be flooded on the decision of a presumably American-owned power company: "my country, sold or drowned, a reservoir; the people were sold along with the land and the animals . . ." *Surfacing* is so carefully put together it would be rewarding to follow through any of the

---

*Compare the metaphor in Adrienne Rich's "Diving into the Wreck."

strands, what she does with water, fishing, the notion of pictures, from pictographs to childhood drawings (personal pictographs), the camera, the illustrations the heroine does for pseudo-European fairy tales.

The protagonist lost herself at some point, she is not sure when. The secret must be in her past. "I have to be more careful about my memories, I have to be sure they're my own and not the memories of other people telling me what I felt, how I act, what I said." She has become disassociated from her history, emotions, body. Part 2 begins:

> The trouble is all in the knob at the top of our bodies. I'm not against the body or the head either; only the neck, which creates the illusion they are separate. . . . If the head extended directly into the shoulders like a worm's or a frog's . . . they wouldn't be able to look down at their bodies and move them around as if they were robots or puppets.

Much later she realizes, "At some point my neck must have closed over . . . shutting me into my head; since then everything had been glancing off me. . . ."

At first she believes her father has gone crazy; she interprets the bizarre drawings she finds as proof. She imagines him "bushed" lurking on the island watching them, potentially dangerous. Then finding a letter from an archeologist thanking him for photographs and drawings of ancient pictographs, she put that together with a map studded with crosses and decided he has left something there for her. She becomes obsessed with decoding the gifts that each of her parents, strong in love and integrity, must have left for her. She has always been good at survival—recognizing edible plants, knowing how to catch a fish and kill it—but survival alone is not enough when all that survives is a remote cold head. She dupes her companions into an expedition to a mark on the map, where she should find a pictograph; the quest is futile. She has forgotten that the land was flooded years before and the ancient shore drowned. On route she finds a dead heron hung up by "Americans" who turn out to be Canadian Met fans. Why did they kill a creature that could not harm them, that they could not eat? "To prove they could do it, they had the power to kill. Otherwise it was valueless; beautiful from a distance but it couldn't be tamed or cooked or trained to talk, the only relation they could have to a thing like that was to destroy it." This is her turning point. She does not find proof of her father's sanity, a legacy of connection she must have; but she identifies herself as dead victim. She begins a social withdrawal, refusing to continue the social and sexual games. She will not tell Joe she loves him and then stops sleeping with him, will not placate him.

She goes alone to another map entry and dives into the cold deep waters of the lake. There she encounters something: not the pictograph but a figure at once her dead father and the dead fetus: the abortion she did not want that cut her off from herself, turned her from lover to object. After the failure of logic, terror accompanies vision. The spot marked by her father is a sacred place where she may learn her truth, how she died. Here presumably is where her father drowned, as she senses he wanted to, the heavy camera pulling him down. His body finally surfaces.

Now she needs to make herself alive again, to heal together her animal and conscious selves. She has sex with Joe for the specific purpose of conceiving a child to replace: 1) the dead fetus, 2) the dead experience of giving birth to an actual child who was the property of her husband. Just as dying was stolen from her mother by the hospital, so the hospital stole from her the experience of giving birth. She goes through the pain she could not feel before, into the primitive and irrational, into the inhuman in order to be born again as a self. She hallucinates, i.e., enters another more integral reality for her in which she experiences her body as part of the landscape (Atwood's position no. 4) and then sees each of her parents again. Each gives her the gift of presence. She then assents in their deaths and transformations. They cease to be the vehicles for her self exploration and become the people they were in their own now ended lives. She relinquishes them.

From her ritual of integration she returns to daily life. Cannily she looks at Joe, who has come back after the others have left. She decides they must do better, they must learn to communicate. "But he isn't an American . . . he is only half formed, and for that reason I can trust him." She is going back to Toronto, presumably pregnant with the child she wants, and what she has in her teeth she sums up like this:

> This above all, to refuse to be a victim. Unless I can do that I can do nothing. I have to recant, give up the old belief that I am powerless and because of it nothing I can do will ever hurt anyone . . . The word games, the winning and losing games are finished; at the moment there are no others but they will have to be invented, withdrawing is no longer possible and the alternative is death.

One trouble I have here and I think Atwood still has, is how to translate this particular rhetoric into any kind of action. What will the protagonist do? If position no. 4 involves being no more a victim or victor, how does one get there in an oppressive society except as a stance in one's head? To remain in the inner landscape is to drown, not to surface—to go mad or die. Can a victim cease being one except through some victory? Easily she renounces the victor games; she has never been anything but a victim. Atwood says yes, but I wonder even in her own terms. Women dislike the idea of winning, of gaining power, even of trying to grasp power as a stage to freedom. Yet her heroine cannot stay in the woods. She can choose a man who opts to be a loser rather than a winner at her expense, but how does *she* stop being a loser after deciding to? Atwood distrusts the glib merely fashionable politics of David, but provides no alternatives. The totems stay in the water, the woods, the base of the spine; the modern woman will go back to the city. No one except her heroines is even faintly likeable in these novels. Susanna Moodie may in death become Canada, but a crazy old lady on a bus has little to offer even if she had a hand grenade in her purse, and Atwood hasn't even given her that.

To cease to be a victim, each of her protagonists fights an entirely solitary battle. Their only allies are the dead, the forces in nature and the psyche, their own life energies. Yet they must live among others. Somehow the next step is missing. I don't believe one woman can single-handedly leave off being a victim: power exists and some have it. Atwood seems to me still to rest in an untenable coyness about what it will mean in the daily world to attempt to take charge of one's life—as a Canadian, as a working person (none of her protagonists have money), and as a woman.

Atwood is a large and remarkable writer. Her concerns are nowhere petty. Her novels and poems move and engage me deeply, can matter to people who read them. As she has come to identify herself consciously, cannily, looking all ways in that tradition she has defined as literature of a victimized colony, I hope that she will also come to help consciously define another growing body to which her work in many of its themes belongs: a women's culture. With her concern with living by eating, with that quest for the self that Barbara Demming has found at the heart of major works by women from the last 150 years (*Liberation*, Summer 1973)* with her passion for becoming conscious of one's victimization and ceasing to acquiesce, with her insistence on nature as a living whole of which we are all interdependent parts, with her respect for the irrational center of the psyche and the healing experiences beyond logical control, her insistence on joining the divided head and body, her awareness of roleplaying and how women suffocate in the narrow crevices of sexual identity, she is part of that growing women's culture already, a great quilt for which we are each stitching our own particolored blocks out of old petticoats, skirts, coats, bedsheets, blood, and berry juice.

---

*"Two Perspectives on Women's Struggle."

III

Afterview

Afterthoughts

A Conversation between Ira Wood and Marge Piercy

In the New York Times *front page review of* Vida *Eleanor Langer says, "Almost alone among her American contemporaries, Marge Piercy is radical and writer simultaneously, her literary identity so indivisible that it is difficult to say where one leaves off and the other begins." I'd like to start this interview with the question, what has your politics got to do with your infamous passion for cats?*

I get on very well with cats. They almost all recognize me. Nothing feels more pleasant to the fingers and palms than the fur of a healthy cat. I like their sensuality and their independence; I see myself mirrored in them. We have our anxieties and our moods and our fierce appetites and our razor sharp curiosity. Often both men and women, but especially men, project onto cats what under patriarchy they have learned to fear in women, which is why cats were burned when the witches were burned all over Europe in the millions. Women and cats were viewed as equally sexual and equally evil. What cannot be broken to obey must be destroyed, by that reasoning. Cats are seen as sneaky. They are considered without loyalty because they have a will and life of their own. But cats form intense passionate attachments and loyalties. I always knew with my old cat Arofa how long I could stay away from home—at what point she would simply refuse food and go on a hunger strike until I reappeared.

Why is sex so important in all your writing?

Well, in some sense that seems to me like the question about why I like cats. Though I suppose that relation might be clear only in my mind. That is, besides all the other reasons I gave you for liking cats, I also like them because I learned a lot about basic mammalian behavior from watching my cats. I've learned a whole lot about people by learning what's basically mammalian. I like sex because it's one of the ways that people leave off operating so much with forebrain. If I like poetry because it ties all the different ways of knowing and being together, sex does the same thing. It operates from all those different levels of minding. All the way down to the reptilian, farther down than that, all the way down the spine. As a novelist, sex has to be important to me because it's one of those touchstones of character. For me, if I can grasp a character sexually or show a character's sexual behavior, often I've shown you a lot about that character. It's a way in for me as a novelist and it's a way in which I can display a character to you and a lot about the kind of relationship between characters. Much that goes on between people can be revealed in the sexual relationship, the power relations, the affectional relations, the aggressive relations, the competitive relations.

A great deal of your writing has to do with pleasure. You don't resist pleasure? You write about it, and yet you're political and you're not ashamed of pleasure. I've heard people remark that they didn't know the two were compatible?

What an extremely peculiar view of the world they must have. The reason I am political is because I want there to be a juster apportionment of the world's pleasure and less unjust apportionment of the world's pain. Power per se is fairly uninteresting to me, except as I observe it distorting peoples' characters. It's never represented much temptation to me. I've never gone after power and when I've wielded it in the minute ways that people on the Left occasionally have access to a tiny bit of it, it has been something I've always been very happy to share and always felt that was best apportioned by lot. I don't have a puritan streak in me, although I'm fascinated by all the different ways people are and certainly I've written about a number of very moralistic and quite puritanical characters. I think that there is in any of us numerous other people that we never live out, and our opposites are as fascinating as what we are. In fiction you get to live out all those little pieces of you, that never really come into your life at all. I think that I trust and respect our basic biology. I feel respect for the bodily processes and for the essential daily work of life support, a respect I think has been missing in a lot of male writers.

I know you hate it when people ask about influences, but give a real answer for once. You hate it because you think it's all too academic, the influence chasing, and indicates that only literature begets literature, which only refers to other literature.

An honest answer, huh? All right, in the beginning there were the romantics, Byron and Shelley and Keats, and also Whitman and Dickinson. That was the beginning, at fifteen. My earliest passions. Then came Eliot. Then came Blake and Yeats and Joyce, Joyce and Yeats and Blake, intense and burning passions. I discovered Muriel Rukeyser very early, when I was a senior in high school, and I loved her always. Always. Then came William Carlos Williams and Neruda and Vallejo. But all this is a gross simplification, because I was always reading so much. I left out Pope. I left out Wordsworth. They were both terribly important. As were Edith Sitwell and Edward Arlington Robinson. I loved Elizabethan lyrics and Wyatt. Just as I put in a lot of time reading fairy tales, tales of all sorts, the basic stories, I put in a lot of time with ballads. Childes ballads and the variations. Ginsberg liberated my imagination at a critical time, 1959. My reading style was heavily influenced by Black poets in the late sixties—not that I imitated what they did, which would have been silly and meretricious, but that they inspired me to figure out how to put my poems across: Sonia Sanchez, June Jordan, Don L. Lee.

I want to ask you as I look through the table of contents of Breaking Camp, *why it doesn't seem as organized as the later books. But I'm sure there was an order you had in mind?*

Breaking Camp has the least structure of any of my books. It was my first collection and it's the only one that really is just a collection of all I'd written up to then that seemed good enough. A lot of it is apprentice work. Basically the only arrangement is moving from the Midwest to New York, from loneliness and a lot of casual and false starts to a commitment that was to endure at least a while, and from the wholly personal to the public fused with the personal. That's about it. It contains sequences such as the one beginning with "The miracle" and going through "Landed fish," a sequence about death: the death of friends, of my favorite uncle, death in the newspaper, death of another poet, Bernie Strempek, whom I had known in college, the possible ways I could comprehend of assimilating death into my life and going on.

In Breaking Camp, *there are many poems about death, but few in the books since then. How do you account for this apparent great interest in mortality and then apparent loss of interest?*

One of my closest friends, someone I really loved, died when I was twenty-four and she was twenty-three. For some years afterward I felt a terrible urgency in all close relationships, as if anyone I cared for might die or vanish at any moment. Any disagreement was something that had to be thrashed through at once, because if I or my friend stayed angry, we might never have the leisure, the time, the life remaining to clarify ourselves. I was terrified, too, that I would die before I had done some little of what I felt I had to do. Keats's sonnets about early death were haunting me then, but I was not precocious. Working out how to do what I wanted to do in prose especially but also in verse took me years and years;

then even after I was writing well, what I was writing about was unacceptable and impermissible for social and political reasons. One of the reasons I wrote that elegy for Strempek was not only because I liked him, but because of the selfish fear I had of suddenly dying young as he had—as I mention in the poem I had just been in an automobile accident like the one that killed him—and not ever doing the work I felt driven to create. I think the theme of death faded from my poetry after I began to experience a sense of future, of posterity—not in direct lineage but in my work. First in political work and then in my own writing. I think too that living in the country and becoming heavily involved with the land, the seasons, the cycles has made me move gradually toward seeing death as part of the whole.

Who was Louis Sullivan and why did you start the book at his grave?

Louis Sullivan was a very great architect who never got to build most of the buildings that were in him, as I feared I wouldn't get to create in public visible form my art. He was defeated by the beginning of the American vision of empire that led us into foreign conquest and made us create bank buildings as temples to money, that Roman design that marked our cities. Right after college I felt very consciously Midwestern and I was searching for populist roots, Midwestern heroes, and some kind of history that led to me. The Chicago anarchists, Emma Goldman, Eugene Debs. Sullivan's books are interesting too, by the way. Toward the end of *Breaking Camp* are some of the first antiwar poems I wrote. The two gasman poems are about how little getting high changes the structure of capitalism. "The peaceable kingdom" is a poem I still respect even though it's dated to 1965–66, that phase of the war in Vietnam and the Hiroshima day demonstrations we still have every August. *Breaking Camp* is the only collection that has a number of rhymed poems in it, even a sonnet or two.

Going on to your next book Hard Loving, *that is divided into four distinct parts. "Walking into love," that's one long poem or six short poems in a sequence. What does the part title mean, "The death of the small commune?"*

Hard Loving begins with that sequence of six poems called "Walking into love," that is not falling but proceeding carefully and slowly; they were written to someone in SDS I was working with. At the time I wrote the poems in *Hard Loving* I lived in a matrix of four relationships all of which were equally important to me and all of which were bound up with the political work we were doing. A number of the poems in all of the sections are about the antiwar movement and about being in SDS as well as about personal relationships.

"The death of the small commune" is about the end of SDS and the disintegration of what I consider one of the best schools for organizers that existed in this century, but I wrote it in personal terms because that way I could deal with it, and that way readers could enter it more easily. It's a poem that I think has touched a lot of people and I think casting it in personal terms worked. I was dealing all the way through the book with both the personal and the political and the attempt to fuse them that was characteristic of the New Left. I was dealing with trying to love and live in more open ways and trying to help each other to grow, to reach, to take chances. In "The death of the small commune," that whole section, I tried to put those innovative struggles in the context of the kind of relationships that I felt were common in the larger society, both exploitative relationships and flimsy bonding, friends who aren't friends, neighbors who aren't neighbors. In "Loving an honest man" I separated out the poems to my husband from the others because the imagery was different and because I though they'd make a better sequence by themselves. The last section "Curse of the earth magician on a metal land" contained my overtly political poems. "For Jeriann's hands" is one of the earliest poems in which I talk about some of the specific problems of creativity in women. In that case there is no difficulty in creating but the problem is in finding a place for what's created in the world afterward. I feel *Hard Loving* is in my own voice. A lot of the poems I still feel close to, some of the love poems and some of the political poems. "Crabs" I think is marvelous and I'm surprised it hasn't been more anthologized; it's the first funny poem I ever wrote.

"Community" uses the imagery of the Pentagon demonstration of October, 1967, just as "Address to the players" is a covert elegy for Che Guevera. A lot of people who read these poems nowadays never know that subtext. "Morning half-life blues" I actually began in a very crude version when I was sixteen and working at Sam's Cut-Rate Department Store in Detroit. Finally sometime in 1968 I took it out and finished it. "Learning experience" came from the fact that I taught for a year and a half at Gary Extension of the Indiana University when I was living in Chicago. Most of the kids who went to school there were Black and/or working class. We were expected to maintain a flunk rate of about one-third of our classes. I felt as if we were punishing the kids for having attended lousy high schools where they didn't learn to write or speak standard business English. Pretty depressing. The time of the war in Vietnam I was no longer teaching. But in that poem "Learning experience" I was imagining how I would feel even further complicity with the system if I were still teaching when the universities were being used to determine who would go to Vietnam and get shot and who got to stay on campus and survive. "Half past home" came out of remembering the building that's actually described in it, the Home for Incurables that I used to pass as I went to my secretarial job in Chicago every day.

As I look at the dates of each book, I see that 4-Telling *came after* Breaking Camp *and* Hard Loving. *How did you happen to want to write a book with three male poets?*

Well, it didn't get put together at that point. It had been put together much earlier. Only *Breaking Camp* had come out. It was conceived of as an enterprise with three editors of *Hang-*

ing Loose at a time I was publishing a lot in that magazine and I was close to them personally and politically. We did a lot of readings and we hung out together. I think the project started when the publisher of a fancy small West Coast press approached us about doing a book together. He diddled around with the manuscript for a couple of years and finally refused to publish it, unless several of the poems he thought improper were removed. I remember he objected to "Song of the fucked duck" because the title wasn't ladylike.

You wouldn't change it, even to get published then? You hadn't been published much at that point.

I wasn't tempted. It just seemed so weird. That whole business of what people call four-letter words. It's a class thing. I was saying "fuck" years before I learned to say "sexual intercourse." That streetwise emotive language for the simple things of life is the basic urban language for me. Using Latin names for parts of the body and using medical language to talk about body functions seems peculiar. It feels awkward and as if you're putting somebody on. You're trying to clean up what you think is dirty by using language that belongs to the laboratory or hospital, because you think the lab or hospital is cleaner than your own bed.

So what finally happened to the book?

By the time we were done with him I had put together *Hard Loving*, it had been accepted and I was writing the first poems that were going to go into *To Be of Use*. I was very heavily involved in the women's liberation movement and no longer as close to the *Hanging Loose* poets. However, the Crossing Press which was then also called Newbooks accepted the manuscript in late 1969 and by the time the book came out in 1971, I'd been in the women's movement for a number of years and I'd had some kind of political disagreement with every one of the editors even though Dick Lourie and I became friends again years later. I admire the work of the other poets. I like their work and they have strong individual voices, but I would have been more comfortable by the time the book was finally published in a group volume with women such as *Mountain Moving Day* Elaine Gill edited for the Crossing Press that I was included in.

To Be of Use is very purposefully structured. What did you have in mind with the three different sections?

To Be of Use I put together as a book of feminist consciousness. I didn't include a lot of love poems. By that time I had written some Cape landscape poems, but I didn't put them in either. The first section begins in exploitation and dependence and goes through the very difficult work of trying to bond with other women, moves through rising anger into fuller consciousness into being able to take action, and ends with a poem rejecting masochism called "Burying blues for Janis." That's one of those sequences in which I come up against people's desire to experience all poems as autobiographical. I remember reading an essay by an academic writer in which "She leaves" was used at length to interpret the rest of the book autobiographically, assuming that in my sweet naivete as a song sparrow I just warble out the poems and let them fall where they may. Actually "She leaves" is about *she*; I wasn't leaving anybody. It was about the walking out of old marriages that I saw happening a lot. The midsection "The spring offensive of the snail" is composed of poems about what you do after you've raised your feminist consciousness but you don't want to remain there hung and angry in reaction. It's about rejoining the Left on your own terms, about trying to be with men again and about trying to communicate and work with other women and with men. The last section "Laying down the tower" is one of those state of my own art sequences which I've done twice, the second being "The Lunar Cycle."

"Councils" in To Be of Use *seems like an odd poem. It's written for a male part and a female voice. Have you ever read this at a reading with somebody else doing the male part?*

Yes, I have. I did that poem a whole lot at one time and I used to get a man to read it with me. It's just that sometimes it's so awkward to try to find someone to read it and not ham it up or mumble, that I think I finally gave up on that. But for a while I did it a lot whenever I was reading to mixed audiences.

How do you respond to people who call you a man-hater?

By biting their ankle. Next question.

Seriously. You run into that a lot?

Usually from people who have never read much of my work. Come on, it's hopeless. I get flak from a number of lesbian feminists because most of my sexual relationships have been with men. Now the truth is, I rarely flirt with men I don't know. Men are accustomed to a certain burring of sexuality with many women. I used to do that myself to survive when I was much younger, before the women's movement. I would—not intentionally but unconsciously—create a sort of hidden sense that I found most men attractive, whether I did or not, simply because they would be kinder to me. Since I came to understand what was involved, I ceased doing that, quite consciously, and I couldn't summon up that kind of behavior today if I wanted to. I don't tend to smile a lot in situations where I feel on display—public situations. I speak directly and straightforwardly and bluntly, and that lack of subterfuge and lack of middle-class women's mannerisms is perceived by some men as hostile, just as Black behavior which is simply straightforward is perceived by some whites as hostile.

Unlike some separatists I don't view men as biologically impaired. I believe sexism is culturally conditioned and that if you change the culture, you will change the kind of behavior which people with the various sorts of genitalia will consider appropriate. What I hate in men is what I consider ugly, brutal, violent, mean behavior—behavior damaging to women, to men they consider inferior, to children, to other living creatures with whom we share our biosphere.

When I write in my novels about how men behave toward women, I am writing the truth out of the characters I have created and a truth I think many readers recognize. To ask that the portraits of all men in my fiction be flattering is to introduce a requirement never foisted on men about the women in their fiction.

Frequently when I go into a place, because I'm a feminist, people assume I'm a lesbian. I never correct that silent assumption. There's no reason why I shouldn't be a lesbian if I fell in love with a woman again. I believe it is very necessary for the possibility of loving another woman to be open to women, just as the possibility for living chastely without any entanglements has to be open, or there is no sexual freedom at all. But then I'm a pluralist in sexuality as in most things. I want people to make many different choices and flourish in them, and to respect the choices they don't make in their own lives as well as those they do.

To Be of Use *I just heard was going out of print. Is that right?*

It will be printed almost in its entirety by Knopf in my new and selected poems, *Circles on the Water*. I have left out maybe six poems from the whole book and I'm putting the rest in. All the other books I selected about a third of.

One question while we're on To Be of Use. *When we first met you did a number of Tarot readings, but we haven't read the Tarot in a while. When you wrote that sequence did reading the Tarot have a larger part in your life?*

I go through periods in which I read the Tarot a lot. A year and a half ago, I read it a number of times. Anyhow, I probably used the cards a lot more in the early seventies, late sixties than I do now.

What did it mean to you? You're not a person who has a great mystical side, you're very practical, pragmatic, political, upfront person. What does that element represent?

The Tarot has always appeared to me to be an incredibly rich treasure of images that have been in Western cultures and particularly heretical Western culture for a long time. I find that contemplating the cards moves those levels of my brain that begin the vibrations that become poems. I also find it a way of contemplating symbolism common in literature and in our culture and thereby trying to encounter my own meanings and penetrate the layers of meaning in the use of imagery and symbols.

Living in the Open *was the book just coming out when you and I met. That was my introduction to you, having not known you at all. I read* Living in the Open *and assumed that everything you said there was you and it scared me quite a bit.*

Why did it scare you?

Well, because I didn't understand what you were saying, "no more lovers, no more husbands, no masters or mistresses, contracts, no affairs, only friends, no more trade-ins or betrayals . . . you are not my insurance, not my vacation, not my romance, not my job," that's heavy stuff to read written by somebody you're considering getting involved with. . . .

It's my impression that in the body of your work your novels as well as your poetry, you never define what you would imagine to be the ideal family. I have the impression that you consider friendship more important than family or standing in the traditional place of family?

I am very interested in the voluntary families that people create; not just the communes but the informal social webs by which a great many people survive and flourish. A lot of my adult life I have been trying in one form or another to create alternatives to the nuclear family.

For me the family under patriarchy is at best a workable compromise. At worst it's a place where people torture each other in intimate ways, where life is wasted in petty tyranny and petty reprisal, in spite that often consists in refusing to do something you want to prevent somebody else from doing what they want, refusing to enjoy, refusing to take chances or to permit others to take chances.

Yet I'm a deeply social person. I like being alone. It's important to me to have space on my own, my space to work, my own room. In my later life I've become accustomed to having a study of my own and my own bedroom, whether or not you sleep there with me. But I work alone. When I finish work for the day, I want company. I want to talk. I want exchange, communication, intimacy. We've talked a lot about each of our need for intimacy. I guess I feel a lot of family life as it's lived precludes solitude on one hand and real intimacy on the other.

Friendship is my paradigm for the good relationship. If you like someone, you will also love them better. If you love without liking, there's a chill at the core of it that easily turns into possessiveness, jealousy, competition.

What were you doing when you put Living in the Open *together?*

A lot of the poems in *Living in the Open* were of the same age as the poems in *To Be of Use*. A number of years had gone by between *Hard Loving* and *To Be of Use* when I had trouble finding a publisher for the Tarot poems. An editor interested early on had involved Lucia Vernarelli in making woodcuts for the poems. When that deal fell through, I felt obliged to honor the commitment. That made finding a publisher hard. But I held out the more personal poems from *To Be of Use* as well as the poems rooted in the Cape landscape that I'd begun to write in 1971. The first section of *Living in the Open* was mostly composed of poems about the Cape. The first poems were written in New York, among the few I wrote while I was ill. The others form my earliest exploration of the Cape. The middle section's title, "The homely war," came from a long poem about why as a feminist I still have relationships with men; the poems in that section are about trying and failing and sometimes enjoying my connections with other people. The last section, "The provocation of the dream," is about the feminist vision. *Living in the Open* is the first of my books that I did with Knopf and it's the first one I think is totally pleasing physically. All the poetry books I've done with Knopf have involved a real cooperation with my editor, Nancy Nicholas, and with the design people. Virginia Tan has worked on all four of my books at Knopf and I'm deeply grateful for her patience. In every case, I've been quite firm about what I wanted and it's taken several attempts for me to feel that the cover was doing what it needed to do for the book.

What a strange title for The Twelve-Spoked Wheel Flashing?

That's my solar book as my lunar book is *The Moon Is Always Female*. It's built around the sequence of a year, each season as an emotional as well as a literal season. The seasons of political ferment and activity, the seasons of loving and friendship, the seasons of the land. It's the wheel of the sun and *The Twelve-Spoked Wheel Flashing* is the wheel of the year which turns but doesn't return to the same place, which is an image that's haunted me for a long time: the wheel that turns but doesn't return.

What was that strange story about the cover of The Moon Is Always Female?

I had given the book that title in manuscript, *The Moon Is Always Female*, and Nancy Nicholas, my dear editor at Knopf, didn't really like the title, and we were quibbling about it at the same time I kept talking about wanting either a cat in the moon or a cat jumping over the moon. The first sketches for the cover displeased me, lacking cats and moons. I think it was probably Virginia Tan herself who found the brush and ink drawing that came from an old Chinese scroll, and there was the cat in the moon and some Chinese lettering which when translated said "The moon is always female." So Nancy gave up and said, so be it. So there was the cover and I got my title.

The country comes up again and again in your poetry, yet your novels seem to be based in the city, no?

I grew up in center city Detroit, although there were short periods of my childhood spent outside the city. But the great bulk of the first thirty-four years of my life was spent in cities. After I left home when I was seventeen, except for my college years in Ann Arbor, a small pleasant city, I lived in urban centers. I don't think I spent more than four days at a time out of the center-city until 1969, when I spent a month on the Cape working on *Dance the Eagle to Sleep*. We spend two days a week in Boston a fair amount of the year now, after all. I think probably what you're getting at is that I have written more fiction based in the city, whereas more of my poetry for the last four books is based in the country. I guess the themes of caste and class that interest me are at their harshest and clearest in the city in our society, and thus I tend to use that setting to explore those themes.

I never knew you when your life was completely based in the city. Have you changed?

In New York I used myself as pure instrument. Even though I believed in mortality certainly because I had lost people close to me and kept losing friends who died or were killed then, nonetheless I treated myself as a totally renewable resource. I slept little, smoked heavily, pushed myself. I didn't consider my body as something that had to be protected or conserved. I thought my energy inexhaustible. I would get up at six, write for four hours, go to three political meetings and a demonstration, make forty phone calls, cook supper for a gang of ten and dance all night and get up the next day and do it again. So I thought. In that extremely political, even overly politicized environment, I tended to treat myself as a tool, which is partly the way I was treated by others. When my health broke, when I came to the end of my energy and had to face my limits, I learned to live in a different way. I had to learn to live so that I would last. I had to learn to be gentler, easier, quieter, to be a political person and go on living my life in a useful manner but to survive my own commitments.

I think I probably told you the way I learned about the B vitamins was by passing out on Broadway and getting stepped on and then discovering I was anemic. That was after an operation where I lost a lot of blood. I'm a nutrition nut now.

Take your yeast, take your vitamin E, take your C!

I had to learn to live in the world in a more careful and healthier way. Of course I'd destroyed my lungs by smoking plus the help of all those nice gasses the government used on us in demonstrations in the late sixties and early seventies. Almost coughing to death, choking on my own lungs, you might say impressed me. I almost died. It left me with a violent allergy to tobacco—a bloody nuisance, but even a little tobacco smoke makes me rotten sick—enough and I'm sick with a fever in bed for a week.

Are you a more productive writer now since you moved to the country?

Vastly. Less interruptions. I can control interruptions better. And since we've been in a relationship, I've become more productive.

Have you become more productive since you've become older and more experienced? For instance, the two of us can sit down at our desks at 8 o'clock and you will leave your desk at 12 having two or three pages to every one I might write. Is that something that I can look forward to with age?

If you consider it something to look forward to, yes. It is the case that a certain kind of mastery comes with experience. You have to have something to look forward to, right? There are lots of problems difficult for the apprentice writer which an experienced writer doesn't think about anymore. You simply solve them, they are in your repertoire of easy solutions, and the problems that provoke you are other. I think there is a constant dialectic between what I can do and what I aim toward in my poetry, beyond what I know how to handle already. There are periods when I am pushing myself and periods when I am exploiting what I can do. Those kinds of epicycles go on, they move forward, you don't return to the same place. Living in the country put me in touch with the land and with the seasons. You know living here you pay attention to the moon. If you want to go oystering, those sweet treasures of the local oysters, you have to watch the tides and the moon, and planting you watch the moon. I've become much more regular in my period since I've lived here. Paying attention to the moon aligns you. We've often noted how people in the city think it's nice weather if it doesn't rain. Well, if you're growing things, and it doesn't rain, it's a disaster. We depend upon our well for water. We're constantly aware of how much it's raining, what the weather is, how cold, and how warm and whether there's likely to be a frost. We're aligned to the weather and the seasons and the climate in a very direct way.

I've never been to a poetry reading of yours where you didn't read some political poems or try to talk to the audience about political issues. Now I know most poets ordinarily get nervous before a reading, but you must get doubly so because you're going to be looked at as trying to talk to them about something political as well. Do you have any fear before poetry readings, a purely political fear as well as nervousness about reading?

Well, I worry about whether I've chosen the right poems for the right place. I worry about whether I can reach people. We had the experience of being in a small college last week in the south where we had supper with the faculty and they kept saying, The kids here are all born-again Christians, and they'll eat you alive, and I felt that they were trying to make me afraid, as if they were daring me to reach the students.

It was incredible though that they were telling us stories before the reading that seemed like college had gone back fifty years, but your readings were so well attended, there were so many people who came up to you afterward, that I think that that really shows that you're right. I think that I would always tend to make my program fit what I thought the audience was. But you don't do that, you make the audience fit you, what you want to say, and you always seem to find people out there for whom you express, and for whom your poems give voice to their ideas. I see it time and time again.

But it's not true, Woody, that I don't try to reach the audience. I'm not going to change my politics but I did no overtly sexual poems that night. I decided that that was probably not going to work there. There are some audiences where I'll do poems like "Snow in May" which is a poem I really love, one of my best lyrics from *The Twelve-Spoked Wheel Flashing*, but it's also a poem where there's cocks and balls. I didn't do any poems there with overtly sexual events or even imagery in them because I felt that if I did that they wouldn't hear anything else. Not that I changed the politics or read less feminist stuff. There's other places where you do overtly sexy things and then the audience gets on your side and you can hit them with the politics. You try to play them. There are places where you can do a lot of the economically political poems and men like that and then you start doing the feminist poems and you have to work to get them across; you've bought them with the others. You have to set the feminist poems up in the program. I'm not going to omit them, I'm not going to ever not say what I've come to say, but I'll do more or less love poems or sexual poems or nature poems as I judge the audience.

People have asked you but you always decline; how come you never read fiction?

320

I have on occasion when there is no other way to do a gig I want and they insist on it but I write my poetry to be read. Poems are arrangements of sounds and silences and they go very well aloud. Fiction makes me feel that, in being a little bit of an actor playing different roles, I feel as if I am hamming it up or not hamming it up enough. The performance seems separate from the writing.

Do you think this is true just for you or have there been fiction writers you've enjoyed hearing?

I remember hearing Toni Morrison read powerfully and Alice Walker and Dorothy Parker, years ago, and Grace Paley reads wonderfully. If I wrote only fiction, I would doubtless read my fiction, but since I write poetry and that's for reading aloud, it always seems to me that it's like working twice as hard to read the fiction aloud, plus I don't write many short stories. It's always a problem trying to pull a piece to read out of a novel, some little excerpt that works on its own. I remember trying it in the very late sixties and early seventies and having trouble managing to stop and start the excerpt and not have to explain for twenty minutes and then read for five minutes.

I want to talk about theme. You are always writing poetry during the time when you're writing a novel. A novel takes two or three to four years to write, and you will at the end of that time have a book of poetry ready because so many poems get written while you're writing a novel. Do they criss-cross, the themes of the poetry and the novel?

Yes. Sometimes I'll be aware of a poem which is also the same germination as the novel. I can think of a couple of examples. "The sun" that ends the Tarot sequence "Laying Down the Tower" in *To Be of Use* is the same vision that was the beginning seed of *Woman on the Edge of Time*; and the poem "The curse of the earth magician on a metal land" is the same vision which was at the beginning of the germination of the seed for *Dance the Eagle to Sleep* which is a phrase taken from that poem. Those are the most obvious examples, and in fact

I took the title *Braided Lives* of my most recent novel from the poem, "Looking at quilts." But there are less obvious relationships also. I have a whole sequence of poems about choice that you can follow from book to book about what it means to be able to choose in your life. The poem "For Inez Garcia" from *Living in the Open* is concerned with what it means as a woman to revenge oneself on a rapist. What is honor from a woman's point of view? Honor has been defined from a male point of view. What does it mean to choose not to endure having been raped? That's one of the first poems in which I think I am concerned with choice in the ultimate sense. I notice the same theme in "For Shoshana-Pat Swinton" from *The Twelve-Spoked Wheel Flashing* where in a political and historical context I'm asking once again what it means to choose to acquiese in decisions on the part of the government you feel to be wrong, or to resist, to cooperate with punitive and politically repressive grand juries or to resist. Of course, that's centered on a political fugitive, as *Vida* was to be. "A gift of light" circles around the same questions. Those same concerns occur in "In Memorium Walter and Lillian Lowenfels" in which I am talking about two people who lived very political lives and who were friends of mine, and it's a celebration of their choosing to remain so alive and so political into old age. In "Memo" from *The Moon Is Always Female* the poem deals with the choice of resistance rather than suicide and despair, and in a number of the Lunar Cycle poems I'm concerned with those ultimate decisions. Of course you could say that my novels follow through lives the effects of such decisions. In "Right to life" the choice is whether or not to have a baby. In "The sabbath of mutual respect" it's the free choice of love object.

As a poet and fiction writer, I think you're really lucky. I'll write a novel over the course of two years and at least 100 small but significant things will happen to me during that time, an automobile accident, a political meeting where I'm enraged, I'll put on and lose twenty pounds; all these things and I have to fight myself not to put it in but to stay on course with the fiction. But you as a poet can use these things to feed you in very specific ways. Do you do that? Do you store them up or write them all out?

Sometimes I respond to things immediately with a poem about them and sometimes I respond to something that happened fifteen years ago with a poem about it. It works both ways but you know that little translates directly. We've gone through this experience of your saying who is that poem written about, and I say well, it's not really about anyone in particular. It's sort of an amalgamation of two or three people and things I was thinking about and so forth. Certainly my autobiographical impulse has primarily played itself out in poetry rather than in fiction. But when I see reviewers as they want to do especially with women's books looking at one or another of my books and making up a sort of narrative which the poems are supposed to express, that makes me feel like banging my head on the wall. It's amazing how naive they assume you are. Everything you say just gushes from you freely and the order in the book has to have some relationship to your life, where there usually is little. I will put together love poems in a sequence that may have had their irrelevant genesis in three different relationships, and somebody will analyze the sequence in terms of some personal autobiographical trauma. It makes the angels throw up.

Two Christmases ago when you asked me what I'd like as a present, I said that I'd like some reference books. You thought about that as you usually do and you came back with a thesaurus, an English grammar, a dictionary of foreign terms in English and three Peterson's guides, one to trees and shrubs, one to wildflowers, one to birds. How come the Peterson's guides? I've heard you recommend field guides to other young writers. Could you elaborate?

I think it was Isaac Babel who talked about city Jews and how alienated we get from the land. He felt that you had to learn your own landscape and put roots down and learn names and somehow acclimate yourself. I remember being impressed by that, when I was reading a lot of Babel when I was twenty. But I would also answer it from a totally other angle which is that just as politically when there is no vocabulary for discussing your situation, when you're a woman before there is language of feminism, trying to understand what it's like to be a woman, you have no concepts, no vocabulary for even understanding your own situation. Similarly, in the natural landscape, you don't begin to observe until you have some vocabulary, some set of criteria to apply, some kind of grids to put down. People who have never done bird watching at all don't know what birds look like. They have no idea of the relative size. They have no way of looking at the different kinds of birds that are in their landscape or what they are doing there. To understand why a warbler has one kind of beak and a finch has another kind of beak. Why the different kinds of ways of flying happen: the darting flight, the soaring flight, the hovering flight. You walk through a field and there's nothing in it. If you begin to look at wildflowers, you begin to see how every two or three weeks the whole field changes, the succession of bloom, and then you begin to look at the individual flowers and see how they are put together and the way the leaves are attached. Once you begin to identify trees, you begin to know how wet or how dry a spot is, how windy or how protected, what kind of climate, and you begin to expect what kind of animals live there and what they eat. You begin to understand the landscape. Until you begin to analyze the landscape, you are not experiencing it. I'm sure I make mistakes like any amateur, but by god if I say Fowler's toad, I have identified a Fowler's toad in the landscape or at least suppose I have. I don't use details decoratively, or I may use them decoratively also, but I also use them truthfully in the sense of responsibility toward the landscape. People who like natural history sometimes relate to my poetry, because it's truthful in that sense. It's responsible in that sense.

I've asked you this many times, but how did you get that way? I mean you grew up in Detroit, you lived in New York, Brooklyn, San

Francisco, Paris. I have lived in less urban places than you have. Where did you come to love nature so much? How did you develop that interest?

My mother who was a child of the slums, of extreme poverty, taught me to love natural beauty. She grew a lot of flowers in a tiny urban yard in Detroit. We had a lush backyard for the tinyness of it, for the extreme industrialization of the landscape. Because of the depression in Detroit, there were holes in the development, in the urban landscape, where nature still existed. It was an interesting landscape that I grew up in. I've tried to suggest it in a couple of my novels, something of the Gary in *Going Down Fast* and the description of the landscape to the south of Detroit, down river, in *The High Cost of Living*, that section where Bernie and Leslie go. In spite of the industrial development, there were pockets in the neighborhood when I was growing up where there were still pheasants and rabbits, at the same time that it was intensely industrialized and there were street gangs. It was a strange combination. Of course enormous rats lived in the alleys where we spent a lot of time. Travel to me was always intensely exciting and for a working class kid, I got to travel a lot. My father drove all over Michigan to repair heavy machinery, and in the summer and sometimes even when I was in school, my mother and I would go with him. We stayed in those sort of cheap hotels a commercial traveler would go to, but some of them had charm for me—for instance, I remember the vines on the porch of the Winona Hotel in Bay City, which were full of Isabella wooly bear caterpillars, of which I was inordinately fond. Still am. My mother couldn't drive and we didn't have the car anyhow, so we'd just sort of walk around and amuse ourselves as best we could. There are specific smells that to this day I associate with certain industrial landscapes in Michigan. It was a pleasure to escape from school and Detroit and home.

We also went regularly to Cleveland, where some of my mother's widely scattered family lived. Also Pennsylvania, where my father's family came from, a small town in coal mining country, where I could get off into the woods easily. I was always attracted by trees and hills, anything semiwild. The low ridgy mountains with their forests, company towns, and the mines hollowing them out from within had a powerful affect on my imagination.

But as an adult, you didn't have much contact with nature until you moved here?

That's an understatement. Except for one period of three or four months traveling around Greece, the closest I got to a tree was in Central Park when we were mounting antiwar demonstrations. Look, I think sometimes the kids who didn't get to see that much in their childhoods that wasn't ugly and grim but who were made aware, usually by their mothers, may value the healing and integrating power of wildness and nature more than people who grew up with a lot of grass and trees. Think of Lawrence and his mining town. The way he writes about flowers and birds and turtles always gets me. I like it much better than when he writes about sex in people. It's much less self-serving (You don't want that orgasm, Frieda, really you don't) and rooted in empathy.

You use that word a lot. It's a value word for you.

But mostly when I'm talking about fiction. It's the prime quality of a novelist. How you enter other people's experiences from the underside or the inside.

Why are you a poet anyhow?

What else should I be, like dead? Poetry is a necessity to me. Even when I have no access to paper or pen or silence, I make up poems. I make up poems for our cats. I say little poems when we're in bed together. I make up little poems for you sometimes when I'm in the kitchen. I say poems to the peas and the day lilies. I make up poems for the houses on the street in Cambridgeport. Those aren't meant to be great or public poems, just the little responses, the little gracenotes of thanksgiving and praise and cursing during a day. They have some slight relationship to the real writing, which is infinitely more intense, concentrated, reaching out to channel far more reality. The little poems of the day are simple, but sometimes in them comes a seed, a flash, that real word that summons real work. The happier I am, the better I work. Out of pain, intense work is produced but often later on, when my actual state is quiet delight.

Often I imagine in different and better times not having to be political. I can even imagine, when I am at the bottom of a long uphill grade, doing something besides writing novels, although I doubt it. But I never imagine living without poetry.

UNDER DISCUSSION
Donald Hall, General Editor

Volumes in the Under Discussion series collect reviews
and essays about individual poets. The series is concerned
with contemporary American and English poets about
whom the consensus has not yet been formed and the
final vote has not been taken. Among those to be consid-
ered are:

Elizabeth Bishop and Her Art
by Lloyd Schwartz and Sybil P. Estess

Adrienne Rich *by Jane Roberta Cooper*

Richard Wilbur *by Wendy Salinger*

Robert Bly *by Joyce Peseroff*

Allen Ginsberg *by Lewis Hyde*

*Please write for further information on available editions and current
prices.*

Ann Arbor   **The University of Michigan Press**